Excerpts from *PAIN AWAITS*

√ The government—politicians—got the country into this financial mess. The government and its employees should be first in line to get the country out. This deduction program should be efficient, expedient, equitable, and above all, simple. It should start and end with two words: No exceptions.

***

√ Regular citizens…did you catch the part about some state employees being allowed to work two jobs in the same office during the same workday and be paid for each? Wouldn't that mean two pensions as well?

***

√ The following information demonstrates to regular law abiding citizens just how ridiculous prison costs can be in many cities and states. There has to be a more economical way to deal with the people who steal from us.

***

√ It should be remembered that "great sacrifice" is required by all to avoid severe financial, economic, and security problems in the near future. All citizens will be asked to sacrifice in some way.

***

√ Most people are aware lightning strikes can cause serious damage, including fire ignition and melting circuits. Most people are unaware of another happening that can cause damage similar to lightening but is far more dangerous.

***

√ Perhaps you've noticed…buy anything today, check the country of origin, and it says, "Made in China." Whose fault is that?

***

√ What can happen if a drug cartel helps smuggle terrorists into the United States and then from the border to any large city? Almost anything.

Terrorists, nearly invisible in a big city, could prepare an ugly attack. An ugly attack such as a "hostage-ransom" situation with terrorists taking over a school and demanding $10 billion or they'll kill 1,000 kids.

The following "three-day terrorist event" suggests where we're headed if we don't get a firm grip on suicidal foreign fanatics. You're not going to like this and it's going to hurt.

Day One is simple. Terrorists enter and secure school. Students forced to third floor. Multiple IEDs in place. Ransom demand of $10 billion. Meaningless negotiations follow. Endless television cameras watch. Recordings of hysterical kids broadcast. Parents' frantic demands and cries broadcast. Negotiations mum. A standoff? No, not even close.

Day Two. Second demand of $10 billion. Noon deadline. Stalled negotiations. Two kids are shown IEDs inside school. At 11:00 a.m. the same two kids walk from school to authorities. Kids, authorities talk. A 12:00 noon, "final demand" issued for $10 billion. Authorities hesitate. At 12:05 p.m. another two kids walk from school. At twenty-five paces, they're head-shot dead. Cameras jolt. Parents' knees buckle. At 1:00 p.m., $10 billion is paid. Terrorists inside school verify payment transfer to foreign bank. At 2:00 p.m. as an anxious nation watches live on TV…the school and all occupants are disintegrated.

Day Three. With trembling hands and sobbing sounds…America records the prior day as its worst day in history.

Who shares the responsibility for this ugly example of a deliberate, unrepairable, unbearable tragedy? Everybody. In no particular order: Drug cartels, they who bring drugs, crime, and killers into our country and neighborhoods. Terrorists, they who have a mindset below that of a rabid dog. Drug abusers, who blindly pay out billions to keep cartels in business. Politicians, who will not tackle the drug problem that operates under their noses. Politicians, who mind their manners when speaking about or dealing with Muslim terrorists. Banks, that launder billions in dirty money, enabling drug trade, torture, and terrorism. American citizens, who have yet to say, "Enough is enough."

***

√ Is there another fierce adversary in American life lurking in the shadows? Yes, there is…and that enemy is inside our gate. That enemy is lethal. That enemy may be unstoppable.

***

√ From special section in book: Add an orange, yellow, or red colored smoke agent to the bomb if feasible. People will fear breathing-in the colored smoke. This should increase panic at site, causing additional injuries.

***

√ Remembering the $20,000,000,000,000 debt…the "best for America" course of action is to reduce funds to unproductive citizens, collect minimum taxes from all, eliminate unneeded subsidies, eliminate US prisons, eliminate unneeded foreign aid, and use those funds saved to improve US infrastructure and security, which benefits all American citizens. It's as simple as that.

***

√ Fewer jobs in the US petroleum industry. More jobs in the Chinese alternative fuel system industry. Who wants that? China.

***

√ One of these days, someone will start welfare benefits at age one and continue them until death at 101 years of age. That would establish a record for the longest uninterrupted career. Unfortunately, the recipient would miss his or her own retirement party.

***

√ There are areas in Mexico where Americans can't go. Soon there'll be areas in America where Americans can't go. It's already happening.

***

√ Is there any doubt there's an economic war taking place? Is there any doubt it's pointed directly at the United States? No doubt.

***

√ From special section in book: Thicker is better. Hard plastic is typical. Folding seats are usually available but they may be limited. Lessor choice is aluminum bench seating. The seat material will be blast splintered and function as shrapnel.

***

√ It's doubtful such a weak and idiotic sign would stop anyone from mischief. A brat would find it invitational. A terrorist directional.

***

√ Our future water infrastructure problems have already arrived, and replacement work is already past due. Our politicians are out sailing.

***

√ Politicians get an A for effort...to get elected. An F for suggesting free education is...free. And, a Z for the end result...which is zip.

**

√ Many of the financial adjustments mentioned there will cause pain, but what choice does the country have today? The country needs money for debt reduction, national security, education, and infrastructure. The country needs to save money somewhere because it needs to spend money everywhere.

**

√ What does this mean? In ultrasimple, numeric-type terms, it means the seventeen-year-old kid sitting back in coach has more advanced electronics in his hand than the fifty-seven-year-old pilot has in his as he guides a 747 across the country.

**

√ Any student who received eleven Ds out of sixteen possible grades probably wouldn't make it to graduation. Why should it be any different with infrastructure? If the infrastructure grades don't improve, infrastructure is not going to make it. When infrastructure fails...we all fail.

**

√ For those illegal-alien immigrants already residing in the United States... there's a simple way to deal with them.

**

√ Readers should pay special attention to reason number one: "Nothing works without the power grid." There is only one statement in the United States that describes a worse scenario: "Everybody is dead."

**

Comments, criticism, or complaints may be sent to
SBSHINEauthor@gmail.com

PAIN AWAITS

SAVING THE UNITED STATES FROM ITSELF

How to permanently fix our economy, reduce our debt,
protect our citizens, enlighten our youth, end our drug culture,
and reestablish America's positive identity

S.B.Shine

Pain Awaits: Saving the United States from itself. How to permanently fix our economy, reduce our debt, protect our citizens, enlighten our youth, end our drug culture, and reestablish America's positive identity.

Copyright © 2018 by S.B.Shine.

All Rights Reserved.

ISBN: 978-0-692-10510-8

Library of Congress Control Number: 2018940802

Editor: Tyler Tichelaar, Superior Book Productions

Interior Book Layout: Superior Book Productions

Cover Design by the Author

Printed in the United States of America

First Edition

2 4 6 8 10 12

DEDICATION

This book is dedicated to YOU.

YOU ... must do the math.

Simple Addition:

$20,000,000,000,000 National Debt

+ National Security Cost

+ Terrorism Prevention

+ Infrastructure Updates

+ Chinese Competition

+ Political Ideology Corruption

+ Media Bias

+ Drug Culture Elimination

+ Entertainment Morality

———————————————

= PAIN AWAITS

Contents

PART FOUR: THE DIRTY DOZEN
Changes for a Lifetime of Making Sense

INTRODUCTION

IT'S MANDATORY the United States avoids a national financial collapse. The first task is to cut spending immediately.

IT'S MANDATORY the United States has superior national security. The first task is to increase all security immediately.

IT'S MANDATORY the United States increases its economic power. The first task is to exploit some sectors immediately.

As you can see from the preceding paragraphs, it'll be extremely difficult to achieve total success when all three tasks are undertaken together, but that effort must begin immediately.

All American citizens, "even after great sacrifice," will still need to find the internal strength of Maximillian Kolbe, and at the same time, be as fortunate as Franciszek Gajowniczek.

Many readers will think the remedies put forth in this book are too extreme. They are incorrect. Many readers will think such remedies will be extremely difficult to implement. They are correct.

Today, the United States is facing serious financial and security problems, and those problems will not go away without serious sacrifice by all Americans.

Serious financial problems call for reduced spending. Serious security problems call for increased spending. Correcting these problems will be more than difficult. People scream for change in every election, but often when the change affects them directly, they scream even louder. Politicians do the opposite. After the election, they quietly forget. These are major problems that must first be addressed in our society before anything else takes place. Likewise, they shall be addressed first in this book as well.

Without going into much detail here, the following three steps should be used to inform all citizens and residents in the United States of the reasons for immediate and substantial changes needed in many common areas:

1. All citizens should be informed in simple, understandable language about the present condition and trend of their country. This would include: the national debt of $20,000,000,000,000, ($20 trillion) the military approaching the size it was in 1940, the 95 million people not working, the previously large manufacturing base that has now shifted to China and other countries, the very large welfare population, the over-capacity prison population, an education system that is good but leaves American students well behind foreign students, the growing drug culture that has the potential to destroy normal American life, and the overall national security problem that is worsening every day.

2. All citizens should be informed of the estimated end result of what life in their country may be like if drastic changes are not made. They should be shown detailed examples of the stupidity that led to the collapse of previously great countries such as: Argentina, England, Germany, Russia, and currently, Greece. By some measures, the United States is already financially worse off than those countries were just before they collapsed. It should be explained to US citizens that history does not lie. History brings deep questions. What exactly happened to Argentina? Are we on the same path? Can we fix America if we start now? US citizens need to understand national problems in order to answer yes to the last question.

3. It should be stressed to all citizens that this forthcoming effort to save the United States is a team effort, so all citizens must endure sacrifice of some kind. All citizens. This will be difficult for some to accept. It should be suggested to those citizens, quietly unconvinced of the necessity of ... all, that they stand in front of a mirror and take a good, long look and say "Mayday" repeatedly, until they recognize the difficult work ahead for everyone. If that doesn't work, then perhaps they should reach out and tap the mirror, "dit dit dit, dah dah dah, dit dit dit." That sound may awaken them before the country sinks to the bottom.

All citizens and residents of America will need to have some understanding of "why" extreme changes are needed before any changes actually occur. This does not mean people will always know beforehand what exact measures are going to be put into place. When advance notice about certain types of change is announced, people often adjust matters, which then reduces the effectiveness of the desired change. That will be clear as you read beyond this section.

Reading this book will not make you happy. But it may save your life. This book will not spare you from the blood, sweat, and tears that must be shed by all citizens if this nation is to return to economic stability and past glory. The task is formidable, and it may not be achievable in our lifetime, although readers should recognize that it's not necessary to achieve complete financial balance at this exact time. That may sound odd considering the theme of this book, but it is true. However, it is necessary that this country, the United States of America, demonstrate to both its citizens and the rest of the world that it is making changes that will immediately lead toward improved financial health. The key word being "immediately."

The policy changes and methods suggested throughout this book have not been written about or discussed in many open forums (at least up until early 2016). Many people will refer to these policy changes as policy madness. They are incorrect. What we see every day from the US government is "policy madness." Our policymakers, the politicians, need to read this book. Unfortunately for all, they won't. They'll run in the other direction. They'll find safety behind closed doors, endless discussion, political correctness, and never making the hard choices that must now be made to save our nation. Why make hard choices that might interrupt the easy life of a politician? Most people don't notice, but a politician's lifestyle doesn't change much regardless of what is happening with the general population. The economy can be good or bad. Employment can be up or down. The nation can be at war or peace. The weather can be sunny or rainy, but politicians will always find a dry place. They should read this book.

There's plenty of danger in the world right now and plenty within US borders. Our politicians appear to be frozen in time or even moving backwards as the world marches forward toward unknown positions. China is rapidly expanding militarily. Russia is flexing its muscles toward Eastern Europe and supplying rogue nations with military equipment. ISIS is cutting off American heads and changing the Middle East in ways not favorable to the United States. Mexico is experiencing an internal war between drug cartels and the government. The drug cartels are decapitating Mexican citizens, which intimidates the citizens and the government. Consequently, the drugs flow into the United States and the money, American dollars, flow into Mexico. The United States doesn't effectively stop the flow in either direction.

Who's in charge of this mess? What will it mean to US citizens when foreign terrorists and drug cartels recognize they can benefit each other?

This book details what can and must be done to safeguard American citizens and America. Much of what is needed is cost-efficient. Other changes, especially concerning the US military, will be very costly. Those changes or improvements are mandatory for a safe future. A very strong military yields many present and future benefits that could be measured in social terms. For example, the youth of America, over time, will find a little discipline goes a long way as they move through life.

Terrorism is spreading across the world. It is now obvious to most Americans that the United States is a primary target. This fact should be everyone's immediate concern. Hundreds of thousands of prime targets exist with literally no defense, and those targets are in every city in America. Shopping centers and schools hold millions of innocent American citizens. Trains carrying oil pass through cities daily. Large airliners packed with people depart city airports flying several hundred feet above crowded streets. Our confidential communications can be intercepted or interrupted. Hundreds of very large power stations make up the power grid. These types of targets, when attacked, can lead to chain-reaction power destruction with serious collateral damage. It's a similar threat with water supply or feed stock. What happens if city water is poisoned with biological toxins and many lives are lost? How fast and far will the panic spread? The panic itself will become deadly.

A "terrorist attack format and plot" has been included in this book. It uses actual dates, places, directives, and know-how to accomplish what could be a very easy and very successful attack within the United States. This attack plan was formulated during the month of May 2015 and would have been executed on November 21, 2015 if it had been carried out by real terrorists. Instead, it was developed by this writer for educational-training purposes only. Readers will discover that with little money and limited manpower, such an attack can be executed and change an entire country forever. What happens to America if there are a hundred such attacks? A substantial attack causing many deaths or widespread panic could be accomplished by a single terrorist. What could ten terrorists do? Or a hundred? This writer believes thousands of terrorist types are within this country and that number may increase every day as the government approves more visas, assists refugee programs, and refuses to seal the border. Readers will discover an easy way to seal the southern border and learn that the cost to do so will remain about the same as it is today. Within a relatively short time, other costs associated with today's lack of border control will actually fall. If this can be accomplished, wouldn't it be wise to do so as soon as possible?

If it is impossible to prevent most terrorist attacks, then other methods must be pursued and implemented that go a long way toward reducing or discouraging future attacks. This book covers those direct and indirect methods and goes where others fear to tread. Some proposals that follow will be deemed unpopular, unnecessary, impossible, or too expensive. Unfortunately, future events will determine the validity of proposals found in this book. Readers may judge beforehand.

The desire and effort will always be to prevent future attacks. Naturally, for preventative measures, we look toward several groups, including the recently formed Department of Homeland Security (DHS) agency. This agency consists of a collection of agencies and departments, approximately twenty-two, such as the following: US Customs and Border Protection (CBP), US Immigration and Customs Enforcement (ICE), Federal Emergency Agency (FEMA), US Coast Guard (CG), Domestic Nuclear Detection Office (DNDO), US Secret Service (SS), Transportation Security Administration (TSA), and US Citizenship and Immigration Services (CIS). These appear to be the main departments within the DHS. Some names will be familiar to knowledgeable readers.

Total personnel at DHS has now reached approximately 250,000. This writer believes the DHS has become another federal government agency that is too complex to be very efficient. Many of its departments have bloated personnel numbers. Nevertheless, this writer suggests more personnel are needed as soon as possible and into the future. Together, the last two sentences may sound a little complicated at best, but there is a way it can be done. In fact, it can be readily accomplished and with little increase in the independent department budgets. An explanation will follow.

In order to better protect citizens in everyday life and to reduce possible terrorist attacks here and abroad, many additional uniformed workers will be needed. This need will greatly affect all law enforcement agencies. The same can be said in regards to all military branches of the United States. Some new measures or methods will need to replace the old. Some old measures and methods will need to replace the new. For this writer, the last sentence is critical for the survival of this country. It may not make sense to readers right now, but it will shortly. It is not the type of methodical change that can wait until after a major terrorist or military event. It needs to be installed and practiced now.

The many extreme recommendations that follow in this book are all necessary in order for the United States to survive in this world. The many practical solutions offered should be immediately installed in the name of common sense. All matters mentioned throughout this book are directly or indirectly connected. They cover many different aspects of American life, but all are related to the economy, security, and financial health of the nation.

For the most part, America's future is in the hands of the American people, not the politicians. But the people must recognize that strength. The people must take a firm grip and accept responsibility for the future. The politicians may be the leaders, but they will back away from introducing severe reforms as suggested in this book. Somehow, it has to happen. It's often said, "When the going gets tough, the tough get going." Will those words ring true? Will Americans respond in today's world? Only time will tell. How much time do we have? Very little.

PART ONE: FINANCIAL
Saving Money for the USA IMMEDIATELY

Chapter One

Adjustment for All Government Paychecks

REDUCING THE AMOUNT of money paid on all government paychecks is the most immediate way to cut spending and improve this country's financial deficit condition. It should be simple to implement if handled as a deduction. It will serve as a wakeup signal for Americans that much sacrifice is needed by all. It will demonstrate to the world that the United States is serious about improving its financial position. This financial improvement will be an important observation for friends and adversaries alike.

The reference here to "all government paychecks" refers to all federal, state, and local governments and any related branch or department.

Cutting the wages of any working group or any retired group is always problematic for those most affected, including their immediate families. For that reason, we will first look at the current benefits provided with government jobs. A comparison with similar work in the private sector may demonstrate important differences that would support reducing government wages regardless of the overall financial health of the United States.

Michael Roberts, an expert in government careers, has done many studies and written many articles that point out some advantages of government jobs over private jobs. Article excerpts follow:

ARTICLE FOUND AT: http://govcareers.about.com/od/StartingOut/a/The-Pros-And-Cons-Of-A-Government-Job.htm

ARTICLE WRITTEN BY: Michael Roberts, Government Careers Expert

DATE: AUGUST 25, 2015

TITLE: THE PROS and Cons of a Government Job

> *STABILITY. Unlike the private sector where companies can go out of business, the government never goes out of business.*

FLEXIBILITY. In the vast majority of positions, workers can easily maintain a healthy work-life balance.

BENEFITS. Government benefits almost always exceed private sector benefit packages. Employees often have superior health care plans with lower cost and favorable retirement plans.

TIME OFF. Leave time accruals are generous, and managers tend to be permissive in approving vacation time. Federal holidays are observed. State and local governments sometimes have their own additional holidays.

Many American workers recognize, often too late to take advantage of it, just how lucrative government retirement plans can be for most government workers.

The following article provides information beneficial to those seeking government work, especially if they're just graduating high school:

ARTICLE FOUND AT: govcareers.about.com/od/retirement/fl/How-to-Retire-Young-from-Public-Service.htm

ARTICLE WRITTEN BY: Michael Roberts

TITLE: How to Retire Young from Public Service

In government, having the option to retire young is fairly common. Retirement systems are generous when it comes to counting age and service time toward retirement eligibility. With some planning, government employees can enjoy retirement well before their private sector friends....

Most government retirement systems count eligibility based on age and years of service within that system. Some government employees reach retirement eligibility as early as their 50s. Government employees filing retirement paperwork in their early 50s must have started in public service in their early 20s.

The following information is taken from a related article from the same website, govcareers.about.com, and the same writer:

ARTICLE FOUND AT: http://govcareers.about.com/od/StartingOut/a/The-Pros-And-Cons-Of-A-Government-Job.htm

ARTICLE WRITTEN BY: Michael Roberts

DATE: JANUARY 11, 2015

TITLE: How GOVERNMENT Retirement Systems Determine Eligibility

Many systems use the rule of 80. This means that once an employee's age and years of service total 80, the employee is eligible to retire. Here is an example. An employee begins working for a government agency at age 27. The organization's retirement system operates under the rule of 80. Given this employee's age and the rule of 80, the employee will be eligible to retire at age 53 ½ after 26 ½ years of service. This early retirement age gives the employee plenty of working years left to pursue a second career or come back to public service to double dip. Double dipping is when an employee has retired and is drawing an annuity but is also working and earning a salary in an organization that participates in the same retirement system.

It's very conceivable the average high school student could graduate and obtain an entry level government job at age eighteen. If the employee works until age forty-nine, he or she would have thirty-one years of government service. The employee's age would then be forty-nine. Adding the thirty-one years of work to their actual age reaches the full retirement rule of eighty. The retired worker would be extremely young compared to any private job retirement age, excepting that of professional athletes.

The United States Armed Forces are a special category of government worker. Those who serve in the military are eligible to retire after twenty years. Many stay much longer. Their work is not comparable in most ways to the average government job and their retirement is calculated much differently. Nevertheless, a change from a twenty-year service to twenty-five year service for retirement should be considered. It will not be explored here.

Energetic government workers throughout their work years could have taken advantage of education benefits partially paid by the government. This effort may have helped greatly with promotions while working or obtaining work after retirement. This is a great government worker benefit.

It appears many retired workers return to work right after retirement and work in the same department or a related department and sometimes in the same office or same building. These types of maneuvers—some might admit it's a scheme—make government jobs very lucrative for workers later in life.

There are other favorable retirement rules for those workers who start their government jobs later in life or have relatively few years on the job. Many of these workers receive a good pension, although it is considerably reduced depending on years worked.

It's important all citizens participate in the "personal sacrifice" needed to improve the nation's financial health. It's also important they have a thorough understanding of the ways in which that can be achieved. This will be especially true for government workers and pensioners.

Government workers and pensioners should be the first to experience the needed "financial sacrifice" ... to save the United States.

To make this happen, all individual government checks paid out as a paycheck or pension check and totaling $100,000 or less annually shall be cut or reduced by 5 percent of the gross amount. This means, as an example, any government worker or government pensioner who receives an annual payment or income of $80,000 would see a deduction of $4,000. Likewise, an annual payment of $40,000 would incur a deduction of $2,000. Similarly, all annual payments over $100,000 would be cut by 10 percent. This means, again as an example, any government worker or pensioner receiving an annual pay amount of $140,000 would see deductions of 5 percent on the first $100,000 or $5,000 and 10 percent on the remaining $40,000 or $4,000. The total deduction on $140,000 would be $9,000.

It should be noted that the previous paragraph referred to the change for government workers' pay or pensions as either a cut or a reduction in pay. But the income examples given in the same paragraph referred to the change in pay as a "deduction." A deduction is simpler and preferable in several ways. It's more beneficial to and understandable by the average worker if the change in pay is referred to as a deduction from wages. Workers receiving paychecks are already familiar with deductions because several are listed on all paycheck stubs.

A deduction can be readily changed to a different amount or percentage. It could be canceled at a certain time. Anytime there is a deduction from a paycheck, that deducted amount of money must be sent somewhere. This means the money could be tracked and the worker or pensioner can know the destination of or final use of the funds. Deducted funds could be applied strictly to federal deficit reduction or to a national security project known to the public. In some ways, the use of the deducted funds could be a matter of national pride for the worker or pensioner. This change in pay, or deduction from pay, for government workers should be well-publicized ... very well-publicized. The change should serve as a reminder that government's first responsibility is to safeguard all citizens in all ways, including financial responsibility. It should be an example to all citizens that sacrifice is needed for the good of country.

Many citizens will think this monetary deduction is too much or unfair for government workers. Many will think just the opposite. Either way, all citizens should agree the proposed changes are a serious sacrifice by all government workers and pensioners. This same deduction percentage shall apply to any and all compensation regardless of what name it is termed. Any pay amount designated as a bonus, longevity, commission, comp pay, back pay, overtime pay, holiday pay, or similar shall be included in the overall amount of annual pay.

The check deduction shall be in force for a period of five years. After five years, the government-check deduction shall be reconsidered but without any type of repayment of previously deducted amounts. This possible change would be contingent on the financial health of the United States being improved to the point of having a balanced budget or the deficit being substantially reduced. Unfortunately, that pronouncement will be determined by the United States Congress.

The number of people affected by the deductions will be substantial. The total figure may exceed 150 million. There should be no waivers nor exceptions to the stipulated percentage deductions. That may be difficult to achieve because anytime politicians are involved, they look for the easiest way out or a politically-correct answer. They like to select groups for favoritism because often those groups vote similarly to what the politicians desire. What politicians should realize is that a declaration stating "no exceptions" to the deduction percentage or for particular people is the most expedient way forward. "No Exceptions" is plain and simple.

This sacrifice for the country starts at the top with the President of the United States and ends with the army private experiencing his first day of basic training. These two job slots happen to be federal jobs, but all government workers and pensioners will be included. Again, this deduction includes federal, state, and local government. For the month of August, 2015, federal, state, and local government combined had approximately 21,995,000 employees.

The same percentage deductions will include all citizens collecting Social Security (SS) and disability payments. That number has been estimated at 59,545,343.

It is not unusual to hear comments or stories about some senior citizens being barely able to survive on only Social Security payments. That is understandable with the current cost of housing, food, and utilities. Today, more so than in the past, people recognize Social Security alone will not be enough money to live on in most areas. Unfortunately, the policy of offering "no exceptions" to proposed deductions from government checks will affect people differently. Many will feel additional hardship.

However, there's one possible stipulation that would affect Social Security recipients. That being ... an earlier end to the 5 percent deduction from their government checks. Since citizens paid their own earned money into Social Security over their working lives, this possible alteration seems appropriate. Because of it, the deduction would cease at an exact future date. An end-time of one or two years should be determined in the beginning.

The deduction from Social Security checks, even if capped at one or two years, will yield a bonus to the Social Security Administration and most Social Security recipients. It's well-known the Social Security system is not in good financial condition because of Federal government mismanagement. Constantly, future dates are estimated and then broadcast as to when Social Security will run out of money. Any reduction in or deduction from Social Security checks, whether for a period of one year or two years, could greatly extend the "run-out-of-money" date for Social Security. The run-out-of-money problem would then be solved for a period of time or at least for the near future. That would be great, but it does depend on exactly what happens with deducted funds. Those funds would need to be funneled back into or remain available to Social Security for future Social Security recipients. That is somewhat different than the use of funds deducted from all other government checks. Recipients of Social Security checks would be affected exactly as all government workers and retirees in that 5 percent is deducted from their checks. All government checks participate with deductions that benefit the nation. The difference is deductions from regular government pay and retirement checks directly benefit the Federal deficit or national security needs and the deductions from Social Security checks directly benefit the Social Security system, which indirectly benefits the nation by helping solve the ongoing Social Security deficit problem. The benefit for current Social Security recipients would be twofold: 1) They will experience the privilege of helping the nation's financial problem, at some sacrifice, and 2) They will benefit from Social Security being solvent for a longer time into the future. That benefits all citizens—those collecting Social Security and those still paying into Social Security. Those who become deceased during the one or two years of deductions leave with only the satisfaction of knowing they participated in saving Social Security and the United States from financial ruin.

Earlier in this chapter, government retirement was mentioned, but the following information refers to the "amount paid" on many government pensions. Millions of former government workers are receiving lucrative pensions, and many worked far fewer years than the average worker in the private sector. Many are receiving two government pensions, and some even receive Social Security payments as well. The best way to demonstrate how lucrative some pensions have become is by listing examples excerpted from articles.

Following are details on three retired government workers from *Daily Kos*:

ARTICLE FOUND AT: www.dailykos.com/story/2013/2/17/1187925/-Bankrupting-US-Government-Pensions

ARTICLE WRITTEN BY: porico (as marked)

DATE: FEBRUARY 18, 2013

TITLE: BANKRUPTING US: Government Pensions

> *All of the social justice we want to promote, money we want to spend on society, is threatened by the government pensions that Federal, State*

and Local employees have acquired for themselves. It is laughably easy for one of the existing government workers with a defined-benefit scheme to receive well over $1,000,000 in retirement benefits. Retiring with a defined government pension is like having over $1,000,000 in the bank on the date of your retirement.

The average American worker can only dream about such a possibility.

The "Greatest Generation" and "Baby Boomer" government employees are going to bankrupt us with their pensions.

Here are three anecdotes that illustrate this.

Case #1 – The government lawyer

My Dad retired at age 55 from the Federal Govt with 30 years service. That was 35 years ago. He was a GS-14 lawyer.

He died at age 75. My 80 year old Mom is still receiving benefits to the tune of over $40,000 a year, plus health insurance, so let's say that is an even $50K. So far, in today's dollars, they have received 35 x 50K, or $1.75 million dollars. That is right, $1,750,000 in benefits.

Case #2 – The Assistant Town Manager

My next door neighbor has North Carolina Municipal Employee Pension benefits. He is 60, and retired after 30 years. He will receive $47,000 a year, plus health insurance, so let's call that $60,000 a year. If he lives for 20 years, that is $1,200,000. Oh, and he is double-dipping, working again for the city as a contractor.

Case #3 – The 42 year-old military "retiree"

My buddy retired at age 42 from the Army as a Lieutenant Colonel. He is making about $3500 a month as a retiree. Plus health care. So, let's say his $42,000, plus health care is worth $50,000. He is likely to live to 80. 38 years- $1,700,000 in the benefits.

The following paragraph and several descriptive sentences taken out of context are from an article titled "Mauldin Economics" in the newsletter *Thoughts from the Frontline.*

ARTICLE FOUND AT: www.mauldineconomics.com/frontlinethoughts/how-not-to-run-a-pension-proofing

ARTICLE WRITTEN BY: John Mauldin

DATE: FEBRUARY 13, 2013

TITLE: How Not to Run a Pension

For all the focus on the unfunded liabilities of Social Security and Medicare, there is another unfunded crisis brewing, and this one is in your own back yard. It's coming to you even if you live outside the US; it

just might take a little longer to get there. I wrote ten years ago that state and local pension funds might be underfunded by as much as $2 trillion. It turns out that I was being overly optimistic. New government research suggests that the figure might be as high as $3 trillion. But what if you take into account that retirees are living longer? Oh my. The problems are not universal—some cities and states will do fine, while others are already in deep kimchee. But it's a big problem and getting worse.

This sad story continues just below with mention of two higher cost states and their particular retirement pensions. The examples given may be extreme compared to the average government retirement package, but they do indicate government retirement pensions are considerably higher or more lucrative than pensions for similar work in private sector. Thus, the overall government retirement program's cost is excessive.

It's almost too easy to pick on California and Illinois, but I am going to do it anyway in order to create a teaching moment. Plus, this sorry tale will make us think about the nature of the social contract and the fabric of our society. It would also be funny if it were not so serious.

Other related information mentioned within the same article, "How Not to Run a Pension," was quoted from the *Wall Street Journal* and *Daily Kos* and continues just below:

Let's start with a few paragraphs that appeared in the Wall Street Journal. Carl Demaio writes this week:

Consider California, where just 10 individual pensioners will cash $50 million in pension checks from state and local governments over the next 25 years. Already, some 30,000 retired California government employees pull in pensions higher than $100,000 a year. One retired librarian in San Diego receives a $234,000 annual pension. Beach lifeguards in Orange County are retiring at age 51 with $108,000 annual pensions plus health-care benefits.

Note that those benefits are cost-of-living-adjusted. But the problem is not just in California, it is nationwide.

A 2011 study by the Congressional Research Service pegged the combined liabilities faced by state and local pension funds at over $3 trillion. That is more than all the bonded debt officially listed on state and local balance sheets combined.

The majority of regular American citizens have little knowledge of the mess their cities and states are in concerning government worker pensions. That's too bad because they're going to get the final bill for all those "successful-for-somebody" labor negotiations. When the government negotiators and the government workers (probably their union representatives) sat down to hammer out a wage and pension agreement … perhaps they should have consulted the citizens who would end up paying for the agreed upon … "lousy-agreement." Often, after finalizing lousy-agreements, the negotiators for both sides have their picture taken while shaking hands, smiling, and laughing. The laughter fades sooner than the ink. And the citizens end up paying too much. In some cases … much too much.

Interesting information from the same article continues:

> *Another study by the Congressional Budget Office comes to the same general conclusion….*

> *I must admit, it is fascinating to Google "California pension problems." You can spend hours swept up in the sheer scandal of it all. Hundreds of state employees who are managers and who theoretically get no overtime are allowed to work second jobs in their departments and get paid for them….*

Regular citizens … did you catch the part about some state employees being allowed to work two jobs in the same office during the same workday and be paid for each? Wouldn't that mean two pensions as well? If that is happening … it's even better for certain employees than regular double-dipping.

Continuing with government pension information from the same "How Not to Run a Pension" article:

> *California public sector employees now earn approximately 30 percent more for doing the same jobs as workers in the private sector….*

> *"Double dipping" is my personal favorite of the scams that are being run. Why not retire with your $100,000 pension and then take another job and earn another $100,000 pension?…*

> *Illinois has a $33 billion state budget—and five pension funds that are officially underfunded by almost $100 billion….*

> *Yes, there are the 28 Illinois state troopers who retired at 51 and draw over $100,000 a year. And the politicians get eye-popping amounts, but their retirement fund is underfunded by 74 percent….*

> *Ingram is in charge of Illinois' biggest pension fund, called the Teachers Retirement System. With $52 billion in unfunded liabilities, it's arguably worse off than any state pension fund in Illinois—which is saying something, considering Illinois has the worst-funded pensions in the country.*

There must be laws to prevent what appears to be, at least on the surface, ridicules labor agreements or, at the very least, hardly-workable labor agreements.

If no sensible laws are available for guidance, perhaps regular common sense should be mentioned during labor negotiations.

A Chicago newspaper provides some insight into a recent labor law dispute that was seeking to alleviate pension problems. Information follows:

ARTICLE FOUND AT: www.chicagotribune.com/news/opinion/commentary/ct-chicago-pension-reform-rita-novak-supreme-court--unions-perspec-0811-jm--20150810-story.html

ARTICLE WRITTEN BY: John Schmidt

DATE: AUGUST 10, 2015

TITLE: How WILL Chicago's Retirees Get Paid When the Pension Funds Dry Up?

> *Cook County Circuit Judge Rita Novak's decision last month to throw out the law reforming two city of Chicago pension plans does not answer a central question: How will retired city workers get paid when the pension funds run out of money?*
>
> *I say "when," not "if." Novak acknowledged the undisputed fact that under the law, without the reforms she threw out, the two pension funds will run out of money in 10 and 14 years, respectively.*
>
> *She said that doesn't matter because the Illinois Constitution prohibits any impairment or diminishing of pension benefits....*

New York has a similarly worded constitution. The United States also has a constitution. The US Constitution has Amendments. Perhaps New York and Illinois' constitutions need amendments.

The paragraphs, sentences, and descriptions quoted above came from different researchers, but they all point to two overwhelming problems with many government pension programs. It's obvious many are underfunded. That will lead to a financial disaster, and it could happen at any time. The second problem is also obvious. The amount of money promised and the amount paid out is too generous when compared to private pensions. How did that happen?

Government unions or groups of government workers often threaten politicians directly or indirectly, and the politicians run from the problem. Try to imagine the atmosphere when city garbage workers tell the city council or the mayor they'll let the garbage pile up on the streets for weeks. When that happens, and it does happen, the citizens phone politicians, screaming about the mess. Every day, TV media proudly covers the garbage scene. People see the garbage. People smell the garbage, and they all fear the rats will show up.

Someday, they'll figure out the rats were there first. They negotiated the asinine labor agreements.

Other worker groups use similar tactics. Teacher unions use kids in the same way garbage workers use garbage. Teachers strike, kids pile up on street. Police officers use the blue flu. Call in sick … less citizen protection and less speeding ticket money for the city treasury.

Politicians worried about reelection cave in to unreasonable and unmaintainable worker demands. Does this always happen? No. But it does happen often, and now the cost in most government departments is unmanageable. That has to change. The fastest and most equitable way to control current costs, lessen future costs, and improve government financial deficits is to implement deductions as previously suggested. Namely, to enforce an across-the-board cut or reduction in all government issued pay and pension checks in the amount of 5 percent under and 10 percent over $100,000 annually.

Politicians need to ingest more calcium and borrow some commonsense from business. Costs too high? Then reduce costs or go out of business.

Government welfare paychecks are little different than government pension or work paychecks. The funds come from the same place. Taxpayers.

Many welfare checks are too generous, considering what little effort recipients exhibit to help support themselves. Too generous and too soon … can be said about many government paychecks for labor and pension benefits, but long-term welfare is in a class by itself.

Welfare recipients are a large group of people collecting some kind of government check or benefit that's paid in different ways such as rent direct to landlord. Welfare recipients should participate in the financial sacrifice just like all government workers, pensioners, military personnel, and Social Security recipients.

It should be noted that some welfare payments include money to spend in general, plus payments for food, rent, utilities, phone, transportation, and other services such as health care. All of these types of payments would receive the same 5 percent deduction as any and all government checks paid-out for labor, pensions, or other services. All forms of welfare should be included. This will be a difficult task to sort through and may not be efficiently feasible in certain programs such as "free-phones." Easier to understand might be welfare rent payments to a landlord. Gross rent might be stipulated at $800 for a two-bedroom apartment. Landlord receives check from government entity for $760 and balance of $40 from welfare tenant. The split varies with recipients' other income. Yes, welfare recipients often have other income. After the proposed change of requiring all government check-receivers to share in "saving the United States from financial collapse," there would be a 5 percent deduction from the $760 government check. The landlord would receive a check for $722. The welfare tenant would then be required to tender to the landlord the rent balance due of $40 + $38 or $78. This situation would still be very lucrative for welfare recipients, who would also have the satisfaction of knowing they're helping their country.

The number of welfare recipients in the United States has been estimated at 110,489,000. That rather large number is from statisticbrain.com. Information follows below:

INFORMATION FOUND AT: www.statisticbrain.com/welfare-statistics/

SOURCE: US DEPARTMENT of Health and Human Services, US Department of Commerce, CATO Institute

DATE OF RESEARCH: January 23, 2016

TITLE: WELFARE STATISTICS

The following paragraph explains some aspects of welfare and how and when it started. Some interesting statistics are also included:

> *Welfare is the organized public or private social services for the assistance of disadvantaged groups. Aid could include general Welfare payments, health care through Medicaid, food stamps, special payments for pregnant women and young mothers, and federal and state housing benefits. The Welfare system in the United States began in the 1930's, during the Great Depression. Opponents of Welfare argue that it affects work incentives.*

There are many different reforms, improvements, and qualifications need-ed in the US welfare system. The changes can be called anything the politicians like, but changes are needed now. Those changes will be outlined later in this book under "Dirty Dozen #8 Welfare."

"Welfare Statistics" continues:

> *Total number of Americans on welfare – 110,489,000*
>
> *Total number of Americans on food stamps – 41,700,000*
>
> *Total number of Americans on unemployment insurance – 10,200,000*
>
> *Percent of the US population on welfare – 35.4 percent*
>
> *Total government spending on welfare annually (not including food stamps or unemployment) - $131,900,000,000.*

The total figure of Americans on welfare is maddeningly shocking. How many of the 110 million could work? Maybe 100 million? No, but how about half? Could 55 million work at something? Probably.

A gentlemen, who was not acting, once said, "*We should measure welfare success by how many people leave welfare, not by how many are added.*" Ronald Reagan, President of the United States (1911-2004).

All welfare checks should have a 5 percent deduction so welfare recipients can feel upbeat as regular contributors in the effort to save their country from financial disaster. As with other "government check receivers," if their annual checks are over the threshold of $100,000, then the 10 percent deduction would apply.

Here are additional statistics from "Welfare Statistics":

> *Total amount of money you can make monthly and still receive welfare - $1000.*
>
> *Total Number of US States where Welfare pays more than an $8 per hour job – 39.*
>
> *Number of US States where Welfare pays more than a $12 per hour job – 6.*
>
> *Number of US States where Welfare pays more than the average salary of a US teacher – 8.*

Yes, the last statistic mentioning teachers was quoted correctly. It's hard to believe, but government authorities are involved. They approve pay for teachers and they approve pay for welfare recipients.

Tens of millions of Americans are working hard every day for wages between $11.11 and $17.50 per hour. And they may pay taxes out of those wages.

Tens of millions of Americans "not working at all" receive free money equal to wages between $11.11 and $17.50 per hour. And they may not pay taxes on the money.

It's unknown which group, workers or non-workers, might complain most about a 5 percent pay deduction to help the US reverse its death spiral financial debt. What figure would equal a "death spiral"? About $20,000,000,000,000.

Related information from "Welfare Statistics" follows:

> *Top 10 Hourly Wage Equivalent Welfare States in U.S.*
>
> *Hawaii - $17.50 – Hourly Wage Equivalent*
>
> *Alaska - $15.48*
>
> *Massachusetts - $14.66*
>
> *Connecticut - $14.23*
>
> *Washington, D.C. - $13.99*
>
> *New York - $13.13*
>
> *New Jersey - $12.55*
>
> *Rhode Island - $12.55*
>
> *California - $11.59*
>
> *Virginia - $11.11 – Hourly Wage Equivalent*

The dollar figures above, $11.11 up to $17.50, represent the equivalent hourly wage of either a worker working at work or a welfare recipient watching television at home. Same income for each in the particular state listed. Actually, it's very probable watching TV ... "nets" a greater amount.

There is some choice involved in this curious situation. Why do some citizens choose to obtain their hourly income from working versus others from watching television? Some of those answers are easy and some are not. But falling asleep in front of a TV should not pay much. A small 5 percent deduction from welfare payments is a small start to alleviating this chronic problem.

Additional statistics from "Statistics Brain":

> *Food Stamp (SNAP) Statistics:*
>
> *Year 2014 – 46,670,373 – Total Number of People Receiving Food Stamps –*
>
> *$133.85 – Average Monthly Benefit*
>
> *Year 2000 – 17,194,000 – $76.62*
>
> *Year 1969 – 2,878,000 – $6.63*

Several "in-between" years of statistics from statisticbrain.com have been left out. But the pattern is similar and shows an increase in the number of recipients and the monthly benefit over the years going forward.

The reason for the difference in total number of food stamp recipients, as quoted above (41,700,000 vs. 46,670,373), is unknown. It could be a difference in count date, but it seems more likely a difference in referring to the number of American citizens receiving food stamps versus the number of all residents receiving food stamps.

The number of 110 million Americans on welfare seems extremely high. Too high for America unless the state is truly king and keeper.

Further research reveals similar information:

ARTICLE FOUND AT: www.cnsnews.com/commentary/terence-p-jeffery/354-percent-109631000-welfare

ARTICLE WRITTEN BY: Terence P. Jeffery

DATE: AUGUST 20, 2014

TITLE: THE 35.4 Percent: 109,631,000 on Welfare

> *109,631,000 Americans lived in households that received benefits from one or more federally funded "means-tested programs"—also known as welfare—as of the fourth quarter of 2012, according to data released Tuesday by the Census Bureau.*
>
> *The Census Bureau has not yet reported how many were on welfare in 2013 or the first two quarters of 2014.*

But the 109,631,000 living in households taking federal welfare benefits as of the end of 2012, according to the Census Bureau, equaled 35.4 percent of all 309,467,000 people living in the United States at that time.

When those receiving benefits from non-means-tested federal programs—such as Social Security, Medicare, unemployment and veterans benefits—were added to those taking welfare benefits, it turned out that 153,323,000 people were getting federal benefits of some type at the end of 2012.

Subtract the 3,297,000 who were receiving veterans' benefits from the total, and that leaves 150,026,000 people receiving non-veterans' benefits.

The 153,323,000 total benefit-takers at the end of 2012, said the Census Bureau, equaled 49.5 percent of the population. The 150,026,000 taking benefits other than veterans' benefits equaled about 48.5 percent of the population.

When America re-elected President Barack Obama in 2012, we had not quite reached the point where more than half the country was taking benefits from the federal government.

It is a reasonable bet, however, that with the implementation of Obamacare—with its provisions expanding Medicaid and providing health-insurance subsidies to people earning up to 400 percent of poverty—that if we have not already surpassed that point (not counting those getting veterans benefits) we soon will.

Got it? You've just been enlightened as to one of the reasons the United States is $20,000,000,000,000 in debt. Too many people not working. Too many people living on welfare. Workers earn money and pay taxes. Welfare recipients collect money and don't pay taxes.

A 5 percent deduction from welfare recipients is minimal. It will help cure the deficit just as any government worker's 5 and 10 percent deduction from a paycheck.

The number of state and local employees is approximately 19,257,000 and has been previously included with the 2,738,000 federal employees. Occupations range from the part-time school janitor to the president of a major state university and include all the usual workers you see around any city such as garbage collectors, police, firemen, and typical county services, including the court system.

The government—politicians—got the country into this financial mess. The government and its employees should be first in line to get the country out. This deduction program should be efficient, expedient, equitable, and above all, *simple*. It should start and end with two words: no exceptions.

All people affected by this necessary reduction in payments will loudly suggest many good and valid reasons why they or their work category should be excluded from any deduction from their checks. Their arguments will be noteworthy. Nevertheless, the sacrifice asked of all, a 5 and 10 percent pay deduction, must be implemented and then enforced. No exceptions.

Chapter Two

What Is US Foreign Aid—
World Welfare or Something Else?

ASK ANYBODY AND he'll say Foreign Aid (FA) is good, bad, necessary, ridiculous, expensive, worthy, important, or a bribe. FA does bring up lots of questions from lots of people. Who actually pays for FA? Can we, the citizens, afford it? What kinds of FA are there? How often does the US receive FA? What do foreigners do with our FA? Why, exactly, do we give out FA? Is the aid always used properly? What does that mean? There are at least ten more questions. Maybe a thousand.

Most answers to these questions are quite simple. But if you want detailed answers or a fuller understanding of foreign aid, you'd have to read the equivalent of a book on each FA handout. Most information is available, but it rarely answers the suspicious questions. A poor country might receive a considerable amount of FA. It may be obvious some citizens of that poor country are starving or dying of thirst. But in that country's capital city on any given day, there may be a political assembly or holiday celebration taking place when a black Mercedes limousine stops and the king or top general gets out to say a few words. Did foreign aid, directly or indirectly, pay for that expensive limo? The exact answer to that is generally unknown. It's also one of the reasons many US citizens complain about FA. Money and certain types of aid are fungible. The aid may be financial. The aid may be food for people, but the food could be traded for money, which would then be used to enrich Mercedes-Benz of Germany. Does that type of thing happen very often? Or something similar? Probably. Too often, there is some shifting around of aid, and the wealthy end up wealthier.

It has happened that US aid is used in such a way that the end result is the obtainment of "equipment from China." The equipment could be purchased or traded for in some manner involving US aid. When the people in the poor country see the equipment, it reads "Made in China." It does not say "Foreign Aid from the United States just for you."

Is the United States satisfied that FA is always being used for the exact purposes it was intended? Would the United States still be satisfied if it knew Chinese equipment was being purchased with US aid money, or goods, but used in such a way as to benefit poor people? Or would the US government be upset that the United States' name may be an unknown factor to the average person in the recipient country?

Such is the world of foreign aid. And the United States participates more than any other country. Is that a mistake?

Generally, there are five common types of federal aid, as described in the *Intelligent Economist*:

INFORMATION FOUND AT: https://www.intelligenteconomist.com/types-of-foreign-aid/

WRITTEN BY: PRATEEK Agarwal

TITLE: TYPES OF Foreign Aid

> *BILATERAL AID is assistance given by a government directly to the government of another country. It is when the capital flows from a developed nation to a developing nation. It is often directed according to strategic political considerations as well as humanitarian ones....*
>
> *MULTILATERAL AID is assistance provided by many governments who pool funds to international organizations like the World Bank, United Nations and International Monetary Fund that are then used to reduce poverty in developing nations....*
>
> *TIED AID is one of the types of foreign aid that must be spent in the country providing the aid (the donor country) or in a group of selected countries. A developed country will provide a bilateral loan or grant to a developing country, but mandate that the money be spent on goods or services produced in the selected country.*
>
> *PROJECT AID is one of the types of foreign aid where the funds are used to finance a particular project, such as a school or a hospital.*
>
> *MILITARY AID ... is never altruistic and such aid usually requires said nation to either buy arms or defense contracts directly from the USA....*

Foreign aid has many advantages and disadvantages depending on its type and purposes. Obviously, one party pays it and the other enjoys it or is generally thankful. Although, either, neither, or both can benefit.

The following paragraph and several sentences from Wikipedia.org are taken out of context but help with understanding our foreign aid system: INFORMATION FOUND AT: https://en.wikipedia.org/wiki/Aid

TITLE: AID

> *Aid may serve one or more functions: it may give a signal of dip lomatic approval, or to strengthen a military ally, to reward a government for behavior desired by the donor, to extend the donor's cultural influence, to provide infrastructure needed by the donor for resource extraction from the recipient country, or to gain other kinds of commercial access. Humanitarian and altruistic purposes are at least partly responsible for the giving of aid.*

The previous paragraph is very important. Its last sentence calmly mentions aid for humanitarian and altruistic purposes as being accurate reasoning or, at least, partially accurate. Is that good enough? Should authorities be taking money from US citizens and spending it without exactness? The following information must be considered:

> *Humanitarian aid is argued to often not reach those who are intended to receive it. For example, a report composed by the World Bank in 2006 stated that an estimated half of the funds donated towards health programs in sub-Saharan Africa did not reach the clinics and hospitals. Money is paid out to fake accounts, prices are increased for transport or warehousing, and drugs are sold to the black market. Another example is in Ghana, where approximately 80 percent of donations do not go towards their intended purposes. This type of corruption only adds to the criticism of aid, as it is not helping those who need it, and may be adding to the problem.*

Is it any wonder that American taxpayers have curious questions about footing the bill for foreign aid arranged or approved by politicians?

> *James Shikwati, a Kenyan economist, has argued that foreign aid causes harm to the recipient nations, specifically because aid is distributed by local politicians, finances the creation of corrupt government such as that led by Dr. Frederick Chiluba in Zambia bureaucracies, and hollows out the local economy. In an interview in Germany's Der Spiegel magazine, Shikwati uses the example of food aid delivered to Kenya in the form of a shipment of corn from America. Portions of the corn may be diverted by corrupt politicians to their own tribes, or sold on the black market at prices that undercut local food producers. Similarly, Kenyan recipients of donated Western clothing will not buy clothing from local tailors, putting the tailors out of business. In an episode of 20/20, John Stossel demonstrated the existence of secret*

government bank accounts which concealed foreign aid money destined for private purposes.

If you look at foreign aid over many years you can see that what often starts in a positive atmosphere of good intentions ends up in a troubling situation for the United States. The following was taken from an article in *Encyclopedia Britannica*:

INFORMATION FOUND AT: https://www.britannica.com/topic/foreign-aid
ARTICLE WRITTEN BY: Victoria Williams
TITLE: FOREIGN AID

> *Since the end of the Cold War, the United States has furnished financial aid as part of peacemaking or peacekeeping initiatives in the Balkans, Northern Ireland, and parts of Africa. Foreign aid also has been used to promote smooth transitions to democracy and capital in former communist countries, most notably Russia.*

Russia? US foreign aid for peacemaking and smooth transitions to democracy are heavenly expectations and they look great on paper. But how's all that working out for us here on earth? Russia recently took over Crimea, has troops threatening the Ukraine, and is currently involved in a military alliance with Syria and Iran, including having its military aircraft in Syria.

The above article entitled "Aid" begins with "Aid may serve one or more functions." That statement tells a realistic story about foreign aid. But it should be read with a suspicious mind. Some of those functions could be interpreted quite differently. Consider the phrase, "to reward a government for behavior desired by the donor." Isn't that similar to a pay-off?

Could that mean we actually get something in return for our foreign aid besides just a good feeling? If that is the case, should it be considered good?

When a country distributes billions of dollars in FA, it should get something in return. Something more than a good feeling. Something that is tangible might even be better. Most countries have something that can be used to benefit the United States. If that sounds harsh or a little selfish, then the following three statements should be considered before passing judgement:

1.   The US taxpayer doesn't vote directly to approve any type of FA.

2.   The US government takes money from its citizens in the form of taxes and part of that money is used for FA.

3.   It's not excess money that is passed out as aid. It's tax money, borrowed money, or money from the basement printer.

The government taxes citizens. The government borrows billions every day to continue functioning as a country. The government also prints money whenever it feels like it. Printing money and putting it into circulation has an effect on the value of material goods owned by US citizens. More dollars means dollars are worth less ... relative to all material goods. When dollars are worth less, sellers demand more dollars for goods. Buyers, being the citizens, must pay more for goods. The country is $20,000,000,000,000 in debt; being bankrupt, why give away any money or goods to anybody, especially foreign governments that excessively smile upon US visits?

If the United States can give away money (foreign aid) it really doesn't have, then maybe the recipient nations can give away, back to the US, some assets they really don't need or use.

There's another way to look at US involvement as a donor nation. If, in fact, some countries misuse US foreign aid in any way, then the US should not be involved with those countries in any way. Certainly not with free FA.

When you look at the entire foreign aid scene (some might say "scheme"), plenty of reasons exist to eliminate part of or nearly all aid transactions. That will not be easy to accomplish. FA recipients, in too many cases, are very good at working the system to obtain favorable results. If that sounds as if it's a business for them, that's because ... it is a business for them and a lot of other people. That would be the case on *both* sides of foreign aid transactions.

There may be a way to determine the real need for and the validity of most US foreign aid transactions. It's a bit unusual, but it would be simple to initiate.

1. Implement an immediate reduction of 50 percent or one half the value amount of each and every individual FA transaction.

2. After aid reduction, take a step back. Listen and observe as to what is being said and what actions are being taken by those involved with aid in the recipient country and the donor country. Both.

3. Determine from observation, investigation, and common sense which FA transactions must—not could or should—but *must* go forward and which should cease completely. Those aid transactions that continue need to be equitable for both the recipient and the donor. Not a free handout to the recipient and not a complete giveaway from the donor country. Namely, the United States.

What will this accomplish? It would save a lot of money for American taxpayers. Most Americans would welcome any reduction in foreign aid. It also puts recipient countries on notice to be completely transparent about aid.

A few countries may reject any inquiries from us and turn to another donor. That's fine. They probably weren't trustworthy friends anyway. Fewer aid recipients would also slightly improve the US financial deficit.

Other recipient countries may be very responsive and do their best to demonstrate a worthy need. They may offer something beneficial to the United States in order to continue the flow of aid. If not, the United States should insist the foreign aid transaction needs to be equitable.

If an aid recipient country has copper in the ground and it doesn't need it or mine it, why not trade mineral rights to the United States in exchange for aid? The US government can sell the mining rights to a US company using that money received for any necessary purpose or to replace the taxpayer funds it uses for FA. The mining company, initiating copper extraction, can then employee Americans and citizens of the host country. Everybody comes out ahead. That may already happen to some extent, but why not make it near mandatory for FA? It could be a good deal for both countries instead of a one-way street. It doesn't have to be copper mining. It could be any of a hundred different transactions.

It should be noted that the dollar amount of aid that could be saved is not a huge figure, but every little bit helps toward the goal of moving US finances in the right direction. That small but wise change in handling the foreign-aid-business represents an annual savings of between 15 and 20 billion dollars. The immediate savings would come with the 50 percent reduction in aid. If the United States received something tangible, directly or indirectly, such as specific mineral rights in return, the cost factor of foreign aid could be calculated even more favorably. It may not even be a cost but something closer to the plus side. *That should be the goal.*

The following "foreign aid" dollar figures and their "claimed area of use" are provided by foreignassistance.gov. The figures represent what was planned for Fiscal Year (FY) 2016:

INFORMATION FOUND AT: beta.foreignassistance.gov

> *PEACE and SECURITY - $8.8 Billion*
>
> *ECONOMIC DEVELOPMENT - $3.7 Billion*
>
> *HEALTH - $8.8 Billion*
>
> *MULTI-SECTOR - $0.0*
>
> *DEMOCRACY, HUMAN RIGHTS and GOVERNANCE - $2.9 Billion*
>
> *PROGRAM MANAGEMENT - $1.7 Billion*
>
> *HUMANITARIAN ASSISTANCE - $5.6 Billion*
>
> *EDUCATION and SOCIAL SERVICES - $1.2 Billion*
>
> *ENVIRONMENT - $1.0 Billion*
>
> *$33.7 Billion planned in Foreign Aid for FY 2016*

Please note the category "MULTI-SECTOR" is indicated at $0.00. The four years prior it averaged $3.9 billion each year. A similar dollar figure may or may not be added shortly.

Continuing with the aid explanation from foreignassistance.gov:

> *Today, the U.S. manages foreign assistance programs in more than a 100 countries around the world through the efforts of over 20 different U.S. Government agencies. These investments further America's foreign policy interests on issues ranging from expanding free markets, combating extremism, ensuring stable democracies, and addressing the root causes of poverty, while simultaneously fostering global good will.*

Investments? Or money pits? That whole paragraph is just … tremendous. No, a better word would be stupendous. If for no other reason than, in the dictionary, it's right above … stupid.

When the government says it uses over twenty agencies to manage foreign aid, what does that mean to the average citizen? Nothing. He doesn't know anything about it. But the twenty agencies … these agencies mean everything to a select group of government workers. They employ thousands or tens of thousands of people in high-paid government jobs. For many, the job spans an entire career that ends happily with early retirement. It sounds absurd, but government workers are employed in order to "take taxpayer money and pass it to others" around the world. Of course, they're being directed by the leaders of US foreign aid policy. It's that aid policy that needs to be questioned.

American taxpayers should always get something in return for their money being spent on aid. Cutting the aid dollar outflow in half is at least a start.

In the last sentence of the foreignassistance.gov paragraph above, certain claims are suspect. Claims such as … "expanding free markets." That could mean aid recipients buying Chinese products. "Combating extremism" sounds good, but it doesn't seem to be working in today's world. "Ensuring stable democracies" is a waste of time and "addressing root causes of poverty" often appears to make middle-men very wealthy.

Many in upper government and the leaders of agencies involved with foreign aid will argue "aid is only about 1 percent of the US budget." That may be correct, but the United States is basically bankrupt. The US government borrows money daily. The constant over-spending must stop, and changing how foreign aid is doled out will help a lot.

It would be best if all foreign aid would cease until the United States, at the very least, balances its budget. If eliminating all aid can't be accomplished today, then reducing aid by 50 percent tomorrow is a very good start. That amounts to nearly $20 billion dollars in annual savings for US taxpayers.

Any continuing foreign aid after a 50 percent reduction should be offset by the United States receiving an equitable exchange for that aid. Open minds should make that easy.

Chapter Three

Adjustment for All Government-Paid Subsidies

WHAT ARE SUBSIDIES? More importantly, what are government subsidies and are they really necessary? Do they often interfere with common sense supply and demand? Do taxpayers get their money's worth? Is there a huge cost involved with arranging handouts known as subsidies?

The following is a definition of a "subsidy," along with other comments from Investopedia.

INFORMATION FOUND AT: www.investopedia.com/terms/s/subsidy.asp

TITLE: SUBSIDY

A subsidy is a benefit given by the government to groups or individuals usually in the form of cash payment or tax reduction.

The subsidy is usually given to remove some type of burden and is often considered to be in the interest of the public.

Politics play an important part in subsidization. In general, the left is more in favor of having subsidized industries, while the right feels that industry should stand on its own without public funds.

There are many forms of subsidies given out by the government, including welfare payments, housing loans, student loans and farm subsidies. For example, if a domestic industry, like farming, is struggling to survive in a highly competitive international industry with low prices, a government may give cash subsidies to farms so that they can sell at the low market price but still achieve financial gain.

This all sounds very good on paper, and it certainly helps some people, namely recipients of subsidies, by putting extra money in their pockets, but that extra money comes from taxpayers. American citizens, at least the taxpayers, may or may not benefit from the estimated lower prices or other suggested benefits. Some estimates or suggestions turn out to be ... incorrect guesses.

One type of subsidy, often in the form of a grant, that's well-known and in big demand all the time is the federal "student loan." Often, the interest-rate or other terms are subsidized by the government. Often the loan is forgiven for some odd reason such as the career path of student. This all pushes student loans toward that all too familiar category of money taken from the taxpayer and given to a non-taxpayer. One may grimace while the other grins.

The last point to make about student loan cash concerns the last collector of that cash: the university. It almost appears as if the university raises tuition fees just as higher-ceiling amounts of student loans are being doled out. The student appears to be a middle man. Money flow: taxpayer to government to student to university to endowment fund. Will the flow ever reverse? Never.

Grants from the government are similar to subsidies in as much as the money originates from taxpayer funds. Grants are usually for a defined purpose and do not have to be repaid. Subsidies usually offset some business operating cost. This chapter deals mostly with business subsidies but not exclusively.

It may be that government subsidies have reached the point where they have become too relied upon in particular industries, including farming. Subsidies may be replacing hard work and innovation on the farm and in other industries as well. America, at least in the past, rose to the top of world leadership through hard work and innovation. Not handouts.

Taxpayers should ask themselves: Have subsidies contributed to the curtailment of American leadership in industry or in any other way? If the answer is yes or probably yes, then it's the subsidies that should be curtailed.

Some interesting comments on government farm subsidies follow:

ARTICLE FOUND AT: www.economist.com/news/united-states/21643191-crop-prices-fall-farmers-grow-subsidies-instead-milking-taxpayers

ARTICLE WRITTEN BY: *The Economist*

DATE: FEBRUARY 14, 2015

TITLE: MILKING TAXPAYERS: as crop prices fall, farmers grow subsidies instead

> To this day, to be treated as a farmer in America doesn't necessarily require you to grow any crops. According to the Government Accountability Office, between 2007 and 2011 Uncle Sam paid some $3m in subsidies to 2300 farms where no crop of any sort was grown.

The $3m figure mentioned above is not a lot of money as government spending goes, but the idea of taxpayers paying an individual or a group for not growing anything should be eliminated. It would be interesting to know exactly how the government determines whether someone is "not" growing a particular crop on his land. It wouldn't be a surprise to learn the government operates a department with branch locations solely to police the 2300 non-farmers not growing crops. If such a department includes satellite offices, 100 employees, and travel expenses, the costs would exceed the $3 million handout by $10 or $20 million.

The government could save $20 million by not giving out $3 million.

Other unusual aspects of the government farm subsidy are found in the following two comments from the same *The Economist* article, "Milking Taxpayers."

> *Between 2008 and 2012, $10.6m was paid to farmers who had been dead for "over a year."*

It should be noted the article says "over a year," not "in the year of death" or "within a year." Again, not a terribly large subsidy expense figure, but the end result of "farm subsidies" can be quite extravagant as the next comment demonstrates.

> *American farm subsidies are egregiously expensive, harvesting $20 billion a year from taxpayer's pockets. Most of the money goes to big, rich farmers producing stable commodities such as corn and soybeans in states such as Iowa.*

Again, what is not mentioned is a dollar-cost figure for operating the government departments that hand out taxpayer's money. Would it surprise anybody if the cost to hand out $20 billion in farm subsidy money was equal to or even more than the subsidy amount?

It should also be noted that there are other individuals besides "farmers" collecting farm subsidies, and their occupations are quite diverse. Some very interesting farm subsidy collectors include: very high level federal politicians, rock stars, many large corporations, relatives of owners of major corporations, Wall Street banker types, and other assorted billionaires. Does that make sense?

If the US government is living on borrowed money, isn't it time to eliminate questionable financing or handouts in as many areas as possible?

Earlier, this book stressed that all citizens will need to sacrifice in some way to save the country. Eliminating farm subsidies is ripe with possibilities.

Eliminating "all subsidies" should be another early step toward reaching a balanced budget. Reaching a balanced budget and reducing the deficit indirectly benefits all citizens. Many will not understand that reasoning, and that's unfortunate, but the alternative is still higher deficits and eventual financial collapse. Most citizens will fully understand that as soon as it happens.

Government subsidies appear to have originated a long time ago. Today, they're well entrenched in the government-corporate relationship.

Regular taxpayers, although most don't realize it, pay the bill for subsidies. Supposedly, these same citizens reap the promised benefits. Unfortunately, in many scenarios, the actual benefits to citizens are very difficult to determine.

Readers should ask themselves: Exactly who would know whether large corporate subsidies actually benefit regular taxpaying citizens?

It's doubtful any corporate personnel collecting subsidy money would ever admit citizens may not be benefiting because of subsidy money. And the government workers who earn their living in the subsidy department probably wouldn't risk their livelihood by suggesting there's little, if any, citizen benefit. Workers don't want their departments cut back. If anything, they prefer expansion. More subsidies. More room for promotion.

Politicians usually prefer not to make waves in any established programs, and they receive plenty of donations from corporate friends. Corporate friends with money ... and subsidies. Politicians with donations. A partnership?

The United States hasn't always had a formal government subsidy program, but some form of energy subsidy has been around a long time. Maybe too long.

Information below suggests subsidies are about as old as the country itself:

ARTICLE FOUND AT: cen.acs.org/articles/89/i51/Long-History-US-Energy-Subsidies.html (Chemical & Engineering News)

ARTICLE WRITTEN BY: Jeff Johnson

DATE: DECEMBER 19, 2011

TITLE: LONG HISTORY of U.S. Energy Subsidies

> *Report shows centuries of government support for fossil fuels....*
>
> *U.S. government subsidies for energy are as old as the nation....*
>
> *U.S. government energy incentives back to 1789, when leaders of the new nation slapped a tariff on the sale of British coal slipped into U.S. ports as ships ballast.*

Farming—another thriving industry collecting subsidies that needs to be scrutinized by government scrutinizers. Since there are no scrutinizers except within those exact government departments that actually stay in business in order to hand out subsidies, **farm subsidies should just be eliminated.**

Government subsidy programs will be difficult to eliminate in the United States, but our overall financial survival warrants maximum effort to curtail spending on all subsidies. Farming should be near the top of the long list.

The Cato Institute, a think-tank that appears to be a libertarian and conservative-leaning organization, provides thought-provoking articles about farm subsidies.

The article below makes good sense. Farm subsidies do not.

ARTICLE FOUND AT: www.downsizinggovernment.org/agriculture/subsidies

ARTICLE WRITTEN BY: Chris Edwards

DATE: OCTOBER 7, 2016

TITLE: AGRICULTURAL SUBSIDIES

The U.S. Department of Agriculture (USDA) spends $25 billion or more a year on subsidies for farm businesses. The particular amount each year depends on the market prices of crops and other factors. Most agricultural subsidies go to farmers of a handful of major crops, including wheat, corn, soybeans, rice, and cotton. Roughly a million farmers and landowners receive federal subsidies, but the payments are heavily tilted toward the largest producers.

Some farm subsidy programs counter adverse fluctuations in prices, revenues, and production. Other programs subsidize farmers' conservation efforts, insurance coverage, product marketing, export sales, research and development, and other activities. Agriculture is no riskier than many other industries, yet the government has created a uniquely large welfare system for farmers.

Farm subsidies are costly to taxpayers, they distort the economy, and they harm the environment. Subsidies induce farmers to overproduce, which pushes down prices and creates political demands for more subsidies. And subsidies hinder farmers from innovating, cutting costs, diversifying their land use, and taking other actions needed to prosper in the competitive global economy.

Brief History of Farm Subsidies

Agriculture has long attracted federal government support. One of the first subsidy programs for agriculture was the Morrill Act of 1862, which established the land-grant colleges. That was followed by the Hatch Act of 1887, which funded agricultural research, and by the Smith-Lever Act of 1914, which funded agricultural education. In 1916 the Federal Farm Loan Act created cooperative "land banks" to provide loans to farmers. That developed into today's Farm Credit System, which is a government-sponsored financial system with more than $250 billion in assets....

Many farm programs were enacted during the 1930s, beginning with the Agricultural Adjustment Act of 1933....

Between the 1940s and the 1980s, Congress occasionally considered farm reforms, usually when commodity prices were high, but then reverted to subsidy expansions when prices were lower....

Agricultural subsidies have never made economic sense, but farmer interests have held sway in Congress. While farmers represent just a small share of the population today, the farm lobby is as strong as ever.... As a result, Congress routinely votes to expand the USDA's budget....

Congress did enact pro-market reforms under the "Freedom to Farm" law of 1996. The law allowed farmers greater flexibility in planting and moved toward reliance on market supply and demand. But Congress reversed course in the late 1990s and passed a series of supplemental farm subsidy bills. As a result, subsidies that were expected to cost $47 billion over the seven years of the 1996 law ended up costing $121 billion.

In 2002 Congress enacted a farm bill that further reversed the 1996 reforms. The law increased projected subsidy payments, added new crops to the subsidy rolls, and created a new price guarantee scheme called the "countercyclical" program. The 2002 law increased projected subsidy payments by 74 percent over 10 years.

In 2008 Congress overrode a presidential veto to enact farm legislation that added further subsidies....

In 2014 Congress passed another huge farm bill....

When the 2014 farm bill was passed, supporters claimed that it would save taxpayer money, but the opposite has happened....

All of these subsidies ensure that farm incomes are much higher than the incomes of most Americans. Farm programs are welfare for the well-to-do, and they induce overproduction, inflate land prices, and harm the environment. They should be ended, and American farmers should stand on their own two feet in the marketplace.

Eight Types of Farm Subsidy

1. Insurance. Crop insurance run by the USDA's Risk Management Agency has become the largest farm program with annual outlays of about $8 billion. Subsidized insurance protects against various business risks, such as adverse weather, low production, and low revenues....

Congress channels the largest portion of farm subsidies through the insurance program in order to obscure the identities of the wealthy recipients. Under prior farm programs, news stories often identified the millionaires receiving farm subsidies, which was embarrassing to Congress....

2. Agricultural Risk Coverage (ARC). This program pays subsidies to farmers if their revenue per acre, or alternately their county's revenue per acre, falls below a benchmark or guaranteed level. Generally, the lower are prices and revenues, the larger are the subsidies paid. More than 20 crops are covered, from wheat and corn to chickpeas and mustard. ARC subsidies fluctuate, but they will be about $7 billion in 2016.

3. Price Loss Coverage (PLC). *This program pays subsidies to farmers based on the average national price of each particular crop compared to the crop's reference price. The larger the fall in a crop's price below its reference price, the larger the payout to farmers. PLC subsidies also cover more than 20 crops. PLC subsidies fluctuate, but they will be about $2 billion in 2016.*

4. Conservation Programs. *The USDA runs numerous farm conservation programs, which cost taxpayers more than $5 billion a year....*

5. Marketing Loans. *This is a price guarantee program that began in the New Deal era. The original idea was to give farmers a loan at harvest time so that they could hold their crops to sell at a higher price later on. But the program has evolved into just another subsidy program that delivers higher payments to farmers when market prices are low. These subsidies will cost about $400 million in 2016.*

6. Disaster Aid. *The government operates various disaster aid programs for different types of farmers, from wheat growers, to livestock producers, to orchard operators. In addition to permanent disaster programs, Congress sometimes distributes additional aid after adverse events. Disaster and supplemental aid costs about $1 to $2 billion a year.*

7. Marketing and Export Promotion. *The Agriculture Marketing Service spends about $1.2 billion a year on farm and food promotion activities. The Foreign Agricultural Service spends about $1.4 billion a year on a range of activities, including marketing U.S. farm and food products abroad through 93 foreign offices.*

8. Research and Other Support. *Most American industries fund their own research and development, but the government employs thousands of scientists and other experts to aid the agriculture industry. The USDA spends about $3 billion a year on agriculture and food research at more than 100 locations....*

Six Reasons to Repeal Farm Subsidies

1. Subsidies Redistribute Wealth Upwards. *Farm subsidies transfer the earnings of taxpayers to well-off farm businesses and landowners. USDA data show that farm incomes have soared far above average U.S. incomes. In 2014 the average income of farm households was $134,164, which was 77 percent higher than the $75,738 average of all U.S.*

households. The same year, the median income of farm households was $81,637, which was 52 percent higher than the U.S. median of $53,657.

While politicians claim to support small farmers, most farm subsidies go to the largest farms. Economist Vincent Smith ("A Midterm Review of the 2014 Farm Bill," American Enterprise Institute, February 2016) found that the largest 15 percent of farm businesses receive more than 85 percent of all farm subsidies. Over the years, many billionaires have received farm subsidies because they were the owners of farmland. Prior to the 2014 farm bill, the Environmental Working Group (EWG) found that 50 people on the Forbes 400 list of the wealthiest Americans received farm subsidies. The new farm bill channels the largest share of subsidies through insurance companies, making it hard to determine the identities of recipients....

2. Subsidies Damage the Economy. The extent of government coddling and micromanagement of the agriculture industry is unique. In most industries, market prices balance supply and demand, profits steer investment, businesses take risks, and entrepreneurs innovate to improve quality and reduce costs. Those market mechanisms are blunted and undermined in U.S. agriculture ...

3. Subsidies Are Prone to Scandal. Like all government subsidy programs, farm programs are subject to both bureaucratic waste and recipient fraud. One problem is that some farm subsidies are paid improperly as farmers create business structures to get around legal subsidy limits. Another problem is that Congress and the USDA distribute disaster payments in a careless manner, with payments going to farmers who do not need them. EWG found another boondoggle called the "prevented planting" program, which covers farmers for losses if conditions during a season prevent them from planting some areas. The group found that billions of dollars have been paid to farmers who would not normally have planted the areas included in their USDA claims.

Perhaps the biggest scandal with regard to farm subsidies is that congressional agriculture committees include members who are active farmers and farmland owners....

4. Subsidies Undermine U.S. Trade Relations. Global stability and U.S. security are enhanced when less developed countries achieve economic growth. America can help by encouraging poor nations to adopt free markets and expand their international trade. However, U.S. and European farm subsidies and agricultural import barriers undermine progress on achieving open trading relationships....

Trade liberalization would boost the exports of U.S. goods that are competitive on world markets, including many agricultural products, but U.S. farm subsidies and protections stand in the way of that goal.

5. Subsidies Harm the Environment. *Federal farm policies damage the natural environment in numerous ways. Subsidies cause overproduction, which draws lower quality farmlands into active production. As a result, areas that might otherwise have been used for parks, forests, grasslands, and wetlands get locked into less efficient agricultural use.*

Subsidies are also thought to induce the excessive use of fertilizers and pesticides. Producers on marginal lands that have poorer soils and climates tend to use more fertilizers and pesticides, which can cause water contamination problems....

6. Agriculture Would Thrive without Subsidies. *If U.S. farm subsidies were ended and agricultural markets deregulated, farming would change. Different crops would be planted, land usage would change, and some farm businesses would contract while others would expand. But a stronger and more innovative industry would emerge that had greater resilience to market fluctuations. Private insurance, other financial tools, and diversification would help cover risks, as they do in other industries.*

Another point to consider is that farm households today are better able to deal with market fluctuations than in the past. Many farm households earn the bulk of their income from nonfarm sources, which creates financial stability. USDA data show that about three-quarters of farm household income comes from off-farm sources.

An interesting example of farmers prospering without subsidies is New Zealand. In 1984 that nation ended its farm subsidies, which was a bold stroke because it is four times more dependent on farming than is the United States. The changes were initially met with resistance, but New Zealand farm productivity, profitability, and output have risen since the reforms. New Zealand farmers cut costs, diversified land use, sought nonfarm income, and developed niche markets such as kiwi fruit.

Conclusions

The distortions caused by federal farm policies have long been recognized. In 1932 a member of Congress noted that the Agriculture Department spent "hundreds of millions a year to stimulate the production of farm products by every method, from irrigating waste lands to loaning and even giving money to the farmers, and simultaneously advising them that there is no adequate market for their crops, and that they should restrict production." That sort of folly is similar eight decades later, except that subsidies have increased from "hundreds of millions" to tens of billions of dollars.

> *The Federated Farmers of New Zealand argues that New Zealand's experience "thoroughly debunked the myth that the farming sector cannot prosper without government subsidies." That myth needs to be debunked in the United States as well.*

Again, the article above makes good sense. Farm subsidies do not.

Government subsidies for farming are extensive, but farming is not the only area where subsidies need to be downsized or eliminated. Other industries soak up billions in tax subsidies. **It appears both "obtaining and granting" subsidies has each become an industry in itself.** If thousands of employees in hundreds of government departments do nothing but shuffle applications for subsidies or arrange for payout of subsidies, it's questionable if taxpaying citizens ever get their money's worth. Corporate offices work the reverse. More money please.

The following quotation comes from thinkprogress.org. Think Progress (TP) appears to be a left-leaning or progressive organization that comments on several subjects, including climate, economy, and health.

ARTICLE FOUND AT: thinkprogress.org/climate/2011/11/13/366988/over-half-of-all-us-tax-subsidies-go-to-four-industries-guess-which-ones/

ARTICLE WRITTEN BY: Joe Romm

DATE: NOVEMBER 13, 2011

TITLE: OVER HALF of All U.S. Tax Subsidies Go to Four Industries. Guess Which Ones?

> *Citizens for Tax Justice has analyzed corporate tax rates from 2008 to 2010. The report examines over half of the Fortune 500 companies.*

> *Perhaps it's no surprise that the richest industries get the biggest subsidies, starting with finance and Big Energy. That's how the 1 percent operate.*

> *Notably, 56 percent of the total tax subsidies went to just four industries: financial, utilities, tele-communications, and oil, gas & pipelines.*

Additional information can be found in the "Cheat Sheet" article below:

ARTICLE FOUND AT: www.cheatsheet.com/business/high-on-the-hog-the-top-8-corporate-welfare-recipients.html/?a=viewall

ARTICLE WRITTEN BY: Sam Becker

DATE: MAY 7, 2015

TITLE: THE 8 Biggest Corporate Welfare Recipients in America

> *In the U.S., it is rather commonplace to see welfare recipients demonized, people on food stamps ostracized, and anyone on any form of public assistance is often made to feel guilty that they need help. They are called lazy and incompetent, with little regard for circumstance or economic*

hardship. Sure, there are some people that take advantage of the system. But there are millions that desperately need help, and social welfare programs are the only thing standing between them and poverty.

That demonization seems to shift, however, when it comes to giving assistance to big business. According to The Cato Institute, corporate welfare handouts shot all the way up to $92 billion as of 2002. Most of those subsidies were secured by companies in industries like energy—which are some of the most profitable entities in the history of the world. As one writer at Forbes points out, cutting these huge subsidies would be a great way to help balance the national budget, but it is never put into action, and much less even considered.

The above article goes on to quote data from a subsidy tracking group named "Good Jobs First." Their data reports the top states receiving corporate subsidies. But another article from "Good Jobs First" is being inserted here which will also serve to identify lucrative subsidy states:

ARTICLE FOUND AT: www.goodjobsfirst.org

ARTICLE WRITTEN BY: David Nicklaus

DATE: MAY 11, 2016

TITLE: DESPITE SUBSIDIES, St. Louis Retailing Is a No-Growth Sector

Area governments have provided more than $2 billion of subsidies to retail developers in the past couple of decades, but metropolitan St. Louis has the same number of people working in retailing as it did in 1990.

New York and Washington were the top two states for handing out corporate subsidies, with New York alone topping more than $20 billion across nearly 69,000 individual handouts.

Twenty billion dollars is a lot of taxpayer money for corporate subsidies in just one state. But the interesting figure is the 69,000 "individual handouts." "Individual" refers to individual companies. How many employees, how much time and paperwork does it take for corporate and government personnel to put together 69,000 individual handouts? The costs for arranging subsidies must be in the billions for corporations and the government. Do corporations care? Doubtful. They receive the subsidy and the cost to obtain it is probably a tax write-off. Does the government care? That's doubtful, too. It's just taxpayer money.

Continuing on from the same "Cheat Sheet" article shows where most corporate subsidy dollars end up:

The data also shows that roughly 75 percent of disclosed subsidy dollars have gone to 965 big companies. The total known value of subsidies across the country came out at an estimated $110 billion, although it's likely more.

From its data, Good Jobs First was able to identify the top 100 recipients of corporate subsidies, dominated by transportation and natural resource companies. Here are the top eight companies from that list, and the total known amount in subsidies they are receiving.

Boeing - $13.18 Billion

Alcoa - $5.64 Billion

Intel - $3.87 Billion

General Motors - $3.58 Billion

Ford - $2.52 Billion

Fiat Chrysler - $2.06 Billion

Royal Dutch Shell - $2.04 Billion

Nike - $2.03 Billion

Boeing has become the king of corporate handouts....

The average US taxpayer may or may not recognize the names above. But everyone should recognize all of them because part of our hard-earned dollars went to subsidize those corporations.

In still another article about US corporate welfare, it appears big banks have consistently won the annual subsidy lottery. Another lottery funded by American taxpayers. Who else would it be?

Article found at: bloombergview.com

Article written by: Bloomberg View Editorial Board

Date: February 20, 2013

Title: Why Should Taxpayers Give Big Banks $83 Billion a Year?

The top five banks—JP Morgan, Bank of America Corp., Citigroup Inc., Wells Fargo & co. and Goldman Sachs Group Inc.—account for $64 billion of the total subsidy, an amount roughly equal to their typical annual profits. In other words, the banks occupying the commanding heights of the U.S. financial industry—with almost $9 trillion in assets, more than half the size of the U.S. economy—would just about break even in the absence of corporate welfare. In large part, the profits they report are essentially transfers from taxpayers to their shareholders.

Neither bank executives nor shareholders have much incentive to change the situation. On the contrary, the financial industry spends hundreds of millions of dollars every election cycle on campaign do-nations and lobbying, much of which is aimed at maintaining the subsidy. The result is a bloated financial sector and recurring credit gluts. Left unchecked, the superbanks could ultimately require bail-outs that exceed the government's resources. Picture a meltdown in which the Treasury is helpless to step in as it did in 2008 and 2009.

A fairly recent report describes another taxpayer financed boondoggle, or at least it's shaping up to be another half-baked energy project.

ARTICLE FOUND AT: www.foxnews.com/politics/2015/10/29/taxpayer-backed-solar-plant-actually-carbon-polluter.html

ARTICLE WRITTEN BY: Jennifer G. Hickey

DATE: NOVEMBER 2, 2015.

TITLE: TAXPAYER-BACKED SOLAR Plant Actually a Carbon polluter

Even as the Obama administration announces another $120 mil-lion in grants to boost solar energy, new reports indicate a center-piece of the administration's green-energy effort is actually a carbon polluter.

Located in Southern California's Mojave Desert, the $2.2 billion Ivanpah Solar Electric Generating System benefited from a $1.6 bil-lion Energy Department loan guarantee, and a $539 million Treasury Department stimulus grant to help pay off the loan.

Yet it is producing carbon emissions at nearly twice the amount that compels power plants and companies to participate in the state's cap-and-trade program....

The above figure of $1.6 billion is supported by an Energy Department loan guarantee. That means if the developer fails to pay the loan, for any rea-son, then the American taxpayer will pay it. The $539 million figure is money from the US Treasury Department. A grant. That means the American tax-payer has already paid the debt. It's doubtful the average taxpayer knows this circumstance.

Other problems with Ivanpah exist. A report in *The Desert Sun* relates an unusual problem which appears very important to many people.

ARTICLE FOUND AT: www.desertsun.com/story/tech/science/greenenergy/2015/04/23/ivanpah-solar-plant-bird-deaths/26273353/

ARTICLE WRITTEN BY: James Meier

DATE: APRIL 23, 2015

TITLE: REPORT: IVANPAH Solar Project Kills 3,500 Birds

More than 3,500 birds died during the 377-megawatt Ivanpah solar project's first year of operation, a new report estimates.

If bird deaths are a limiting factor when installing a power plant, shouldn't that be considered early? Shouldn't every developer consider every aspect of every project before final approval, especially when they're using taxpayer money?

Or is it just the opposite? As long as money is available, start something, somewhere…. Hurry before the money changes its mind.

The Ivanpah project, being a solar power system, does not operate at night. That makes sense. But the exact location of Ivanpah is in the sandy desert between two mountain ranges. The weather around these mountains can often produce clouds and wind patterns that may bring dust storms or frequent rain. Clouds or dust particles in the air will reduce the sun needed for solar energy just as darkness does every night.

The Ivanpah location may have not been the most suitable area for such a project. Nevertheless, the project proceeded. Was there a rush to judgment or some financial reason for its site selection?

Subsidy money may be too easy to obtain. If a project is important and necessary and, at the same time, feasible, maybe subsidy money shouldn't be the deciding factor. If the power project makes good sense and the probability of profit is fair, then private money is usually available. **Government subsidies may interfere with good business sense.**

Why must taxpayers, many with good business sense, give part of their hard-earned income to the government to use for a project that actually does exactly the opposite of what it's supposed to do? The Ivanpah project was claimed as necessary because the current power plant produced too many harmful emissions or pollutants. Unfortunately the new, costly Ivanpah replacement power plant gives off double the emissions of the old power plant. Does that make any sense? No. Too often subsidies do not make any sense.

Making good sense or financial sense for any project doesn't seem to be high on the list for deciding whether a project goes forward. It's much more likely to be the availability of money. Your money. From your pocket to some developer's pocket. Often, in the end, after project failure, your pocket's still empty. But some people connected to the whimsical project are able to retire. Often to a resort area. Deep pockets, no doubt.

How many shaky projects like Ivanpah does the government subsidize? The number may be difficult to recognize. You have to watch for early and questioning headlines. And, by then, it's usually too late to make a difference.

When these projects completely fail or just fail to operate as originally intended, such as the Ivanpah Solar System did … who suffers the repercussions? The American taxpayers. Is there a way to stop government subsidy waste? Yes, but only one way.

A well-known example of a complete failure in the energy field is the Solyndra Corporation in Fremont, California. It was going to save everybody money with fancy solar panels. That did not happen, but it's probable that some investors and developers at Solyndra did more than okay financially. Taxpayers and workers at the plant didn't do so well.

On or about May 26, 2010, President Obama toured the Solyndra manufacturing plant touting the benefits of solar energy over other reliable energy sources. Unfortunately for him, his bragging highlights during the plant tour were televised to the American public. The end result is quoted below.

INFORMATION FOUND AT: https://en.wikipedia.org/wiki/Solyndra

TITLE: SOLYNDRA

> Solyndra received a $536 million U.S. Energy Department loan guarantee, the first recipient of a loan guarantee under President Barack Obama's economic stimulus program, the "American Recovery and Reinvestment Act of 2009." Additionally, Solyndra received a $25.1 million tax break from California's Alternative Energy and Advanced Transportation Financing Authority.
>
> Following the bankruptcy, the government was expected to recoup $27 million under the Solyndra restructuring plan, but no money was ever recovered.

If you think about it, there's a major question here. Should the government be in the business of handing out hundreds of millions of taxpayer dollars, collected as necessary taxes from ordinary taxpayers, for risky business deals? Isn't that a "deal" smart business men put together? Is that exactly what happened? Did smart business men smart-talk the government do-gooders into another happy-go-lucky project? Neither side seems to be talking much about the $500 to $600 million in taxpayer money that evaporated in the hot sun.

On or about September 1, 2011, the Solyndra Corporation filed for bankruptcy and approximately 1,100 workers were permanently laid off. The taxpayers lost nearly $600 million because the US government and the California state government chose to hand out large subsidies or issue loan-guarantees to a very questionable corporate gamble. Why would the government do that?

It should be strongly noted that considerable private funds from multiple entities had already been invested in Solyndra. It's unknown whether any of the private funds lost or expended earlier were somehow recouped before, during, or after the government subsidies arrived. If so, then some smart business investors outsmarted the government. How unusual is that?

In as much as government or taxpayer funds are still being used to subsidize hundreds, possibly thousands, of costly green energy projects, isn't it time for "extreme scrutiny" of all proposals requesting a subsidy?

This needed caution goes well beyond just energy projects. All corporate requests for any type of subsidy need thorough investigation and scrutiny.

Admittedly, "extreme scrutiny" of all proposed subsidies would be a difficult and time-consuming task. But isn't that the best way to protect the American taxpayers from subsidy fraud, failure, favoritism, or foolish investment?

Another area of subsidies needs brief mentioning. It's a "touchy" area because it has to do with kids, donations, and government subsidies. At the same time, it has to do with entities that might be sitting on $100 plus million in surplus money and administrators annually collecting millions in salary plus benefits while having their hands stretched out begging for donations from average citizens. *And, please send grant money, too.*

Puzzling, sometimes sad, information from selected comments follows.

INFORMATION FOUND IN book: Makary, Marty. *Unaccountable: What Hospitals Won't Tell You and How Transparency Can Revolutionize Health.* New York: Bloomsbury Press, 2012, p. 129, 131, 132.
SOURCE: GILBERT M. Gaul, "Children's Hospitals Pay Millions to CEOs," Fort Worth Star-Telegram, September 26, 2011.
SOURCE: FORBES.COM, "THE 200 Largest U.S. Charities," November 17, 2010, http://www.forbes.com/lists/2010/14/charity-10_Childrens-Hospital-Boston_CH0036.html.

> *I had heard from pediatricians at one of these hospitals that the institutions do not spend wisely the millions of dollars they raise from small donors in their communities. With one of my research students, I began looking into the finances of these hospitals. In the process, we discovered that some children's hospital CEOs now make over $5 million per year, and some had perks including cars, first class travel, country-club memberships, and special retirement packages worth millions.*

Most of these hospitals are termed "nonprofit" facilities which, to the average citizen, makes the hospital sound deserving of and desperate for money. Money ... so they can maintain services for young patients. Or, at least, that's a typical pitch used when soliciting for donations or grants. Many of these hospitals have "children" in their names and they do specialize in ill children. That name is also beneficial when soliciting for free money from either the government or any donating entity seeking notoriety or tax write-off benefits.

Donations are fine, but sometimes the hospital administrators go too far with fundraising, especially when subsidies are being received. *The objection here concerns subsidies not donations.* Although some use of fundraised money is objectionable, it's the combination of government subsidies, grants, and fundraising efforts that's most bothersome.

> *In one fund-raiser for Children's Hospital Boston (Harvard's children's hospital), children were asked to collect pennies from other children at school. This for an organization that recorded a $111 million surplus that year (2009) as a nonprofit and paid its CEO millions.... Hospital fund-raising is so lucrative that the hospital has 125 full-time fund-raisers—more than the number of primary-care pediatricians there....*
>
> *In 2009, the last year records were available, Texas Children's Hospital recorded a $275 million profit and Children's Hospital of Philadelphia (CHOP) $359 million. That same year, Reuters reported that half of the nation's full-service hospitals weren't even breaking even. Yet CHOP also got a $121 million grant from the government.*

Government grant or subsidy money is originally taxpayer money. Why hand it to CHOP as a $121 million grant when CHOP has a surplus or profit of $359 million? That seems like a prime example of money being taken from the needy and given to the affluent. And, in some ways, it's even worse.

Money from both donations and subsidies may benefit "working adults ... at the hospital" more so than "sick kids ... in the hospital."

Regardless of how any money is used at a hospital it should be remembered that donations are freely given. Subsidies represent money first taken from citizens and then given by government.

As with foreign aid, all subsidies in the US should cease until the federal budget is balanced. Is that possible? Probably not.

Politicians live on donations. The donations come from many sources, including corporations that receive subsidies. Politicians ultimately determine subsidy policy. Thus, politicians are the roadblock to eliminating subsidies.

Different from foreign aid, cutting all subsidies by 50 percent would not easily work. Subsidy dollar amount requests would just increase, perhaps by 100 percent, and government departments handing out subsidies would prefer to stay relevant regardless of the subsidy amount, the subsidy recipient, and even the absolute necessity of reducing government debt.

Many government subsidies interfere with regular supply and demand. More so with corporations than hospitals. "Supply and demand" gives some balance to the functioning marketplace. If cost or price on a product gets too high, buyers tend to buy less of that product. Less purchase of or demand for the product leads to surplus. When that happens, product market price falls; more consumers then purchase the product, which then tends to raise the price. It's sometimes a delicate balancing act. It does not apply to everything, but it should be considered when doling out subsidies. Subsidies can interfere with prices in the marketplace.

Subsidies may also affect competition between similar manufacturers. If one gets a subsidy, the other demands or needs a subsidy. That would apply internationally as well. It's best if the market determines pricing.

Many concerns exist within the government subsidy "business." Subsidies have become a business. The government's not supposed to be in business.

Subsidies have become a racket. The government should not be involved in any kind of racket.

The government should not be handing out subsidies for anything and that especially applies to entities such as corporations, large or small, that are in business to make a profit. When there are profits to be made in business, there's always private investment money available. Private investment money usually requires "extreme scrutiny" of the project or business to assess risk. Risk determines the level and terms of the investment money because personal wealth is involved. That's not exactly the case with government subsidies. The government, or those who hand out subsidy money for the government, use "other people's money." The "other" people are American taxpayers who have no choice in the matter. If they did have a choice, most would say, "No thanks."

Therefore, considering the amount of investment money available, the shakiness of many projects, the frequent appearances of unfair or unnecessary requests, and the nation's massive debt ... all subsidies should cease promptly.

The savings for taxpayers and the US treasury would be in the hundreds of billions of dollars. And as an added bonus, a level and more understandable business playing field.

Chapter Four

Adjustment for the US Prison System

WHEN THE UNITED States has a $20,000,000,000,000 deficit, it seems unfortunate the country must spend a fortune to support a huge prison system. Most people will say there is no choice. Hardened criminals must be locked up for society's protection. Is that always true? Yes. **But is there a way to reduce the cost of incarceration by 50-75 percent? Yes.**

The United States has a prison population of approximately 2 million. Some estimates suggest as many as 2.4 million based on certain criteria. These people are incarcerated in every city and state. There are city and county jails. There are state and federal prisons. Some are fairly dingy and some are almost luxurious. It may be laboriously difficult to know precisely which style serves society best. Although, the cost to society is easily discernible.

Reducing the cost to house 2 million prisoners may appear impossible to the government's Department of Corrections, but there is a simple way to save a lot of money. Anytime the government is involved in a cost-reduction plan, it seems discussion and committee meetings go on forever. The whole process often yields a result that costs more than the hoped for savings. It doesn't have to be that way. A needy partner with experience is the answer. That partner can take control in a short amount of time, leaving the Department of Corrections in an oversight role and better able to assist convicts as they reenter society.

The Obama administration released thousands of convicted drug dealers from prison by claiming the selling of drugs or using drugs is a nonviolent crime. It's as if the government doesn't recognize that many drug users will do anything for drug money, including breaking into houses and committing other serious crimes in order to feed their drug habits. When house break-ins happen, the affected neighborhoods live in fear. It could be any neighborhood, but in some areas, crime has become an everyday way of life. High government officials who make decisions to free criminals usually live in areas not affected much by serious crime. They can also afford elaborate security systems.

The politicians in charge may be desirous of showing some kind of prisoner-compassion or just cutting prison-housing costs, but protecting citizens should come first. Releasing thousands of drug dealers early will save prisoner-housing costs today, but over time, it may cost much more in other ways.

It's widely believed whatever the cost of prisons to society, those costs are necessary. That is generally true, but taxpayers might choose an alternative if they had a choice.

Many taxpayers are familiar with the cost of a hotel room or the cost of a year in college. Without stipulating any figures for hotel or college costs, it's probable most taxpayers would say hotel rooms are expensive but at least guests are provided a nice bed, television, air conditioning, pool, and a fitness room. The same can be said about a college dormitory room. Actually, unbeknownst to most taxpayers, the exact same amenities are provided in many prisons.

The same taxpaying citizens who know something about costs in a hotel or a college dormitory room know much less about everyday prison costs.

Many studies have been completed that identify a fairly wide range in both annual and per day costs to house inmates. As would be expected, big city prison costs are higher than smaller county jails. Perhaps the simplest way for regular citizens to understand prison-housing costs is to compare those costs to a nightly hotel room, but calculated on an annual basis. If a hotel guest paid $100 per night and stayed for one year without any discount, the annual cost would be $36,500.

The following information demonstrates to regular, law-abiding citizens just how ridiculous prison costs can be in many cities and states. **There has to be a more economical way to deal with the people who steal from us.**
ARTICLE FOUND AT: www.nytimes.com/2013/08/24/nyregion/citys-annual-cost-per-inmate-is-nearly-168000-study-says.html?_r=0
ARTICLE WRITTEN BY: Marc Santora
DATE: AUGUST 23, 2013
TITLE: CITY'S ANNUAL Cost Per Inmate Is $168,000, Study Finds

New York City is an expensive place to live for just about everyone, including prisoners.

The city paid $167,731 to feed, house and guard each inmate last year, according to a study the Independent Budget Office released this week.

That number is specific to New York City and is probably the highest in the nation. Other states' average prison costs are shown below as collected in an in-depth study by VERA Institute of Justice.

Source of study: www.vera.org

The study was released on or about February 29, 2012. The following figures are examples of different states' "average annual cost per inmate."

New York - $60,076 - average annual cost per inmate
New Jersey - $54,865
California - $47,421
Illinois - $38,268
Utah - $29,349
Ohio - $25,814
Texas - $21,390
Idaho - $19,545
Oklahoma - $18,467

This sampling of annual costs gives readers an idea of prison-housing costs in several states, from the top of the scale to several at the low end. Typically, costs in any big city are higher than statewide averages, as demonstrated earlier with New York City at $168,000 per inmate annually. That annual figure converts to $460 per day.

Other costs paid by American taxpayers and concerning most prisoners are not evident to the average person. Some of those costs are mentioned in the following VERA Institute of Justice report.

This study is an analysis of the direct cost of state prisons to taxpayers. VERA did not attempt to measure every cost that arises as a result of incarceration.

When a person is in prison, taxpayers may incur additional—or indirect—costs, such as the costs of social services, child welfare, and education, for example. For the most part, these indirect costs are borne by government agencies other than the department of corrections. They are not included in the calculations presented here, however.

Incarcerated men and women also bear economic and social costs associated with prison—as do their families and communities.

It should be noted the VERA study reports on "state" prisoner costs. It appears its study excludes federal prisons.

The following information cites both state and federal prisoner costs.

INFORMATION FOUND AT: https://en.wikipedia.org/wiki/Incarceration_in-the-United-States

INFORMATION FROM: WIKIPEDIA, the free encyclopedia
TITLE: INCARCERATION IN the United States

> *Judicial, police, and corrections costs totaled $212 billion in 2011 according to the U.S. Census Bureau....*

> *In 2014, among facilities operated by the Federal Bureau of Prisons, the average costs of incarceration for federal inmates in the fiscal year 2014 was $30,619.85. The average annual cost to confine an inmate in a residential re-entry center was $28,999.25.*

> *State prisons averaged $31,286 per inmate in 2010 according to Vera Institute of Justice study. It ranged from $14,603 in Kentucky to $60,076 in New York.*

Several different reports show costs to maintain prisoners. The annual dollar amounts vary substantially because one prison may be quite different from another in size, location, function, and the number of prisoners. Information found in *The Washington Post* refers to prison-cost depending on the level of security.

ARTICLE FOUND AT: https://www.washingtonpost.com/blogs/wonkbook/wp/2013/08/13/wonkbook-11-facts-about-americas-prison-population

ARTICLE WRITTEN BY: Ezra Klein and Evan Soltas

DATE: AUGUST 13, 2013

TITLE: WONKBOOK: 11 Facts about America's Prison Population

> *The number of federal inmates has quadrupled since 1980 and now surpasses 218,000. Housing all those prisoners isn't cheap: The average minimum-security inmate now costs $21,000 a year, while the average high-security inmate costs $33,000 a year.*

Several variables need to be considered when determining the cost of prison. Some are easy, such as: state prison vs. federal, city vs. county, or minimum security vs. high security vs. supermax security prison. On the low end, the cost may be as little as $15,000 annually per inmate. On the high end, usually for supermax prison facilities, the cost may exceed $75,000 annually.

Other variables exist, but they are more difficult to ascertain. Information presented at GOLOCAL Prov News refers to inmate cost figures for the state of Rhode Island. Other states may be similar, more or less in cost. Rhode Island information follows below:

ARTICLE FOUND AT: www.golocalprov.com/news/maximum-security-prisoners-cost-rhode-island-200k-each-per-year

ARTICLE WRITTEN BY: Dan McGowen, GoLocal/Prov News Editor

DATE: DECEMBER 13, 2012

TITLE: MAXIMUM SECURITY Prisoners Cost RI up to $200k Each Per Year

> *Rhode Island's most violent criminals cost the state up to $200,000 each in the 2012 fiscal year, according to cost-per-offender data released by the Department of Corrections (DOC).*
>
> *Those figures include salary and benefits for department staff, operating expenses, medical costs, probation and parole costs and home confinement expenses along with overhead and capital costs, Tracey Zeckhausen, a spokesperson for the department, said....*
>
> *All told, the department spent just under $190 million during 2012 fiscal year, and for the High Security Center in Cranston (which houses inmates who require close custody, control, and security and has an average population of 90), the cost-per-offender was $200,215. For the average 632 prisoners in maximum security prison, the cost was $62,730 each. For those in minimum security, the cost was $47,679 per offender.*
>
> *The figures come as the Rhode Island Brotherhood of Correctional Officers (RIBCO) fights to make the public aware of decisions made that allow violent criminals back on the streets far in advance of their expected release dates as long as they behave while in confinement.*

It's safe to conclude the American taxpayer is paying a lot of money to support a lot of bad people. Isn't it time our elected government finds a better way to save prison costs besides putting convicted criminals back on the street?

Is there a way to save money on prison housing costs and continue to house prisoners? Yes, there is a way. There's a way to save as much as 50 percent or even more on the housing cost for many prisoners.

The estimate of 50 percent savings may sound ridiculous and impossible. But that's only because such a program would call for "drastic change" in where we house prisoners. There would also need to be a change in the current mindset of many people, especially politicians and some government labor unions. It should be stressed to those with major concerns that saving money in state and federal government operations is mandatory to avoid major financial problems. It's not only the federal government that needs to cut spending but most states, too.

Should the federal government along with state governments devise a plan to house long-term prisoners in a foreign country? Could that be the perfect answer to help save regular taxpayers from rising taxes?

If such a program, utilizing a "foreign country for maintaining US prisoners," sounds too far-fetched to the average citizen, then he or she should refrain from shopping for merchandise of any kind. This country already uses foreign country goods for just about everything every single day. You can't shop at any large US hardware or department store without increasing business profits for some foreign country—usually China.

This country has about 2 million inmates. Using the following approximate figures, it appears regular taxpayers could save an impressive amount of money if all inmates were housed offshore. But it doesn't have to be all. It could be, at least initially, those hard-core, long-term prisoners. Generally, they are the most dangerous and most costly to secure.

Using an average cost of $30,000 per year for each inmate with an estimated 2 million prisoners, the annual cost is $60 billion. That works out to about $82 per day for each inmate. The $82 figure is probably low, but especially low in certain states and any supermax prison where many per day rates are between $100 and $120. As an extreme example, New York City per day rates are $460.

Most construction projects and many manufactured products go through the "bidding" process. The low bidder often gets the job. Often, bidding is a normal business requirement, and it takes place every day. In the United States, many construction projects have been bid by foreign companies, and after submitting the lowest bid, those companies proceeded to build the project.

Why not use the bidding process for housing prisoners?

The government would simply announce an open bid, seeking a foreign country to provide housing along with regular every day care for an estimated number of prisoners. Certain guidelines and minimal requirements would be stipulated. Let the host country maneuver its bid to obtain the work.

The host country would be in complete charge of all prison operations. Basic necessities need to be provided such as: food, water, and shelter. Quite basic compared to some American prisons that may include team sports, modern facilities, air conditioning, an exercise weight room, libraries, extensive television programming, a swimming pool, individual cells, and other unnecessary conveniences.

Prison should be punishment for crimes against society, not the equivalent of living on a college campus.

Beyond basic necessities, there should be regular health care such as medical assistance or counseling as needed. Any facility would be expected to provide toilets, showers, mattresses, and three American-type meals a day.

Any negotiated agreement for prison housing would be between the US government and the host country's government. State and local governments would abide by the agreement or not participate.

Several stipulations concerning the prisoners would be incorporated into any agreement between the two governments.

1. No US female prisoners will be included for prison housing.

2. No torture or extremely harsh treatment.

3. All prisoner housing payments to host country paid monthly.

4. All past payments for any prisoner that becomes escapee are forfeited.

5. All transportation of prisoners will be provided by US military.

6. All transportation from arrival airport to prison provided by host country.

7. All transportation would be in large groups not individual or several.

8. All prisoner deaths shall be immediately reported along with debriefing.

9. A small US team consisting of prison and medical personnel would visit the host prison unannounced twice a year for inspection and prisoner interviews. Any complaints or recommendations would be noted, acted upon when appropriate, and remedied when possible.

10. Cell phone provided prisoner one hour per week.

The stipulations above are in general terms and may be expanded in order to ensure a reasonable prison operation. The dual goal: The host country adequately fulfills a service for the US government, and the US government saves taxpayer money.

It should be remembered ... prison is punishment for crime. It's best for society if prisoners being released have a strong desire never to go back. Prison life should be a tough life. It's probable ... most prison experiences away from the US would be thought of as a tough life. But isn't that the way it should be remembered by any convict released from jail? They don't want to go back to prison and society should not want them to go back.

Just the idea of foreign prisons may be an added benefit for our society. Besides saving taxpayer's money with prisoners being confined offshore, those same prisoners may try harder to stay within the law. The recidivism rate in the United States is too high. Anything that improves that rate should be welcomed by all.

The following recidivism information from the National Institute of Justice tells a frightening story.

INFORMATION FOUND AT: www.nij.gov/topics/corrections/recidivism/pages/
welcome.aspx

INFORMATION FROM: NATIONAL Institute of Justice

DATE: JUNE 17, 2014

HEADING: RECIDIVISM

> *Recidivism is one of the most fundamental concepts in criminal justice. It refers to a person's relapse into criminal behavior…. Recidivism is measured by criminal acts that resulted in rearrest, reconviction or return to prison during a three-year period following the prisoner's release.*

Additional information follows:

INFORMATION FOUND AT: www.nij.gov/topics/corrections/recidivism/pages /
welcome.aspx

INFORMATION FROM: NATIONAL Institute of Justice

HEADING: NATIONAL STATISTICS on Recidivism

STUDY REPORT BY: Matthew R. Durose, Alexia D. Cooper, Howard N. Snyder

TITLE: RECIDIVISM OF Prisoners Released in 30 States in 2005: Patterns from 2005 to 2010

DATE MODIFIED: JUNE 17, 2014

> *Bureau of Justice Statistics studies have found high rates of recidivism among released prisoners. One study tracked 404,638 prisoners in 30 states after their release from prison in 2005.*
>
> *The researchers found that:*
>
> - *Within three years of release, about two-thirds (67.6 percent) of released prisoners were rearrested.*
> - *Within five years of release, about three-quarters (76.6 percent) of released prisoners were rearrested.*
> - *Of those prisoners who were rearrested, more than half (56.7 percent) were arrested by the end of the first year.*

The information above about repeat offenders coupled with the United States having 2 million prisoners suggests we have an expensive "ongoing problem." If housing prisoners offshore saves taxpayers money and there are secondary benefits such as reduced recidivism, then an offshore program should be initiated immediately.

A United States government offshore prison program could save taxpayers a minimum of $35 billion every year. It could be considerably more.

The following paragraph suggests first steps for such a program to get started in a limited time. Any mention of the usual formation of political committees and endless debate will not be covered here.

After a description of the desired plan for housing prisoners offshore is complete, other nations would be contacted. First, several targeted countries, then as many more as is needed. Interested countries could voice their thoughts in private meetings in order to arrive at a plan that satisfies our requirements and meets our overall objectives.

The main objective for the United States should be to find a suitable host country or countries that can successfully and humanely house many thousands of prisoners at $25 or less per day for each inmate.

That may sound impossible or even ridiculous to some readers, but consider the following made-up example: Today, a foreign country may be already holding 10,000 prisoners of its own and it is being paid nothing. Tomorrow, that same country could replace its own 10,000 prisoners with 10,000 US prisoners and be paid $250,000 each and every day. **Such a business arrangement should attract rapid attention.**

Another more obvious thought would be concerning labor rates in some foreign countries. If a country's labor rates for prison personnel happen to be $2.00 per hour, it should be easy to understand how $25.00 per day per prisoner may be a bargain for both countries.

Another very loose comparison is: If the average cost of a prisoner in the United States is $82 per day and a prison guard is paid $20 per hour, that is a 4:1 ratio. Using the same ratio, it's easy to see a $2 guard equates with $8 per day. Maybe $25 per day paid to a foreign host country is too high.

It should be noted that all prisoners transferred from the US to a foreign country facility should have a minimum of eighteen months remaining on their sentences. Those inmates with less than eighteen months would remain in US prisons. Flexibility on the eighteen-month period may be required.

Removing long-term prisoners to a foreign country location will significantly reduce the population in most prisons. Those short-term prisoners remaining can be transferred to another facility for cost-efficiency. Some older facilities may be closed or sold for commercial use.

Other facilities may continue to be a prison, but a prison designed solely for the final six months of an inmate's term. In this regard, the prison's function would shift drastically to be much more of an instructional facility.

It's possible the six months will need to be "to be determined" (TBD). Some prison personnel would shift away from guard duty to an instructional position, assisting prisoners to be successfully released into society. Prisoners would finish their last six months, but with a dynamic change in atmosphere, along with intense instruction in many areas that will benefit them upon release. This "change in atmosphere" may include anything from ordering their own food selection from a tasty prison menu to learning significant new job skills. This program would be quite extensive with the overall objective being to reduce the recidivism rate, thereby reducing future costs to all taxpayers.

The Six Month Release Program (SMRP) will not only be extensive, but it'll be all important for convicts, society, and the taxpayers who pay taxes to support incarceration. The SMRP will be greatly beneficial to some inmates but less so for others. Some inmates may be quite educated and serving relatively short sentences. The society they return to may be the same society from which they left. Other inmates have been locked up for decades. For them, society will be more than just different. It'll be a different world entirely. Six months will be a short time for them to catch up, so additional help may be necessary. The list below is an example of what will take place during the SMRP. Many subjects, from A to Z, will be basic but still important for anybody to get along well in everyday society. Much of the instruction will center on obtaining, working, and keeping a job in a very competitive world. Here is a typical six-month program curriculum:

A.) Recent news catchup

B.) Language cleanup

C.) Personal hygiene

D.) Manners

E.) Personality

F.) Personal interaction

G.) Promptness

H.) Preparing a meal

I.) Cell phone use

J.) Agreement/disagreement, debate/argue, compromise

K.) The Boss is the Boss

L.) City transportation

M.) Bank/checking account

N.) Family/friends/foes

O.) Reading/writing/arithmetic/computers

P.) Cross-section of basic/typical job introduction

Q.) Job preference/probabilities

R.) Interview dos and don'ts

S.) Interview practice, testing, recommendations

T.) Cross-section of jobs/training

U.) Job selection/knowledge, training, on the job training

V.) Jobs available on Internet/newspaper/signs

W.) Jobs-what they require/preparation to fit requirements

X.) Jobs-probation period/promotion

Y.) Job success/living nearby/apt/relatives/come-go prison bed

Z.) Vocational school possibilities

Some readers will think the alphabet list above is nothing more than a wish list. They are generally correct. It is a wish list, so it will need to be adjusted and expanded. It won't easily apply to some inmates, but others will benefit a lot from it. For some, the program will be a lifesaver because they'll find careers and contribute to society as their neighbors do now. Others will need practice.

Some large employers may agree to work with the SMRP. This relationship could go beyond guidance or instruction at the prison and include future employment that benefits many of those who complete the program.

If 2 million prisoners are in the United States, it can be expected as many as half or 1 million are being held longer than eighteen months, making them eligible to be housed in a foreign country under the suggested plan. Many of these prisoners are held in maximum security. It's probable these higher security prisoners have a higher cost factor than the average of $82 per day. Thus, additional savings are possible for the United States.

This program to house US prisoners in a foreign country will hear plenty of criticism and objections. That's always the case, but still the US government needs to address its overspending in every possible way.

One glaring problem that must be addressed would be the lack of family visitors to any foreign prison. These visits are often the highlight of the month for individual prisoners. One remedy that might suffice would be Skype or a similar electronic setup so the prisoner can have face-to-face contact with family. This visual setup will be an additional cost factor but beneficial for all over time.

Prisoner transportation cost to and from another country will be an early objection. Related to that cost factor will be concern for public safety during any prisoner transportation. But prisoners are transported all the time, and it's rare for the public even to know about it, much less be involved with it in anyway. Objections may arise from remembrance of famous escape scenes in past movies. In numerous movies, escapes are frequent and usually involve planes, trains, or buses, and a far-fetched plot.

The way to alleviate the concerns of safety or cost is to use the US military for transportation. Each month, military pilots log a number of flight hours.

Many flights are international. There's also regular training flights for pilots in advanced flight school. The aircraft used would be transports or cargo planes. This method of transportation is not much different from using commercial flights except travel would depart from the nearest military air base. Regular security safeguards would be taken at all times, especially during flight.

It should be recognized that military flights are routine work for air crews that must keep flying skills current. Flights would take place with or without the additional service of transporting prisoners.

The assigned destination might change, but the time and cost would be about the same, depending on distance. When an Air Force transport plane flies from its base in San Antonio, Texas to another base in Guam, the distance is about 7,200 miles. If the same plane, used as a prisoner transport, flew from San Antonio to Beijing, China, instead of Guam, the distance would be about 7,200 miles. The amount of time, training, and cost for either flight would be nearly identical. In this strict example, one could say the prisoner transportation was free.

Transportation and security for prisoners from arrival airport to prison would be under the control of the host country. US military personnel would not go beyond the airport tarmac.

Returning prisoners would transport back to the United States in the same way. Using an optimum scenario, sometime in the future, 100 prisoners might arrive in the host country at the same time 100 prisoners are due to return to the United States to start their SMRP time. And, our military pilots fulfil their flight hour requirements.

Transportation of prisoners to and from a distant foreign country would initially be thought of as a substantial cost factor. Using the military for double duty reduces that cost to a fraction of usual cost. The military completes its required flight time and the Department of Corrections has its transportation problem solved. That makes the use of foreign prisons much more feasible.

The United States Department of Justice, the Federal Bureau of Prisons along with all individual states' Department of Correction chiefs should immediately formulate a general plan to house US prisoners under foreign control. The plan could be completed in 30-60 days and the transferring of prisoners could start within six months.

The savings for American taxpayers could reach $35 billion per year. The recidivism rate would decrease, leading to future savings. Ex-convicts would have a better chance at becoming productive citizens. The US government would improve its financial deficit. The world would see the United States is quite serious about improving its financial position.

PART TWO: SECURITY
Increasing US Security IMMEDIATELY

Chapter One

The US Military Service Adjustment

THE LEADERSHIP OF the United States' Federal government is elected by American citizens. Its very first responsibility is security for American citizens.

Today, American citizens are worried about their individual security. They're very worried about national security. They're worried about terrorism, safety on the street, the rampant drug culture, and their job security. All important. All serious problems ... and they're all related. Is there one way to solve all these problems completely and at the same time? No, probably not ... but there is one way that will lead to success in all these areas. Great success with national security. Great success with terrorism. Great success stopping the drug trade. Good success changing street crime and improving a weak job market.

If the preceding paragraph is true and accurate ... what glaring reason stands out that would cause this country, a country in serious trouble, to be reluctant to adopt whatever measures are needed to solve these problems as soon as possible?

Politics. Yes, politics. Politicians often get in the way of implementing what's best for the country. The two major parties, Democrats and Republicans, rarely agree on anything unless it's personally beneficial for both of them. They love to tell voting citizens that hope is here and change is right around the corner. After the election, it doesn't matter much whether citizens turned left or turned right. Hope dwindles, change turns to status quo, and politicians breathe a sigh of relief.

When it comes to tough choices, politicians could serve their fellow citizens better if they understood and accepted for themselves the following words:

"The ultimate measure of a man is not where he stands in moments of comfort and convenience but where he stands at times of challenge and controversy."
— Martin Luther King, Jr.

The United States faces numerous challenges right now; controversy abounds, time may be short, and politicians seek comfort.

Other reasons besides politics exist. Broad bold change requires more than just political courage. Change scares people. Change can mean altering a life-style. Usually the older generation, set in their ways, is reluctant to change even if they won't have to change much. Dramatic change will have to come mostly from younger people. They'll resist. They may revolt. People should know that if the country is sliding in the wrong direction, a course correction is needed. Sometimes it must be bold, and often, it is needed expeditiously.

Solving the nation's security problem is mandatory. Remember, national security is always the federal government's number one responsibility. Whatever the costs, it must be paid. It's not just a monetary cost. It's a cost in many ways for many people. Initially, it's the realization we have an ongoing security problem that requires guidance and determination from the nation's leadership. All American citizens need to realize we have a serious security problem and be willing to sacrifice to cure that problem.

Enhancing the nation's military ability will assure our national security. It can also protect our borders, stop the drug trade, reduce terrorism by half, and strengthen the backbones of the country's youth.

Assure national security? Protect borders? Eliminate drugs? Drastically reduce terrorism? Instill discipline in our youth? Is all of this possible? Is it all necessary? Yes. And, the time to start is now.

The United States should immediately double the size and capability of its military forces.

Doubling the size and capability of all US military forces would be a huge undertaking. It's much more than a project. A project is something you start, finish, and then celebrate. Doubling the US military would be life-changing for many, but with lifelong benefits, too. Doubling the military from its present size greatly improves our guard against catastrophic attack, and that improves the future for all Americans. Currently, the military does the following:

- assures national security
- signals the world we are serious about peace and protection
- provides the means to protect much of our infrastructure
- brings the country more friends and less enemies worldwide
- counters the huge and fast buildup of China's military capability

- brings ability to seal the border without great expense
- teaches better interaction between people
- indirectly reduces crime on the street
- teaches proper use of firearms
- teaches responsibility to individuals
- prepares the youth for work through a cross-section of jobs
- improves the physical condition of youth and slows the obesity trend
- improves coping skills
- counters Russia's military buildup
- slows Russia's territorial expansion
- teaches leadership skills
- strengthens the ability to complete a task regardless of conditions
- brings ability to reduce terrorism by half or more
- teaches aspects of self-defense and national defense
- educates youth through foreign travel
- builds character
- teaches teamwork
- brings a feeling of patriotism by serving the nation
- improves the chances for youth to be more productive in the future
- gives full medical coverage to members and their families
- pays bonus money for some members to stay members
- gives education benefits to members
- improves the overall job market
- instills discipline in youth at a time it is sorely needed

Please note the last benefit listed. Discipline is the most important benefit obtained in military service. American youth need discipline. They'll individually benefit. America will collectively benefit.

The many benefits of spending time, even a limited amount of time, in the military has in the past and will continue to serve our youth very well. Likewise, an expanded military will serve our nation well and even better in the future.

The list above includes many intangible benefits for members of the military. Those individual benefits flow through to the entire country over time. The country will benefit economically and financially going forward. This benefit is a very important aspect of any security plan put forth in this book.

Doubling the military in size and capability will cause plenty of controversy. The "added cost" controversy will be front and center ... right up to the time the method of doubling personnel is announced.

Any plan to double the military will be very difficult to introduce, but at the same time, it may find general acceptance by the average American citizen who pays the bill. The magic words disclosing "military duty compliance" must come from politicians, and those words are unknown at this time.

First courage, then wisdom, before thorough explanation will be needed by national leaders to obtain an understanding, followed by agreement, from the general population. It shouldn't have to be this way, but big-change is always difficult and always controversial.

It should be remembered that "great sacrifice" is required by all to avoid severe financial, economic, and security problems in the near future. All citizens will be asked to sacrifice in some way.

The United States' leaders should immediately initiate the following action: double the military's size and capability. This military action-plan would be extensive and quite different from anything in the past. It will be referred to in this book simply as the Military Plan (MP).

The highlights of the MP, without detail, follow:

- All citizens required to serve sometime between ages 18-30
- Service will be designated Domestic Only or International Possible
- Service time enlistment/draft ... minimum of one year
- Some military units will be skilled in extremely different ways of operation
- Some military units will more than double in number
- Some equipment and some systems will more than double in number
- Border protection will be military
- Critical Infrastructure protection will be military
- Energy/power structure and supply protection will be military
- Drug interdiction will be military
- Foreign intervention by US military will be paid for by foreign beneficiary
- Many younger short-term members will be added
- More older long-term members will be retired
- Civilian control of military will continue

All the above areas are somewhat different, some considerably so, from the past, with the exception of civilian control. Some of these areas will be expanded upon with greater detail and explanation.

The most controversial change to be found in the MP will be conscription. Conscription … commonly referred to as "the Draft." In the United States, a draft is when the Federal government sends a notice to American citizens, informing them that they have been "inducted" into the military on a certain date and shall report to a specific location for training. This satisfies young people's requirement to serve their country. It's not an unusual happening in many countries, nor in US history. The draft component in the MP will be different from the draft at any time in the past. Draftees will be provided important choices that should be satisfying to them.

There's one area of the proposed draft that will be quite different from the past. Who is exempt? Only prospective military members under extreme medical circumstance or disability will be excluded from serving in the military. Otherwise, there will be no exclusions from the draft. Exclusion attempts are too often a time-wasting nuisance for everybody. People are not excluded if they are: too fat, married, busy in school, ex-cons, have a bad limp, wear glasses, or wet the bed. If the present day military can accept transgender members, then all others should be able to work together as well.

The draft will include both male and female youth. There hasn't been a draft for many years, so more than a few will object loudly. That's very unfortunate since the objector could serve his country for a relatively short time while remaining close to home. Any "service to country" is something of which most people feel proud.

Generally, women have not been drafted, but they have served in the US Army since 1775. They have been eligible for combat duty since 2013. Today, the Army is made up of about 15 percent women serving in most units. For many citizens, the introduction of a draft, especially a draft including women, will be a shock.

For those men and women who enlist or are drafted, the usual financial, medical, and educational benefits will apply, but they will be limited, depending on length of service chosen. Some unusual but interesting choices would also be included in their military service. Draftees can choose "Domestic-Only" or "International-Possible" service. Certain stipulations would exist regarding the International-Possible choice, relative to length of service. Draftees can choose to serve between one and six years. All service members will go to "regular basic training," which lasts eight weeks. After basic training, members will be assigned a school depending on the length of agreed-upon service. It's expected most draftees will choose the minimum term of one year. Their schooling or preparation for a military job would probably be relatively short … about 1-3 weeks at a convenient duty station. Their job or work would likely not be complex. It may be menial but necessary government service work. Nevertheless, strict military-like discipline would be maintained.

The next duty station for those service members with only a one-year commitment would be as near to their regular residence as possible. That's generally one of the following locations: 1) a nearby regular military base, 2) a nearby military reserve armory, 3) a nearby special-duty assignment. Their service would be Domestic-Only. No exceptions.

The "nearby next duty station" can best be explained by the following example of a new service member from Tucson.

A Tucson, Arizona resident who enters military service for a one-year commitment would complete his or her eight weeks of basic training at any of several training bases. His or her next duty station would be in or around the Tucson area. It may be at local Davis-Monthan Air Force Base. It may be at one of the several Reserve Centers around Tucson. If the service member volunteers for or is selected for a "special-duty assignment" (SDA), he or she would work at any one of a several qualified locations in or relatively near Tucson but still be attached to the AF base or a local Reserve Unit.

Special Duty Assignment (SDA) will be covered later in this book.

Another choice would be open to all draftees or enlistees. New members could serve part-time in a Reserve Unit, but their freedom of choice would be more limited. They would be assigned a training school and start time would be immediate, but active training might start in several weeks or months. Time of service would be six years usually starting with six months active duty time and five-and-a-half years of two-and-a-half days per month training, plus two weeks of yearly training. It's possible the six-year term would be lowered. Some would find this part-time involvement more suitable for their civilian lifestyle while allowing them to serve their country for a period of years.

All service members, being either draftees or enlistees, will find some choice in training or military job preparation. The training school choice or assignment will depend on length of service. One year service members will find only limited or basic job preparation offered as training. At the other end of instruction and schooling might be flight training. Flight school lasts eighteen months and would be a six-year commitment. Other intensive training schools would be available to those who have agreed to serve three, four, or five years. Training, depending on military needs, will almost always be connected to the number of years you serve. A longer time of commitment helps determine whether "qualified individuals" are accepted into selective schools. An easy-to-understand example would be any military member serving two years or less would not be accepted into any intensive training school. These schools usually last for an extended time.

Service members who have agreed to a two-year or longer enlistment will have a choice between Domestic-Only and International-Possible service. This choice will also somewhat affect school assignment or choice. Those members who choose one year of service will be Domestic-Only. It is expected many young men and women will have limited interest in serving, and especially so when being drafted. That lack of interest suggests a sizable majority of new service members will serve the one-year minimum.

Another important choice for draftees or enlistees will be start-date of service. It's expected the earliest time to start military service would be eighteen and the latest thirty years of age. This choice of service time is more important for the individual than one might think. Different personal circumstances may dictate a best time for service, and the member gets to choose that time. An example might be a twenty year old who has just finished two years of college and needs a break from school. He or she can arrange to start a one-year or more military service commitment during the summer months. If the person is away for one year, he or she would return in time for the following year's fall semester. This is very good timing for those who wish to continue college but also need to fulfill their military requirement serving their country. They make the choice.

It should be noted that all draftees, including those who choose one year of service, will have some limited choice as to the branch of service. They will be given two branches to choose from upon induction. The draft will provide personnel to the Army, Air Force, Navy, Marine Corps, and Coast Guard. All draftees can choose to become enlistees and the exact branch they wish for a minimum of two years and as many as six years, depending on training school application and acceptance.

An alternative plan for prospective service members would stipulate any person choosing a one-year commitment be assigned to the Army to provide the majority of security personnel. That possible scenario will not be discussed here.

Below are five examples of young citizens fulfilling military requirement:

Betty is eighteen-and-a-half years old and receives her draft notice in the mail. She has finished high school with very good grades and she is mechanically inclined. She prefers a technical school over college. She reports to the induction center and learns she is eligible to serve as little as one year but chooses to enlist in the Air Force for four years because she wants to work in avionics. She is assigned to an avionics trade school as soon as basic training is finished. She chooses International-Possible.

Mark is eighteen years old and receives his draft notice. He is upset because he's recently been accepted at a major university. As a hobby, he loves boating with his father. He reports to the induction center for initial processing. He signs an agreement to postpone his military obligation until he graduates from college or sometime before he turns thirty. He now has time to decide whether he wants to fulfill a minimum one-year commitment after college or a two- to six-year commitment with an unknown-at-this-time school or possibly Officer Candidate School (OCS). He could also decide to join ROTC while in school. His father advises him to join Navy ROTC at school and become a naval officer after school. Mark has choices for his future.

Fred is nearly nineteen and has just graduated from high school. He receives his draft notice, which he hoped would never arrive. He has a job, but it's only part-time. His girlfriend is starting community college, but Mark is not ready for another school. He reports to the induction center. He chooses to serve the minimum time of one year. He's given a choice of the Army or Coast Guard, and he chooses the Army. He leaves for basic training in thirty days and will serve Domestic-Only. His father tells him it is the best thing he has ever done.

Wayne is eighteen and a half and has just graduated high school. His girlfriend will turn eighteen in one month. She must finish a four-week summer school course before she can receive her diploma on July 1. They wish to get married and start a family as soon as possible. They both have part-time jobs. Wayne reports to the induction center. He discusses his choices with advisors. He chooses to enlist for six years in the local reserve unit. He will leave for basic training in September. His girlfriend, knowing her draft notice will arrive within the next few months, intends to join the same reserve unit in July and hopes to leave for basic training sometime in September. They both hope to be assigned technical schools for advanced training. They both made choices that fit their future plans.

Jerry is twenty-two years old and working in what he calls a dead-end job. He left high school one year early and did not graduate. He does not have to serve in the military because the draft has recently been reintroduced for eighteen year olds. He wants to enlist in the Air Force and change his life. But he's told he's not eligible because he failed to finish high school. It's suggested he enroll in regular high school courses at night to finish school and then apply for a one-year enlistment. During this year of service, Jerry can consider enlisting in the Air Force, and if approved, receive additional schooling. Jerry agrees to follow the counselor's advice and looks forward to the possibility of working in the Air Force.

Regardless of military service requirements, all youth should be required to complete high school.

These five examples demonstrate a wide variety of choices are available to people. They can choose to serve only domestically, for as little as six months active duty reserves or a one year total commitment, arrange for technical training school, start their service anytime between the ages of eighteen and thirty, and they have some control over which branch of service to enter and where they serve. These personal choices will be an extremely important aspect when introducing the draft.

For some citizens, serving their country will bring opportunity and pride. Others will show little interest, but they will have considerable choice. That choice should be greatly appreciated. In the past, little choice existed in duty station or job assignment. Orders were orders.

Whether service members had choice or not, over the years, the US military forces have defended the country and its allies on land, at sea, and in the air. The military's job is to train constantly for many different types of warfare and adapt to whatever the threats are at the time. Climate is another variable the military must contend with as well. Certain weather conditions can make a big difference for men and the operation of their equipment. Korea was bitter cold and mountainous. Viet Nam was hot and wet. The Gulf War was hot and sandstorms blinding.

Our enemies use these different weather conditions to equalize our mechanized force as well as employing unusual tactics to their advantage. In Viet Nam, booby traps were a problem. In Iraq, IEDs were a threat to life and limb. Battlefield conditions vary from region to region and military preparedness must adapt as necessary for long-term survival.

A great statesman with foresight, Benjamin Franklin, said:

"By failing to prepare, you are preparing to fail."

A true statement in all matters, but vividly so in warfare or terrorism where a lack of preparation can cause death. Surprise in next duty-station is one thing, but surprise on the battlefield is dangerous.

Surprise is difficult to eliminate, so preparation against any kind of attack must be extensive. Our military must have foresight along with the ability to overcome any new threats swiftly as they emerge. Unfortunately, it's often the element of surprise that serves as a first alert. The events of 911 were a surprise.

Terrorism is an active threat today, and it's getting close to home. Most would say it's here and growing. In Europe, terror problems are frequent and should be a clear warning to the US. At the same time, in many Middle East countries, there is obvious and considerable support for terrorism.

Nuclear weapons are another threat. They can be delivered a long distance by air. Today, you can add small nuclear weapons to that threat. Small weapons mean delivery methods change. Some Middle East countries have nuclear weapons now, and some are in the process of obtaining them. These same countries may be experts in terrorist tactics. What could this mean?

If you add the last three paragraphs together, you get…surprise, terrorism, and nuclear weapons. A very lethal combination.

That lethal combination comes with a very serious question: Is the United States and the US military ready, willing, and able to defend themselves successfully against any surprise attack by any terrorist especially if that terrorist intends to detonate any size nuclear weapon?

Are you afraid to answer that question? You should be because the most likely answer is no, and that is scary. If you take the question apart and just focus on the individual elements, the "no" answer is easier to understand. Ask yourself a few short questions:

Are the authorities in New York City "ready, willing, or able" to prevent, deal with, or recover from any nuclear terrorist attack? They think so, but is there *really* any success after a nuclear detonation? Even a small blast? Are authorities ready or able everywhere? New York City is about 500 square miles. It has about 9 million people unless you count the immediate surrounding area, which would bring the total to 20 million.

What if the target is Dayton, Ohio? Dayton is small compared to New York City, but it has a large Air Force Base. Does that make it a target? Are Dayton authorities as ready and able as New York City's? Authorities being: USAF, city police, county police, FBI, Department of Homeland Security (DHS), and others. Who's in charge?

Is the United States "willing" to defend against any attack inside or outside of its borders? Most citizens would say yes. What if these same citizens were asked to spend more of their money for needed security updates? Is the federal government willing to go the extra mile to make sure common citizens are safe? The federal government, generally referring to the Obama administration of the last several years, severely cut back military personnel and certain equipment. Is it possible the US military is willing to defend at any cost to itself, but the federal government is not willing to defend at any cost? It's the federal government that cuts military expenditures, not the military.

Exactly how do you stop or defend against a "surprise" terrorist attack anywhere but especially within the United States? There are soft targets and hard targets. About a million of them. "Surprise" brings up the "unknown" factors: type of target, location, time, explosive, size, method, means of movement, and more.

How do the "unknowns" become known? Surprise is a terrorist tactic, and in order to get ahead of it, security people need to crack the unknowns.

Let's return to the main question above: Is the United States and the US military ready, willing, and able?

Thankfully, there is some good news. Many terrorist attacks have indeed been interrupted before they took place. Usually, almost always, it's the intelligence gathering net that alerts authorities to a possible attack. That same intelligence factor has been under assault in the United States in recent years. When critical work being done by the National Security Agency (NSA) was disclosed to US citizens and to the world, many people objected and the politicians took sides publically, which eventually harmed US intelligence. The United States also reduced its intelligence ability by stepping back from the Middle East. That includes eight years of the Obama administration's strained relationship with Israel. Israel's leaders, different than many leaders in the United States, understand they must have the best intelligence possible in order to survive.

Electronic intelligence is of primary importance to prevent surprise terrorist attacks or attacks from other adversaries. Relations with China or Russia can change fast, making electronic surveillance a daily necessity. Rogue nations such as North Korea or Iran openly profess their wish to put an end to the United States. If there's any way to hear what they say behind closed doors, it should be done.

The United States should and must quietly lead in electronic listening.

It appears there's considerable concern about possible terrorist attacks on US infrastructure. Most importantly, the energy or power grid could be attacked on a relatively small scale but with damage and outages spreading out from the original attack location. Damage can be repaired, but what happens if damage spreads 100 miles in multiple directions? It could take weeks or months to make repairs. What if onsite repair equipment is also damaged? Americans are used to getting food, water, gasoline, or whatever they want when they want it. That may be a spoiled brat concept, but it is quite real, especially when the kids are hungry. At some point, it will become quite dangerous. Any widespread or extended time loss of power would render regular American life unsustainable.

It's of paramount importance that US infrastructure is well-protected from terrorists at all times starting today and forever. It doesn't matter whether the terrorists are part of a well-known international group such as ISIS, al-Qaeda, Hezbollah, Hamas, or a small individual terrorist cell already operating inside the United States.

The military should be assigned to protect all critical infrastructure, but especially assets such as the power grid, water supply stations, airports,

and bridges. This may sound extreme to many, but compared to a poisoned water supply or an extended blackout ... any military presence should be welcomed.

A large scale infrastructure collapse within the United States and caused by a terrorist attack is nearly unthinkable because of the high number of regular citizens that would be affected. But what if a similar thing happened on the battlefield in a foreign country? What if the US military power grid or power source, especially the communication aspect, was incapacitated during battle? Communication loss would cripple American military forces.

An unusual "fallback" way that would help support military field operations should be initiated immediately. It's unknown to this writer exactly how it would be implemented, how long it would take to become operational, and whether it's even possible in today's age of push-buttons and voice activation. But an attempt at creating this new "ability to operate" system, just in case of a worst-case-scenario event, could prove all important for America.

This idea or proposal should actually apply to *all* aspects of everyday American life, but here it will be concerned with military communications.

All branches of the military should immediately create a small but specialized unit that incorporates a very different method of handling everyday operations, but especially, the communication function. It would be expected the "new" equipment personnel would come from the communications section and remain under that same command.

For illustration purposes in this book, this new, small unit will be designated PICO. PICO could stand for Pigeon Communication because years ago the military did use pigeons for communication. But pigeons are not being suggested here.

The mission of this new PICO unit would be to operate communications today exactly as a military combat unit would have operated in the 1940s. Readers should pause and reread that last sentence.

Under "blackout" circumstances, a PICO unit could become most important on the battlefield as the only way to communicate. What happens if an EMP or similar event takes place near military field operations and all modern sensitive electronic circuits are fried? How would one communicate?

Many may think the burned-out-circuit scenario is improbable. Yes, it may be improbable ... just as was the incredible success of 9/11. Or, Army Major Hasan, appearing as a fine young man, serving our country, but also serving his religion, easily killing and wounding 30 soldiers on an Army base in Texas. Improbable? Yes. Impossible? Obviously not.

Disregarding for a minute the seriousness of losing all electronics, even losing a single circuit or system, could prove a disaster. It's not just system loss itself but the battlefield situation in which soldiers may find themselves at the time and their ability to remedy the problem. Some ground operators of modern electronic systems are lost when just the lights go out. An even more pressing problem might be the loss of an aircraft electronic system in flight.

Related to losing electronics is another flight problem. In the last several years articles have appeared about pilots losing their flying skills because of automation in the cockpit. Studies have demonstrated when one of the computers assisting the aircraft is shut off the pilot is sometimes at a loss concerning exactly what to do to maintain safe flight. This could be even more of a problem if the avionics interruption is sudden or extensive.

Automation or electronics has reduced the overall flying skills of pilots which has been verified in testing. Numerous articles are available about this modern problem including one from 'New Science' mentioned here:

ARTICLE FOUND AT: https://www.newscientist.com
ARTICLE WRITTEN BY: Paul Marks
DATE: NOVEMBER 20, 2013
TITLE: 'COCKPIT COMPUTERS are Sapping Pilots' Ability to Fly'

> *"Who's flying your plane? Pilots' manual flying skills have become dangerously eroded because they rely too much on automated systems. That's one conclusion of a leaked report on air safety commissioned by the US Federal Aviation Administration (FAA)."*

The point is … we all rely on electronic systems and if all or any important part fails it's a serious problem and must be remedied fast. A pilot must find an airport and land without delay. Electronic systems failure on a factory floor may shut down one piece of equipment or all equipment being used. But when all circuits in a wide area are affected at the exact same time a speedy recovery could be months or even years. An unimaginable situation. And, it may be even more acute on the battlefield.

An out-of-the-ordinary backup system that does not use modern sensitive electronics is needed. That would be the function of PICO.

The avionics example applies to any aircraft in flight. It could be military, commercial or private. A blip in one of the onboard computers is one thing but if all circuits on all aircraft are fried because of an electromagnetic pulse (EMP) or similar event there will be a huge problem. That's obvious for planes in flight, but the problem goes well beyond aviation.

Besides the need for pilots to maintain expert flying skills, they need to be ready for unusual or sudden equipment failures during flight. That's why they have backup systems on aircraft. It's the same for all personnel who are operating critical equipment, including communications. They need backup systems. That could mean backup systems well beyond present day backup systems. Military communications must function well enough to get the task-at-hand successfully completed. In battlefield operations, failure means lives lost.

The following is a rough estimate of what a PICO unit might look like on paper. An old US Army training type company will be used in this example:

Charlie Company – 200 personnel – 4 Platoons + HQs

Communications (Como) Section – 20 personnel (part of 1 platoon)

PICO unit – 6 cross-trained personnel (part of 20 in Como section)

After some very old-specialized training, the PICO unit would be fully operational. The unit may also adjust its personnel numbers up or down, depending on progress or need. All PICO members would stay active in the "new" field of "old communications," including when training in the field.

Usually, personnel go through training until they learn the trade. But adapting to communications in the 1940s will be quite different. Experienced trainers may be scarce. After the unit is operational, other platoons + HQs would each assign one person to work closely with the six members of the PICO unit. That one person would be the communications (como) contact in each platoon when and if needed. All PICO personnel would regularly train in order to stay proficient in "communication methods from the past," just as if they were operating on the battlefield during World War II.

A fully operational PICO unit means personnel would use old equipment, understand how to use it, and train with it in different situations. Their training exercises would include their single contact in other same-company platoons and eventually spread to larger groups. Individual platoon PICO members would carry the old-style phone while on field maneuvers and use it to communicate with their PICO contacts in other platoons. "Old style" phones are not loaded with modern electronic circuits that could be "fried" with an EMP or similar type attack.

Plans would be in place to install additional "old" equipment upon short notice wherever needed. If there was ever a sudden or extensive failure in regular como, the PICO unit's job would be to maintain some communication in order to allow chain-of-command continuity.

The example above, in very simple terms, describes how an Army company might create and operate a PICO unit. A good test might be to move from a company-size exercise to a battalion-size exercise. And finally reaching an unannounced exercise where a military base's entire communication system is shut down, making it very difficult for anyone to operate. Often when all power is lost and there's no como, it's funny … for about five minutes. But that should never happen in a military situation. The military could be in a very hostile environment, so there aren't five minutes of fun to enjoy anytime. Como isn't just a casual phone call to the Mess Hall. It could be a Forward Observer calling in coordinates to an artillery crew that must lay down a barrage of fire to stop the advance of an enemy about to overrun a bogged down infantry platoon. The PICO unit could find itself involved in providing the last means of defense by coordinating communications on the battlefield.

The PICO unit would be similar in all military branches, allowing for the distinction of land, sea, or air. There's still some use today of communication with military flags, heliograph flash lamps, and Morse Code, but it's limited because of the availability of sensitive electronic equipment. The Navy at sea, as the Army on land, may need to expand the use of light signal equipment or hoist flags for como between ships if modern equipment fails. Sounds silly, but what if it's the only way to communicate? Preparation for the unexpected is necessary.

The PICO unit's mission should be easy to understand. Provide como between all military forces in any way possible when high-tech electronic communication equipment fails. The mission is usual. The remedy is unusual. Complete success will be difficult.

It should be recognized that a military PICO unit may never be needed. That would be preferable. But preparation for disruption is beyond wise.

Modern electronic equipment is great to use in military or civilian operations, but any major problem can be very swift and quite extensive. Worst-case scenarios must be considered.

Today, some nations have large advanced nuclear weapons and the means to deliver them to any target. But it's unlikely any major country would use such weapons because they fear instant retaliation. But what about small unstable nations? What about rogue nations or terrorist groups who seem convinced that dying is the way to live forever? If men could quietly plan to fly an airplane full of kids into a building, then they can do anything regardless of the horror caused. Would they act any differently with nuclear weapons? Doubtful.

Most people are aware lightning strikes can cause serious damage, including fire ignition and melting circuits. Most people are unaware of another happening that can cause damage similar to lightning but is far more dangerous than lightning because it can cover a much greater area. It could be the equivalent of a million lightning bolts at the same time. An EMP event.

EMP was mentioned earlier but only briefly. The following EMP information should be understood by all:

INFORMATION FOUND AT: https://en.wikipedia.org/wiki/Nuclear_
electromagnetic_pulse

> *An electromagnetic pulse is a burst of electromagnetic radiation. Nuclear explosions create a characteristic pulse of electromagnetic radiation called a nuclear EMP or NEMP.... The resulting rapidly changing electric and magnetic fields may couple with electrical and electronic systems to produce damaging current and voltage surges. The specific characteristics of any particular nuclear EMP event vary according to a number of factors, the greatest of which is the altitude of the detonation.*

What does all this EMP talk mean for the average American citizen? It means "nothing works" after an EMP event. What can be done about it before an event takes place? Some individual preparation is possible, but it's a government responsibility to prevent, prepare for, and respond to an EMP event. But prompt government action is often the equivalent of pulling your own teeth.

Average citizens don't understand much about an EMP event. They don't know how drastically life would change. Federal politicians do know or they should know about EMPs. Information has been in front of them for years. It's their responsibility to act and to protect the American people. How many times must they be reminded?

An unstoppable geomagnetic storm or nuclear attack could strike the US mainland without notice. Either are EMP events. An attack could come from a major adversary or troublesome rogue nation with a nuclear weapon and the means to deliver it. Same for a terrorist group. In a worst-case scenario, if a large nuclear bomb detonated at an optimum altitude, the US population would be rendered nearly helpless. Why helpless? Electronic system shutdown. The nation would be as quiet as a mouse, except for the screaming.

Today, almost everything is electronically controlled from city water pumping stations to gasoline pumping stations. People either need water to live or gasoline to travel some distance to find water. It's probable cell phones would cease working. Bank computers would freeze up one way or the other. Citizens could be left with a nonfunctioning power-grid. What follows would be instant panic and time accelerates panic into deadly chaos.

The United States government has known for ages about the severe consequences of either an EMP attack or a geomagnetic storm, often referred to as solar flares. Most people would think by now the United States would be completely prepared for any EMP event, whether it be natural or man-made. It doesn't appear so. The federal government has formed commissions to collect data and committees to discuss data. The same information is passed back and forth numerous times. Despite all of this, we end up with little protection for US citizens. Allocated funds for EMP protection are not remotely comparable to funds spent concerning global warming which, even if it's real, is a very slight change over many, many decades of time.

Additional information from the same website as above follows:

INFORMATION FOUND AT: https://en.wikipedia.org/wiki/Nuclear_ electomagnetic_pulse

TITLE: NUCLEAR ELECTROMAGNETIC pulse

> *The United States EMP Commission was created by the United States Congress in 2001. The commission is formally known as the Commission to Assess the Threat to the United States from Electromagnetic Pulse (EMP) Attack.*

The federal government has been aware of this potential disaster long enough that all known protection should already be in place. A formal investigating committee was started in 2001. That's more than fifteen years ago. It's as if they're waiting for a disaster before taking sufficient action. Continuing with information about the 2001 "commission" that was formed:

> *The Commission brought together notable scientists and technologists to compile several reports. In 2008, the EMP Commission released the "Critical National Infrastructures Report." This report describes the likely consequences of a nuclear EMP on civilian infrastructure.... The United States EMP Commission determined that long-known protections are almost completely absent in the civilian infrastructure of the United States and that large parts of US military services were less-protected against EMP than during the Cold War. In public statements, the EMP experts on the EMP Commission recommended making electronic equipment and electrical components resistant to EMP—and maintaining spare parts inventories that would enable prompt repairs.*

The government commission's report hasn't been a secret, but still, it hasn't caused politicians to act with any haste. What does it take? There's plenty of critical comment about the country's lack of preparedness and what could happen without protection from an EMP event. Again, what does it take? Hopefully, not an actual EMP event. Here's a previous EMP event example:

ARTICLE FOUND AT: www.forbes.com

ARTICLE WRITTEN BY: Peter Kelly-Detwiler

DATE: JULY 31, 2014

TITLE: FAILURE TO Protect U.S. Against Electromagnetic Pulse Threat Could Make 9/11 Look Trivial Someday

> *In 1962, during the depths of the Cold War, the U.S. military exploded a nuclear weapon high above an atoll in the Pacific Ocean. Dubbed Operation Starfish, this exercise was part of a larger project to evaluate*

the impacts of nuclear explosions in space. The missile, launched from Johnson Island, 900 miles from Hawaii, was armed with a 1.4 megaton warhead, programmed to explode at 240 miles above the earth. It detonated as expected. What was not entirely expected was the magnitude of the resulting electromagnetic pulse (EMP).

The EMP was powerful enough to affect the electric grid in Hawaii, blowing out streetlights, and resulting in telephone outages and radio blackouts.

Readers should note the difference in current nuclear weapons compared to those available in 1962. Today, they're much more powerful and destructive. And today, nearly all equipment operates with sensitive electronics. Our modern society needs EMP protection more than ever. Ugly EMP information follows:

ARTICLE FOUND AT: https://www.centerforsecuritypolicy.org/category/homeland-security/infrastructure-and-emp/

TITLE: INFRASTRUCTURE AND EMP

With the end of the Cold War, the threat of a massive bipolar nuclear exchange has, thankfully, abated. However, one of the most frightening consequences of nuclear proliferation among rogue states and, potentially, terrorist organizations, is these bad actors' ability to create unimaginable devastation without massive stockpiles of warheads or ICBMs.

One of the most terrifying of these is an EMP attack. An electromagnetic pulse (EMP) is generated when a conventional nuclear weapon is detonated high in the earth's atmosphere over a desired target; the pulse radiates a powerful current that disables and "fries" all electrical equipment for thousands of miles. This kind of assault would, in effect, reduce our technology based society to pre-industrial modes of communication and subsistence—and leave hundreds of millions without food, money, or transportation.

What was just said? Something about like this: Rogue states, terrorist organizations, and nuclear weapons equal fried circuits, no food, and millions of dead Americans.

Why would the US government hesitate approving and installing maximum or super-maximum protection against any EMP event that could end our lives? It can't be money because it spends more on unneeded projects every single month.

The following article contains information every American should know and understand. It was written by two men ... both extremely knowledgeable in international politics, intelligence work, and the EMP threat.

Article found in: The Wall Street Journal
Article written by: R. James Woolsey and Peter Vincent Pry
Date: August 12, 2014
Title: The Growing Threat From an EMP Attack

A nuclear device detonated above the U.S. could kill millions, and we've done almost nothing to prepare.

In a recent letter to investors, billionaire hedge-fund manager Paul Singer warned that an electromagnetic pulse, or EMP, is "the most significant threat" to the U.S. and our allies in the world. He's right. Our food and water supplies, communications, banking, hospitals, law enforcement, etc., all depend on the electric grid. Yet until recently little attention has been paid to the ease of generating EMPs by detonating a nuclear weapon in orbit above the U.S., and thus bringing our civilization to a cold, dark halt.

Recent declassification of EMP studies by the U.S. government has begun to draw attention to this dire threat. Rogue nations such as North Korea (and possibly Iran) will soon match Russia and China and have the primary ingredients for an EMP attack: simple ballistic missiles such as Scuds that could be launched from a freighter near our shores; space-launch vehicles able to loft low-earth-orbit satellites; and simple low-yield nuclear weapons that can generate gamma rays and fireballs.

The much neglected 2004 and 2008 reports by the congressional EMP Commission—only now garnering increased public attention—warn that "terrorists or state actors that possess relatively unsophisticated missiles armed with nuclear weapons may well calculate that, instead of destroying a city or military base, they may gain the greatest political-military utility from one or a few such weapons by using them—or threatening their use—in an EMP attack.

The EMP Commission reports that: "China and Russia have considered limited nuclear-attack options that, unlike their Cold War plans, employ EMP as the primary or sole means of attack." The report further warns that: "designs for variants of such weapons may have been illicitly trafficked for a quarter century"....

What would a successful EMP attack look like? The EMP Commission, in 2008, estimated that within 12 months of a nationwide blackout, up to 90 percent of the U.S. population could possibly perish from starvation, disease and societal breakdown....

> *The cost of protecting the national electric grid, according to a 2008 EMP Commission estimate, would be about $2 billion—roughly what the U.S. gives each year in foreign aid to Pakistan....*
>
> *What is lacking in Washington is a sense of urgency....*

This article by Woolsey and Pry should be a severe wakeup shock to American politicians just as it would be to American citizens if they ever read it.

At least on the surface, it appears the US government currently spends more money to protect Pakistan than it does to protect American citizens from a life-ending EMP event. Does that make any sense?

Apparently, few political leaders expect any attack that qualifies as an EMP attack. Maybe they're guessing right. Maybe they're guessing dead-wrong. But why take the chance? Government money is wasted every day on meaningless projects. An EMP attack is meaningful. An EMP attack in the US could far, far surpass Pearl Harbor or 9/11. It's as if our leaders don't realize once an attack takes place you can't go back and prepare for it. You may not recover from it. Try to imagine the chaos. Accordingly, the United States could cease being "united." It would be every man for himself. A lack of food, water, and warmth. What does one do? Kill the enemy? The enemy is now the neighbor standing next to you, fighting for the same scarce resources you need to survive.

An EMP event is no longer a threat solely from Russia or China. Both countries are more than adventuresome and have full ability to execute an EMP attack. That's reason enough to be on the safe side rather than nearly ignoring the unearthly EMP possibilities.

There may be an even greater threat from smaller nations. They now have capabilities they didn't have in the past. They have nuclear weapons or the means to obtain them. They're also not shy about threatening to use them on the United States. Maybe the threats are empty promises, but it's never good to find out after you guessed wrong.

Increasingly, terrorists demonstrate their ability to cause destruction with no regard for innocent lives. Often they're very intelligent warriors with money to burn. A dangerous combination. Would they ever seek to obtain a nuclear weapon? Would they use it? Could they manage to bring a weapon into the United States? Political leaders say that would be very difficult. Political leaders are always right until they're deadly wrong. Then there's something from politicians called ... reasonable excuse. Their verbal backbone.

How would an adversary bring a nuclear weapon into the United States? Probably not through the front door. There may be sensitive alarms at major checkpoints.

But what if a small foreign freighter entered New York Harbor on a routine visit? Another entered Boston Harbor? Another the Inner Harbor of Baltimore? This probably happens every single day. Each freighter, at about the same time, launches a small boat after dark. The small boats are operated by suicide terrorists and are carrying what's known as a suitcase-nuke. A portable, tactical device capable of inflicting considerable local death and destruction but also nationwide fear and psychological damage. Each boat's mission would be to stay out of trouble until 10 a.m. when all city buildings are full of people. Then, bring the bombs ashore or maneuver them as close to the city as possible. Political leaders would say that particular scenario would be very difficult to accomplish. They may be right, but the scenario sounds so easy ... they just might be wrong.

The regular citizen may not know exactly what damage this type of bomb detonation would cause in or near a downtown area, but most know the outcome would not be good. People would die. Much electronic equipment in the area would be knocked out. There would probably be long-lasting contamination and surely widespread chaos. Not just in the cities, but chaos across the country. **The question spreading like wildfire ... who's next?**

If or when a small nuclear device is detonated in the United States, it's not only electronic equipment that ceases to work but people as well.

Consider the following "rapid-fire," worst-case scenario starting at 10 a.m. Monday: small nuclear device detonates in three East Coast city-harbor areas causing mass confusion, city panic, harbor shutdown. Tuesday: *all* US harbors/ports closed. Next day: all harbors and harbor city areas a mess. Next day: ships backing-up. Next day: food and goods shortage starting, shelves emptying fast. Next day: widespread confusion, anger, and chaos. Sunday: much praying, severe anger, panic, chaos, and killing. Next day: What next day?

The point of the above scenario is twofold: Anything is possible when a suicidal adversary is deliberate, and the United States needs to prepare accordingly.

The safeguarding of electronic equipment with some kind of shielding and backup measures should be started immediately. These preventative and backup measures go well beyond military base communications and a PICO unit. An EMP event could directly affect the entire country in many fatal ways.

Regardless of whether an adversary ever executes an EMP attack, there's always the threat of a geomagnetic storm. This phenomenon is unstoppable. It could do as much or more damage as any adversary, and no amount of discussion, pleading, or logic will have a preventative effect. Only credible preparation will help.

The US government should disregard cost and immediately take all action possible to lesson damage from any EMP event. At the same time, citizens need to prepare for the aftermath of and the recovery from an EMP event. **More preparation equals faster recovery. Less preparation equals little recovery.**

Chapter Two

The Grid: Our Infrastructure.
The SDA: Our Protection.

THE "GRID" REFERS to the electrical grid in the United States. See below:

INFORMATION FOUND AT: https://en.wikipedia.org/wiki/electrical_grid

SOURCE: KAPLAN, S. M. *Smart Grid: Modernizing Electric Power Transmission and Distribution; Energy Independence, Storage and Security; Energy Independence and Security Act of 2007 (EISA); Improving Electrical Grid Efficiency, Communication, Reliability, and Resiliency; Integrating New and Renewable Energy Sources.* Alexandria, VA: The Capitol.Net, 2009.

> *An electric grid is an interconnected network for delivering electricity from suppliers to consumers. It consists of generating stations that produce electrical power, high-voltage transmission lines that carry power from distant sources to demand centers and distribution lines that connect individual customers.*

The grid is the basic part of US infrastructure that sustains American life. The country's infrastructure is vast, ranging from seaports in Long Beach to water supply lines in Oklahoma City to bridges in Boston. It all sustains American life, and it all must be kept operational and secure.

Operational and secure sounds easy because it has been easy. That is changing. From time to time, there have been weather interruptions and mechanical breakdowns, which usually infuriate people. But those inconveniences are explainable and thus understandable. What about something more sinister? What about terrorism? Does anybody understand terrorism and infrastructure?

The first responsibility of the US government is the security of US citizens. That goes well beyond personal physical protection. National security, being a broad concept, includes the economy, government, transportation, and many other areas. The military forces are part of that national security whether in a foreign land or in our neighborhoods. In the past, adversaries were mostly thought of as distant nations usually expounding a much different ideology than that of the United States. That has changed over the years. Adversaries are no longer solely large distant nations. Adversaries with determination, knowledge, and the means to carry out destructive acts now include individuals and small groups of people—some located within US borders. They may be illegal foreigners or foreigners who have become legal residents. They may live here but have strong allegiance to terrorists groups such as al-Qaeda or ISIS and no allegiance to the US.

If US citizens are ultimately protected from adversaries by the US military, and part of those citizens' national security includes operational infrastructure, and adversaries are now inside our country, then the US military should protect our infrastructure as part of overall citizen protection.

The military would not operate alone in protecting infrastructure. It would cooperate with local police, corporate onsite security, and the US Department of Homeland Security (DHS).

All of these entities working together may sound like overkill, but it won't be ... after an effective working format is worked out. Most of the "working together" is spelled out with leadership and planning. All groups would bring a different ability and individual excellence to any assignment. "Different abilities" could be something as mundane as a person's sleeping habits such as: police officers work eight hours before heading home and army personnel may be at a job site 24/7.

Additional protection for infrastructure generally refers to "critical" infrastructure. It appears the federal government is aware of the importance of critical infrastructure since it is seriously mentioned by the DHS just below:

INFORMATION FOUND AT: www.dhs.gov/critical-infrastructure-sectors

TITLE: CRITICAL INFRASTRUCTURE Sectors

> *There are 16 critical infrastructure sectors whose assets, systems, and networks, whether physical or virtual, are considered so vital to the United States that their incapacitation or destruction would have a debilitating effect on security, national economic security, national public health or safety, or any combination thereof.*

The sixteen critical infrastructure sectors, without description, follow:

- Chemical
- Commercial Facilities
- Communication

- Critical Manufacturing
- Dams
- Defense Industrial Base
- Emergency Service
- Energy
- Financial Services
- Food and Agriculture
- Government Facilities
- Healthcare and Public Health
- Information Technology
- Nuclear Reactors, Material and Waste
- Transportation System
- Water and Wastewater Systems

Looking over the list, it's difficult even to imagine what would take place if any one of these sector's operations was interrupted or shut down across the country. Even across a region. Or even in a small part of a state, especially if a large city is affected. People would be upset. But upset for how long? How long depends on how long the shutdown exists. That may depend on how wide is the area affected. If city-wide, help is nearby. If statewide, the state will need a lot of neighboring states' help. If the problem is region-wide, then national help is needed fast. If the shutdown problem is countrywide ... there is no help. It's mandatory the problem is avoided before it happens.

How long would people be upset? In a worst-case scenario, people would not be upset very long. Instead, they would be killing each other.

All of the infrastructure areas mentioned are singularly very important, but they're also all related in many ways. Readers should take another look at the critical infrastructure list. Pick any one category. If that infrastructure's operation is interrupted or mostly shut down by some act of terror, it would affect all other categories. Some drastically. The easiest to understand is energy or power. When power is shut down, "everything" comes to a stop except your horse. Nearly all electric power flows through the grid. Previous discussion covered an EMP event. Such an event could be very widespread. But it doesn't have to be an EMP disaster. It could be a local, but major, power station that's connected to the grid, which is connected to just about everything.

Smaller events that disrupt power are happening more often in recent time. Cyber-attacks are frequent and increasing. They can come from an individual, group, or country and they can be initiated from anywhere. This is becoming a huge problem with possible severe consequences. But other physical attacks also have the ability to shut down electric service in wide areas as well. Recent articles cover incidents, and there's much talk about related concerns. Is that one of the problems? Plenty of discussions upstairs and lots of friendly talk at the water cooler? More action is needed before the lights go out.

It often seems remedies are slower to materialize when remarks from business people, politicians, and law enforcement have a wide disparity. The actual reporting may be an example. The reported number of cyber-attack incidents varies a lot, and it may be the same for physical attacks. It's also possible there's a general feeling that less disclosure to the public is preferable.

Often, physical attack incidents are attributed to youth vandals. That may be probable and it's actually preferable to other possibilities.

The following articles should be of interest to all:

ARTICLE FOUND AT: www.forbes.com

ARTICLE WRITTEN BY: Loren Thompson

DATE: AUGUST 19, 2015

TITLE: FIVE REASONS the U.S. Power Grid Is Overdue for a Cyber Catastrophe

> As other major industries one by one fall victim to hackers, the U.S. electrical-power generation and distribution system seems remarkably insulated from cyber threats. A March 24 story in USA Today reported that out of 362 attacks on the power grid over the last four years, only 14 were cyberattacks and "there has never been a successful attempt to cause a power outage through a cyberattack in the United States."

> However, a big attack is coming. The intelligence community has noted a rising incidence of assaults on the industrial control mechanisms used to operate the grid, more and more of which are linked in some fashion to the internet. Industry officials admit that data bases recording the frequency of attacks are unreliable because there is no standard definition of what constitutes a cyberattack and utilities are reluctant to report vulnerabilities. Chances are, the networks supporting grid operations are probed every day by outsiders, often with nefarious intent....

> Here are the top five reasons why "the big one" is coming.
> 1. Nothing works without the power grid.
> 2. The current grid has numerous vulnerabilities.
> 3. New technologies make the danger worse.
> 4. Industrial financial incentives are weak.
> 5. The regulatory structure dilutes oversight.

The bottom line is that the U.S. power grid will remain vulnerable to cyberattack for the foreseeable future ..."

Readers should pay special attention to reason number one: "Nothing works without the power grid." There is only one statement in the United States that describes a worse scenario: "Everybody is dead."

Couple reason number one with the last phrase in the article, *"the U.S. power grid will remain vulnerable to cyberattack for the foreseeable future."*

The combination of "nothing works" and "we're vulnerable" is beyond frightening. It is very frightening, and it is very dangerous. And ... we are at risk now.

The government and all citizens must pay whatever the costs are to protect the power grid. That would include substantial preventative measures, a strong management plan for a long power interruption, and a ready-to-go recovery plan for a 6-12 month period. The average citizen will be unable to endure any extreme life struggles that may be the result of a long power grid shutdown.

Another article with some different but troublesome figures follows:

ARTICLE FOUND AT: www.cnn.com

ARTICLE WRITTEN BY: Rene Marsh

DATE: OCTOBER 21, 2015

TITLE: CONGRESSMAN: NATIONAL Power Grid Frequently Attacked

The energy sector is calling for improvement in notification and information sharing from the federal government in the face of ever-increasing cyber and physical attacks on the nation's electric grid, industry experts said before a House panel on Wednesday....

America's electric grid is being modernized through an increased use of "smart grid" technology which includes more digital IT technology. However, a more modernized system also means more interconnectivity and more access points for intruders....

"In just one month, the PJM interconnection—which coordinates electricity transactions in 13 states and in D.C.—experienced 4,090 documented cyber attempts to attack their system," said Rep. Suzanne Bonamici, D-Oregon. "That's more than five and half attacks on their electrical power system per hour."

The PJM Interconnection operation is located in Pennsylvania. On a daily basis, it deals with numerous companies as a large wholesaler of electricity. If the 4,090 number of attempted attacks on its system is accurate, most sane people would agree, there is a significant problem with hackers, and this problem has the potential to wreck the system.

Now is the time to take all preventative actions. The FBI, DHS, corporate security, local police, and the US military should be involved in some manner. Some legal authority should take the lead and formulate a best remedy. This is not suggesting an Army platoon investigate Internet hacking, but it is saying that a competent team to prevent system intruders is necessary. That would include international investigation, prosecution, and the elimination of any type of threat. Don't wait until thirteen states being served by PJM are crippled by a total power shutdown. Prevention is always best, but a fast response and an early recovery are also necessary. The overall task will be extensive.

It's obvious cyber-attacks against the grid are increasing, but so are on-site attacks. Physical attacks have happened at power stations, transformers, and even electric lines across the country. These attacks could take place at any location, but particular installations are more critical than others. These locations need electronic and physical security. It shouldn't be that way, but terrorism has come to the United States, and it must be dealt with by any and all means.

One of the more notable physical attacks occurred on April 16, 2013. It was not only a serious attack but also a sophisticated attack because it was well-planned in advance and little evidence was left behind. Authorities are at a loss as to what really happened, especially concerning motive.

The following article appeared in the *Los Angeles Times*. It provides some factual detail and some interesting comment about the attack.

ARTICLE FOUND AT: www.latimes.com/nation/la-na-grid-attack-20140211-story.html

ARTICLE WRITTEN BY: Richard A. Serrano and Evan Halper

DATE: FEBRUARY 11, 2014

TITLE: SOPHISTICATED BUT Low-Tech Power Grid Attack Baffles Authorities

> *WASHINGTON—They came after midnight, two or more armed individuals so deft that they cut telecommunication cables in an underground vault and outsmarted security cameras and motion sensors at the power substation in a remote corner of Santa Clara County.*
>
> *At daylight, FBI agents began poring over time-lapse photographs from the surveillance cameras. But the photos revealed only staccato muzzle flashes from a semiautomatic weapon and sparks as shots hit rows of transformers. There was not a face, not a shadow, of who was doing the firing.*
>
> *The shooters disappeared into the gloom minutes before the first police car arrived.*

The military-style raid on April 16 knocked out 17 giant trans-formers at the Metcalf Transmission Substation, which feeds power to Silicon Valley. The FBI is still working the case, and agents say they are confident it was not the work of terrorists.

What they do not have is a motive, fingerprints or suspects.

But theories are piling up. Was it a modern-day Monkey Wrench Gang bent on eco-terrorism? Was it a test of the vulnerability of the U.S. electrical grid? Was it a dress rehearsal for a larger attack to come?

Was it an inside job by disgruntled Pacific Gas and Electric Co. em-ployees? Was it related to the bombing of the Boston Marathon across the country only 13 hours earlier? Was it aimed at killing power in Silicon Valley, as one official wondered, "maybe somebody trying to knock down service to Google or something"?

The Metcalf substation incident doesn't sound like teenage vandals. Kids and most other law-breakers blab to someone about their dirty deeds and someone quietly informs the police. Secrets are exposed. Evidence is found. Arrests are made. The damaged facility is repaired and everything gets back to normal. But that was yesterday's bad guy. It's not today's terrorist. Terrorism is here and it's different from noisy crime. Terrorism could be the quiet, friend-ly guy next door or the smiling, hard-working tech guy at the shop.

The article mentions the Metcalf grid incident in Santa Clara County be-ing executed at the same time as the Boston Marathon bombing. Maybe the two incidents were related. Maybe not ... but what if the perpetrators believe in the same anti-American ideology? Does that make the incidents indirectly related? Foreign influence was absolutely involved in Boston. That's terror-ism. The question remains today ... was Santa Clara terrorism?

The damage at the Pacific Gas and Electric (PG&E) unit was over $15 million. That doesn't sound like a prank. Apparently, the seventeen giant transformers are cooled by oil. At least one, maybe several, lost its cooling ability when over 50,000 gallons of oil leaked onto the ground. That usually leads to a transformer's complete destruction. Some believe that is exactly what was intended. If all transformers burned up because of lost coolant, it would have been a critical situation in Silicon Valley.

There's something else not talked about in public reports. Is it possible the shooters were depending on rifle bullets causing sparks when hitting steel, thereby starting an oil fire? What if the shooters had used explosive-type ammo? What if they would have used an RPG (rocket-propelled grenade)? Tens of millions of RPGs have been produced and they are quite common throughout the world, including within terrorist groups. If transformers be-ing cooled with 100,000 gallons of oil had caught fire, it's probable the entire substation would have been destroyed. The facility may be called a substation, but it is quite large and quite complex. It's also located in a sparse area about 100 feet off a major highway. A car could drive up in the middle of the night and stop for as little as one minute. Two men could step out quickly and fire two or three RPG rounds into specific targets such as oil-filled transformers. The end result could easily be the entire electric transmission station being destroyed. The facility would then need to be completely rebuilt. Would that take one year, two years, or three years?

The above scenario may sound far-fetched but … is it really? It appears fairly easy to accomplish compared to destroying the World Trade Center in New York City.

Silicon Valley is home to hundreds of high-tech companies, including many world-class institutions. They're involved in everyday operations around the world. Necessary working connections exist between Silicon Valley and strategic locations everywhere. What happens if Silicon Valley can't function normally for six months? Would there be related interruptions or other upheavals around the world? Are some Silicon Valley companies interconnected with super-critical operations around the world? Were the Metcalf attackers seeking to cause an international incident? The answers to these four questions: something similar to an electronic ice-age, yes, yes, and unknown.

As usual, frank discussion, swift action, and effective prevention methods are called for to protect important infrastructure such as the Metcalf Transmission Substation. That should be acutely clear to everyone after such an attack. But why wait until after an attack? Prevention is always clear then.

Shortly after the April 16, 2013 shooting attack, PG&E indicated the substation would be safe from terrorists, vandals, or intruders of any kind.

After any attack or near tragedy, it's always calming for the public to hear authorities claim they're taking immediate action to ensure against any future problems. But often that "immediate action time" exceeds the calmness respite. Around the Metcalf area, it must have been disconcerting for area residents to read the article below.

ARTICLE FOUND AT: www.nbcbayarea.com/investagations
ARTICLE WRITTEN BY: Scott Pham and Cheryl Hurd
DATE: AUGUST 27, 2014
TITLE: NEW SECURITY BREACH at Metcalf Substation, Site of 2013 Sniper Attack

> More than a year after a major sniper attack at an electrical substation near San Jose, a new security breach has PG&E asking the public for help.

> *PG&E officials said burglars stole construction equipment from the Metcalf Substation. The security breach happened at about 2 a.m. Wednesday along a fence line at the station, with burglars cutting through in three locations.*

It appears PG&E officials, police, and government investigators may have been treating the April 2013 sniper attack as some kind of unusual accident. One year and four months passed after a very serious shooting attack. Nearly 500 days. Isn't that more than enough time for discussion, action, and installation of adequate preventative measures at such an important facility as Metcalf?

The August 2014 facility intrusion did not cause any shutdown of electric service. What it did do was demonstrate the unfortunate fact that authorities, those charged with service to and security of American citizens, are not doing their job sufficiently.

In today's world of surprise terrorism, even doing an adequate security job may not suffice. Going beyond what we normally think is required.

Apparently, the second Metcalf attack or, as authorities say, intrusion, has had an effect on installing preventative measures to safeguard both the facility and citizens in the region. An NBC Bay Area news report provided an update on some overdue security work at Metcalf. Citizens can judge for themselves the progress, or lack thereof, at Metcalf.

It appears authorities often lack an understanding of the word "critical":
ARTICLE FOUND AT: www.nbcbayarea.com/news/local/PGE-Makes-Security-Upgrades-at-Metcalf-Substation-297045201.html
ARTICLE WRITTEN BY: Tony Kovaleski, Liz Wagner, and Mark Villarreal
DATE: MARCH 20, 2015
TITLE: PG&E MAKES Security Upgrades at Metcalf Substation

> *Construction is underway on security enhancements nearly two years after a sniper attack crippled the facility and six months after an NBC Bay Area investigation exposed potential security vulnerabilities at some of PG&E's critical substations.*

> *Pacific Gas & Electric Company (PG&E) is in the process of improving security at an electric substation in south San Jose nearly two years after snipers attacked the facility. The company has begun to install more security cameras, better lighting and concrete fencing around the facility's perimeter to protect the critical infrastructure responsible for powering much of Silicon Valley....*

> *Last summer, NBC Bay Area discovered that many of the improvements PG&E promised had failed to materialize. The Investigative Unit*

made 14 unannounced visits to nine substations in northern and central California and found that many security vulnerabilities still existed at the locations more than 18 months after the attack on the Metcalf facility.

The story above ... and the following question are repeated too often in the United States: What does it take for politicians and various authorities to get off their collective duffs and initiate frank discussion that leads to swift action in installing effective prevention methods that would greatly improve critical-infrastructure security?

The sniper-shooting incident at Metcalf was two years in the past before moderate prevention efforts were completed. What took so long? It's as if authorities were waiting to see whether the April 2013 sniper attack was comparable to what's known as "the 100-year flood." When it comes to national security, authorities should not be waiting, guessing, hoping, wishing or praying. While they waited and hoped, adversaries were preparing another attack. And, there was another attack. It was sixteen months after the first attack, and it was successful.

If authorities were banking on the 100-year mark ... they missed by ninety-eight years.

As of this writing, all investigations at Metcalf are ongoing. The progress is unknown. Urgency is unknown. Site reinforcement such as cement fences, additional cameras, and a number of guards are said finally to be in place. These added measures are fine and dandy, but they could have been completed within thirty days of the first attack. Apparently, the attitude needed to accomplish an immediate "hardening" of the site was slow to materialize. But there was something immediate on April 16, 2013. The sniper attack itself. The Metcalf attack should have served as an immediate warning to all US authorities that extraordinary protection may be needed at 25,000 critical infrastructure sites. The key word being "extraordinary." Extraordinary calls for extra protection. More than regular. Beyond ordinary. But still, the nation awaits.

Many political authorities will resist spending scarce money to protect against the remote possibility of an unknown infrastructure attack. Vote money is always more important. But the risk factor for any possible attack taking place should always be calculated by security experts. They should recognize that a surprise terrorist attack and its consequences provide a serious threat today.

Infrastructure, such as electric power stations, is always important. Dams are too. There are as many as 87,000 dams in the United States. Most are small or very small. Many others are large structures necessary to sustain regular life in very large areas. It would be difficult, but not impossible, for terrorists to enter critical areas and then use enough explosives to destroy a large dam. If that did happen, the ramifications would be more than severe. The easy part of "recovery" might be the five years it would take to build a new dam.

Political leaders and infrastructure site management should start with the following question: What would life be like in this area if this particular infrastructure were seriously damaged or destroyed? Using any dam as an example would be a good start.

It's unknown whether Metcalf management ever calculated what life would be like if a long-term shutdown happened in the region. It further appears Metcalf management presumed there could never be another attack or intrusion at its substation so why not take two years to reinforce the site. The second attack must have changed their lethargic thinking.

Another example of reluctant management might involve a high profile infrastructure target such as an airport. The airport authority may feel an obligation or receive public pressure to strengthen the airport perimeter. Airline management, being non-owners of the airport but trying to maintain their own budget, may quietly suggest perimeter reinforcement is not needed and too expensive. Upon completion of any upgraded security, including additional security personnel, the added cost would probably mean airline landing fees increase. Airlines would then be forced to raise ticket prices and customers would complain. Nobody wants any of that, but everybody wants security.

In an earlier chapter, I discussed doubling the size of the military, stipulating all would serve, but most for a single year and only domestically. These service members would preferably be stationed close to home or possibly live at home. Recruiters and reservists live at home.

However, these short-termers may be "one big answer" to safeguarding the nation's critical infrastructure. And get it done without breaking the bank.

Critical infrastructure is … critical. Therefore, protecting it is critical. That protection would be an important job, and some training would be necessary, but military short-termers could play an important role here at home. Military service is thought of as protecting our nation against adversaries. Anyone, especially a terrorist group, attacking homeland infrastructure is an adversary.

How would this work? The Metcalf substation will be used as an example: The substation would easily qualify as a critical infrastructure location, thereby making the site available for federal assistance. Namely, guard duty.

The main criteria used to qualify any infrastructure as critical infrastructure would be: 1) If the infrastructure were destroyed or severely damaged, would it make the surrounding area or another area served by the infrastructure un-livable or unusable, and 2) Would the repair or replacement of the destroyed or damaged infrastructure exceed thirty days?

Using federal assistance in the form of military guard duty does not mean Metcalf internal security, local police, or DHS personnel would not be in-volved. The military security role would be limited. It can and would provide physical onsite protection on a 24/7 basis. It would function exactly as secu-rity functions at any military base around the world. One exception might be the operation of a front gate or entrance. Who is allowed to enter a restricted area would be determined solely by facility management.

Critical infrastructure guard-work would not be suitable for all service members. General selection would come from volunteers among those serv-ing the minimum one-year enlistment. Besides the usual military discipline that greatly benefits our nation's youth, those members selected to protect vital assets may also feel genuine pride as "protectors of the homeland."

Selected members would be part of the SDA (Special Duty Assignment) personnel protecting critical infrastructure. Important work in an important unit serving the United States. And, it would look good on any resume.

It's probable that nearby Military Reserve Units would be involved with this special infrastructure guard duty. Personnel from reserve units typically serve part-time each month for six years. They generally meet for training on Friday evening or Saturday morning at an armory that houses their equip-ment and provides shelter when needed. Often, they convoy to a field loca-tion and set up a complete functioning military field base before returning to the armory on Sunday night. This exercise provides two days and two nights in the field. All of these individual reserve members have been trained in particular jobs and function as any full-time military unit, except on a part-time basis.

The Metcalf guard duty assignment could operate exactly as reserve mil-itary members do when in the field. The number of guards needed would vary depending on the infrastructure being secured. At Metcalf, that number might be as few as six or eight. Number TBD. They would operate the same as border patrol duty or military base security. The security team could rotate daily or camp on site for several days before replacements relieve it. It could rotate with others who are fulfilling their duty at a nearby armory. Scheduling and logistics would be worked out as needed to accomplish the mission. That mission: to secure the site with 24/7 security to prevent or counter any kind of attack.

Critics will suggest many reasons against any plan that has military service members protecting infrastructure. Simple reasons such as:

1. It's more of a private security matter than federal.

2. It's too costly.

3. It's not needed because a security breech is rare.

4. It would not be effective.

5. Guards are too young for a serious job.

6. One-year service members learn little being guards.

There are critics for every plan, especially if it's new or different. But critics are necessary as they help arrive at a best course of action.

Here are simple answers to each of the above criticisms by number:

1. The Federal government's number-one job is to protect US citizens.

2. Military members are paid regardless of what they're doing.

3. Rare, yes, but if it happens, it could seriously change the country.

4. Service members protect military bases so it must be effective.

5. Battlefield deaths are serious and most are very young.

6. Members learn about authority, discipline, responsibility, leadership, teamwork, and law enforcement practice.

Obviously, much more could be said, but it doesn't need to be covered here. Certain infrastructure sites, if ever destroyed, would result in many American deaths and change the direction of the country. Infrastructure is at risk now. If the infrastructure is at risk, then the United States is at risk. Certainly, recent history demonstrates what is possible in this dangerous world.

The attack on September 11, 2001, was one of the most successful attacks in world history. It may be arguable whether the attack was actually an attack on infrastructure or not, but DHS does list "financial services" as a critical infrastructure. Therefore, New York's financial district qualifies as critical financial infrastructure. What makes a structure critical is often the aftermath of its destruction. Reconstruction is not always a remedy. Rapid reconstruction is a rarity. There may be no good remedy at all, thus making "more than adequate" prevention most important.

Answer #3 above reads, "Rare, yes, but if it happens, it could seriously change the country." Did the country change forever after 9/11? The answer to that varies a bit, but yes is the most complete answer. It appears many things did change and they're quite permanent: American citizens now feel vulnerable, the US has spent a trillion dollars because of 9/11 and that money is not recoverable, increased security costs are ongoing and will continue forever, American citizens must now put up with inconveniences such as airport searches because they have no choice in today's world.

The DHS was created after 9/11 and at least partially because of the attack. It's another bloated and permanent federal agency that's often too cumbersome in its operation. Is DHS necessary? Yes, many of its departments serve a vital service in national security and during natural disasters.

The United States can't afford another large, successful terrorist attack. It's not affordable financially or psychologically.

The US economy remains relatively weak after the 9/11 event, compared to its earlier history. And US citizens, having been among the freest in the world, feel less secure today than yesterday.

Readers should try to imagine the magnitude of the 9/11 attack, but with a change of target. What would have been the immediate aftermath and the long-term effects if instead of the World Trade Center (WTC) buildings being obliterated, a large nuclear power plant had been? Or a large dam producing power for tens of millions of people living in cities downstream from the dam?

If these type targets suffered a similar fate as the WTC, that region of the country might be unlivable today. A formerly vibrant, densely populated area of the United States could end up a wasteland for decades.

If it's feasible to help protect particular critical infrastructure locations with armed forces personnel on site, then it should be started immediately.

The 24/7 physical security would work well at the Metcalf Transmission Substation. Less so at super-busy sites such as New York's financial district.

Many facilities are certainly not critical infrastructure but are substantial public-access locations that may be targets for terrorists. These areas also need adequate security at all times. From time to time, extensive security is required, and those times increase with every incident. Locations considered "public-access" would not qualify for federal security assistance, nor would such assistance be very workable in our society. We are not a police-state, but our everyday freedoms decline with every additional terrorist attack.

Locations such as sports stadiums, shopping centers, schools, or any natural gathering place for people are easy targets. An attack on these locations by terrorists or any adversary is different than an attack on a power station or dam facility. People can be seriously affected in all cases, but most crowd-gathering places are usually not critical to keep the US physically operating normally. These places have less security, easier access, and are comparably quite public. They're referred to as soft-targets. People are the target, not the facility.

The immediate and ongoing financial effect on the country may be great when critical infrastructure is destroyed, but psychologically, the long-lasting effect from mass casualties is equally devastating. The psychological damage reaches every state and may last forever. All Americans feel violated and will be reminded of it often. When a school is attacked, causing a large number of casualties, the security will increase at all schools. That is already happening across the country because of past incidents involving American citizens. These criminal citizens, usually individuals, end up in jail or deceased. They're completely eliminated from society and can never again execute an attack. Nevertheless, schools still increase security. People, and especially parents, see the additional security every day and are reminded of what happened somewhere in the United States. Recent notorious events such as the Sandy Hook Elementary School in Connecticut or Virginia Tech University shootings were major incidents focused on soft-targets. These attacks are now part of American history, but they will forever be a reminder of our need for security. The school attacks weren't necessarily terrorism, but the end result was about the same.

When a major terrorist attack happens against any one of millions of soft-targets, it's a very bad day all across the United States. Citizens are reminded terrorism is never 100 percent preventable. The military just can't be present at soft-target sites to deter terrorism. They can be involved in alternative ways.

The repercussions from a soft-target terrorist attack will be many and varied. Much anger, sadness, and fright will pervade the entire country. The ongoing security cost will increase, and society will feel the financial pain. When would that end? Never. Look at the airports today.

Soft-target terrorism has been around a long time, but it's found its way into the United States during the last two decades. Soft-targets are easy. Hard targets may have reinforced facilities or other high security measures in place, including guards around the perimeter. Are those higher security measures enough? Think about that question. Whatever the answer … it's not guaranteed. Terrorist methods evolve. Terrorists have more patience than Americans. And terrorists could be working inside our secure facilities as trusted employees just waiting for orders from above. Time will tell.

It should also be obvious to authorities that terrorists may switch from a hard-target infrastructure facility to a soft-target location. Soft-targets are easy and readily available. They're usually "public people places," making any attack successful with a high casualty count. High death counts brings wide notoriety.

Other attacks may have other motives and repercussions. It's not always physical damage to critical infrastructure, financial loss, or a high body count. It could be considerable psychological damage to society, and that can last forever.

The following pages provide a **"rough overview of a terrorist plot"** against a soft-target in the United States. A fair amount of detail is included because its author believes a terrorist attack's success or failure often depends on strict attention to detail. In this presentation, the terrorist's objective is to produce "immediate, long-lasting, and nationwide psychological terror." The paper was originally presented by the author for a past project, but it is now approved for release. Actual locations and dates were used at that time but are now past. Very minor changes or omissions were needed for this paper to be included in this public book.

Terrorist Attack Paper
By: S.B. Shine

The purpose of this paper is to develop a terrorist attack with a high probability of success within the United States. Here, in this educational exercise, the desire is that the "success" of the attack (from the terrorist's viewpoint) not be measured by the number of casualties nor the amount of structural damage done, although those measures always add to overall shock. The goal here is to develop and demonstrate a terrorist attack that is fairly easy to execute and that "success" be measured by the immediate extensive notoriety, the adverse effect on present and future American entertainment, the added layer of economic security costs going forward, and the escape of the bombers as compared to the 9/11 hijackers.

BASIC CHARACTERISTICS of this terrorist attack

The attack operation team totals fourteen men. This includes eight members in the Middle East (ME). They will be known as ME1, ME2, ME3, ME4, ME5, ME6, ME7, and ME8. The other six team members are the attack team (AT) already located in the United States (US) as members of terrorist cells or possibly "lone wolves" and probably of Middle-Eastern culture. They will be known as US-AT1, US-AT2, US-AT3, US-AT4, US-AT5, and US-AT6. These US-AT members are located in different regions of the United States and do not know each other or do not know each other on a working basis.

The attack will be a bomb/IED attack.

The attack will be in six separate US locations.

The attack will take place at 3:11 p.m. EST on November 21, 2015.

The attack to be described demonstrates the usual terrorist intentions: surprise, panic, chaos, and suggests, "We can strike anywhere, anytime."

The attack will be an explosion in an area crowded with only Americans.

Please note:

The excessive amount of attack preparation detail presented, some very minor, is included for several reasons. Often, a mission may fail on a single, overlooked detail. It is also very important that much care is taken so no suspicion, not even a minor item, is raised concerning a possible attack. If authorities pick up just a hint of trouble about the attack date, the attack area, or the attack event itself, their focus would immediately center on the "exact" target. Any suspicion would bring additional and "next level" security to the target location, which could easily mean mission failure across multiple sites. Much attention is given to travel security. All communication with the six attackers (US-AT1 through 6) is person to person and on a need-to-know basis. Physical appearance of the actual attacker is stressed. Much of this writing will appear as "instructions" to the bomber. Different designations and abbreviations will be used throughout and may make this writing difficult to follow, such as: team members (ME or US-AT) airport codes (SLC, ORD, MPS), cities (MPLS, NYC, SLC).

DESCRIPTION of eight Terrorist Team members in the Middle East, including Title, Duties, and Requirements

ME1 - Leader. Fundraising. Sole contact person for any US-based "cell leaders" (not US-ATs) who may recommend prospective US-AT members but *never* any talk about any attack plans.

ME2 - Logistics Expert. Research Specialist for plan needs in US.

ME3 - Travel Expert. Assists with Visa needs. Makes most travel arrangements. Instructs traveling team members about travel security aspects. Research Specialist for plan needs in US.

ME4 - Bomb Maker Expert. Has ability to teach bomb techniques to ME6-7-8. Research Specialist concerning explosive material in US-designated areas.

ME5 - Expert in covert methods and activity. Research Specialist concerning US security.

ME6-7-8 – Fluent in English. Driver's license. Educated. Ability to travel legally to Europe and US with valid Passport and Visa. Ability to carry/use three different credit cards. Ability to work closely with ME2-3-4-5 for attack plan understanding.

DESCRIPTION of six Terrorist Team members already located in the US

US-AT1 through 6 – Fluent in English. Ability to follow instructions exactly and improvise when necessary.

INFORMATION about US-AT members

The six US-AT members will be chosen from approximately twelve men. The six members are unaware of each other and thus will have no communication between them. The only contact available for them will be *from* their single ME partner, being ME6, ME7, or ME8. All communication mentioning the attack is face to face. Each of these six attackers believes he is the sole bomber at a single target and won't know the actual target until 3-4 weeks prior to attack date.

FIRST MEETING in Middle East

On or about May 21, 2015, the ME1 through ME8 members gather in a Middle East location six months prior to the target attack date of November 21, 2015. The first month will consist of ME1 through ME8 doing extensive research on US locations and putting together the basic outline of the future attack. ME6-7-8 prepare for their US meetings with and selection of US-AT members. Travel plans and documents will immediately be arranged for ME6-7-8 to travel from a Middle Eastern city to a European city to a United States city.

TRAVEL flight itinerary for ME6-7-8

The departing travel dates to the US through Europe depend on the amount of preparation work accomplished by ME1 through ME8 during the initial four to six weeks of planning. Estimated flight dates between 6/21/15 and 7/6/15. Date 7/4/15 excluded for security reasons. ME6-7-8 do not travel together. They do not travel on same day. They do not travel on the same airline between Europe and the US. They do not travel to same European city or same US city. All tickets will be purchased using separate credit cards. All tickets will be full-fare round-trip tickets with open-date return.

ME6 will fly to Rome from Middle East. Different airline Rome to Los Angeles (LA) airport (LAX). One day lay over in LA and a visit to any local university grad school for brief inquiry and collecting some printed info. This is to help establish reason and interest in coming to US if needed. Flight from LA to Salt Lake City (SLC) airport (SLC). Rental car arranged in person at airport.

ME7 will fly to Paris from Middle East and from Paris to New York City (NYC) airport (JFK). No continuing flight beyond JFK. SAME ROUTINE visiting local university as ME6.

ME8 will fly to London from Middle East and from London to Chicago (CHI) airport (ORD). No continuing flight beyond ORD. SAME ROUTINE, visiting local university, as ME6 and ME7.

SELECTION of US-AT members by ME6-7-8

ME6 work. ME6 will interview *separately* two different cell members located in the general SLC area. It should be that no cell members know each other or at least do not know of each other's individual meeting with ME6. ME6 will select one of the two for the upcoming attack. The other will be told he may be contacted later. At this point, neither prospective member knows anything concerning the attack. Daily meetings with each may last several days or a week. Casual meetings at first. ME6 is interested in general appearance, conversation in English, confidence, apparent ability to improvise, following directions, timeliness, ability to keep quiet, and willingness to alter appearance, such as shaving. As a test, ME6 may ask the potential US-AT member to set up a 100 percent covert meeting/talk between the two (ME6 and US-AT candidate) and let him do/say/handle everything. As an example, if the candidate drives ME6 to a public park and picks an outside area to chat or strolls to a picnic table among many tables as a place to sit with a sandwich, that would be a good sign. Other ME6 observations of the candidate at such a meeting: does he check for a wire, does he say a lot of words with his hand shielding his mouth in multiple manners, head turning different directions, hand gestures pointing toward anything for no reason or an occasional laugh? All "meaningless" movements done so it appears conversation is fun and friendly instead of a serious discussion. ME6 makes selection of US-AT1. Initial work in SLC area is concluded.

Please note:

Concerning the above-mentioned "conversation" detail – In-room bugs are common, but there are also listening devices that can pick up sound waves of speaking from many miles away. Nearby lip readers are common, but there are also sight devices as small as a quarter that can read lips from many miles away.[1] It's important for speakers to interfere with line-of-sight or listening when possible.

ME6 then flies from SLC to Minneapolis (MPLS) airport (MSP) to interview and select his second US-AT team member who is located in the general MPLS area. ME6 uses exact SAME ROUTINE in selection process as he did in SLC. ME6 will be working with two separate team members. One in SLC area and one in MPLS area. ME6's MPLS selection becomes US-AT2. ME6 is now the sole ME connection for US-AT1 (SLC area) and US-AT2 (MPLS area). ME6 changes return ticket from LA to Rome for new routing of MPLS to Rome. Rome to Middle East.

1   Intevac, Inc., Photonics Div., Santa Clara, CA, www.intevac.com.

ME7 work. ME7 drives to an area northeast of NYC to interview and select US-AT3. ME7 then drives to southwest of NYC to interview and select US-AT4. ME7 uses SAME ROUTINE of interview/selection as detailed under ME6. ME7 uses return ticket to fly from NYC to Paris. Paris to Middle East.

ME8 work. ME8 drives to an area northwest of Chicago to interview/select US-AT5. ME8 then drives southeast of Chicago to interview/select US-AT6. ME8 uses SAME ROUTINE as detailed under ME6. ME8 uses return ticket to fly from Chicago to London. London to Middle East.

APPROXIMATE DATE AUGUST 1, 2015

The US team of six members is now complete. They are located in six different regions of the US. Each is unaware of his counterparts and has no knowledge about the attack plan. They have been instructed to continue a normal routine for the next ten weeks until ME6-7-8 return to US with final instructions for attack. They are to maintain explosives in their possession or obtain additional explosives if needed. No discussion with anyone about ME6-7-8 meetings. No investigative work of any kind online. All relevant info will be provided in person by ME6-7-8 at a later date.

The Middle East team, ME1 through ME8, is now back together at Middle East location. They have ten weeks to rehearse, perfect, and finalize all details of the terrorist attack. The next contact with US-AT1 through US-AT6 will be when ME6-7-8 return back to the US on or about October 15, 2015.

DECISIONS and DETAILS of attack plan by ME1 thru 8

Clothing for US-AT1 through US-AT6 on "Day of Attack." All clothes for US-ATs purchased new after ME6-7-8 return to US. Coat - Medium weight. Length to hip. Color brown, tan, or gray. No red, black, camouflage, or Army green. Exterior fabric - not shiny. Lining fabric - strong but appears easy to remove. Baseball hat - color to be determined. Shirt - long-sleeved. No bright colors. Pants - Blue Jeans. Belt with large non-descript metal buckle. Gym shoes - No bright colors.

Appearance of US-AT1 through US-AT6 on "Day of Attack." No beard. No long hair. No bald. No sunglasses.

Coat Alteration for Explosives - Coat alteration is an integral part of plan. Coat to be made similar to a suicide vest. The liner will be altered or replaced so it can conceal explosives. Explosives will be located under each arm and less toward the back. Liner reattached "except" at the vertical center back of coat. Following the length of the wearer's backbone, the coat will be free of a liner. This vertical strip would be six inches wide from collar to tail. This is so the coat can be easily split later with a box cutter into two identical halves. Coat will contain two bombs, each with separate mechanism to detonate. One bomber, one coat, two bombs.

Bomb/Explosive to be used - C-4 or Semtex. More explosive than TNT and not very sensitive. Stats show a 20 lb. charge of TNT would have a Mandatory Evacuation Distance of 110 ft. and a Preferred Evacuation Distance of 1750 ft.[2] Speed of Expansion rate near 26,500 ft./second.[3] The attack being planned would use a smaller charge estimated in the range of 2½ - 5 lb. (each side of coat), but the explosive to be used is also somewhat more powerful than TNT. Depending on the actual placement of the bombs and surrounding structure, you can expect a sizeable number of casualties. Injuries extensive.

Add an orange, yellow, or red-colored smoke agent to the bomb if feasible. People will fear breathing in the colored smoke. This should increase panic at site, causing additional injuries.

Detonation by remote connection such as cell phone. Cell phones are convenient.

Please note:

"The remote controlled IED is the terrorist's first choice of bombs today. That's because they are so easy to construct and deploy."[4]

"The signal engages a relay connected to a blasting cap, which in turn detonates explosive material. Often the vibration function is the part terrorists use to trigger bombs."[5]

PRECAUTIONS

There are some precautions to take with explosives besides the obvious. You may not know the age of the explosive or the atmosphere it has been stored in over time. Shelf life could be important as some explosives loose strength with age. Use material less than five years old. However, be

2   The National Counterterrorism Center, 2014 Calendar, Methods and Tactics, Bomb Threat Distances, www.NCTC.gov/site/technical/Bomb_Threat.html

3   Tom Harris, How C-4 Works, C-4 Plastic Explosives, Science, http://science.howstuffworks.com/c-42.htm

4   Howard Melamed, CEO, Cell Antenna Corp., Coral Springs, FL., quoted by Christa Miller, Cell Phone Bombs, www.officer.com/article/10250461/cell-phone-bombs

5   Christa Miller, Cell Phone Bombs, www.officer.com/article/10250461/cell-phone-bombs

aware that more recently produced explosives have a "taggant" (added ingredient) added. This taggant may allow a chemical vapor to be picked up by a sniffer prior to detonation. After explosion, a taggant may allow the explosive's origin to be determined. A taggant is similar to a fingerprint.[6]

For detonators, use foreign made batteries *without* a brand name if possible. Counterfeit batteries may be *best* since they often lack any fail-safe mechanism. "Batteries are designed to be 'fail safe.' Although, some batteries made overseas lack 'fail safe' feature and best to use."[7] Fail safe could interrupt rigged detonator operation.

Finished bomb and detonator device should be hard-wrapped for added vapor seal. Keep explosive material away from clothes to be worn on day of attack. Use gloves. Wash yourself with bleach.

TARGET SELECTION CRITERIA

Terrorist cell currently located in general area. Explosive availability. Northern half of US. Extensive television viewership. Large number of American people. Large city nearby. US team members (US-AT1 through US-AT6) have ability to be inconspicuous at target and surrounding area. Alternate target nearby.

PRIMARY TARGETS

1. **Level Edwards Stadium** in Provo, UT; Game – Fresno State Univ vs Brigham Young Univ; 63,000 seats; Time Zone MST; Temp 36°; large city- Salt Lake City, UT 42 mi/46min; bomber US-AT1.

2. **TCF Bank Stadium** in Minneapolis, MN; Game - Univ of Illinois vs Univ of Minnesota; 51,000 seats; Time Zone CST; Temp 26°; large city -Minneapolis, MN - 3mi/10min; bomber US-AT2.

3. **Yale Bowl Stadium** in New Haven, CT; Game Harvard Univ vs Yale Univ; 64,000 seats; Time Zone EST, Temp 40°; large city - Hartford, CT 39mi/42min; bomber US-AT3.

4. **Lincoln Financial Stadium** in Philadelphia, PA; Game Univ of Memphis vs Temple Univ; 69,000 seats; Time Zone EST; Temp 42°; large city - Philadelphia, PA 2mi/6min; bomber US-AT4.

5. **Camp Randal Stadium** in Madison, WI; Game Northwestern

---

6   Microtrace LLC, Taggant Technologies, www.microsolutions.com/
     taggant-technolgies/?gclid
7   Jim Akridge, CEO, (former) Valence Technologies, Austin, TX, www.valence.com

Univ vs Univ of Wisconsin; 80,000 seats; Time Zone CST; Temp 29°; large city - Madison, WI 2mi/5min; bomber US-AT5.

6. ***Ohio Stadium*** in Columbus, OH; Game Michigan State Univ vs Ohio State Univ; 105,000 seats; Time Zone EST; Temp 37°; large city - Columbus, OH 2mi/6min; bomber US-AT6.

ALTERNATE TARGETS *nearby*

A1) ***Rice Eccles Stadium*** in Salt Lake City, UT; Game UCLA vs Univ of Utah; 45,000 seats; Time Zone MST; Temp 35°; large city – Salt Lake City, UT 3mi/6min; bomber US-AT1.

A2) ***Beaver Stadium*** in State College, PA; Game Univ of Michigan vs Penn State Univ; 107,000 seats; Time Zone EST; Temp 35°; large city – Harrisburg, PA 87mi/92min; bomber US-AT4.

A3) ***Kinnick Stadium*** in Iowa City, IA; Game Purdue Univ vs Univ of Iowa; 70,000 seats; Time Zone CST; Temp 33°; large city – Des Moines, IA 113 mi/100 min; Bomber US-AT5.

A4) ***Heinz Stadium*** in Pittsburgh, PA ; Game Univ of Louisville vs Univ of Pittsburgh; 65,000 seats; Time Zone EST; Temp 38°; large city – Pittsburgh, PA 3mi/7min; bomber US-AT6.

Please note:

All Targets are in three different time zones. Most games start at 1:00 p.m. As of this writing game times are listed as TBA. Detonation time is set for 3:11 p.m. EST. This equates with 2:11 p.m. CST and 1:11 p.m. MST.

All 12 detonations should be simultaneous or within a three-minute span. Detonation may be early in one game, such as 1st quarter, but late in another game, such as 4th quarter. NEAR-SIMULTANEOUS DETONATION IS THE KEY.

Game starting times could be adjusted for TV broadcasts and still be workable depending on time zone.

An alternate target could be substituted depending on circumstances.

Television – All games will be televised. Some telecasts will be national. Some regional. Many viewers will watch their favorite teams on pay-per-view.

Temperature – All stipulated temps are an average of the mean temp listed for November and December at the individual stadium location. All appear to be "coat-needed" temps.

BOMB LOCATION and placement in Stadium

Testing in the ME includes a limited mock-up of seats/stands with explosives used. Results will vary. Seat construction is very important. Preferred seat is a slatted or solid folding seat made of heavy metal, hard plastic, or aluminum. Thicker is better. Hard plastic is typical. Folding seats are usually available, but they may be limited. Lesser choice is aluminum bench seating. The seat material will be blast splintered and function as shrapnel.

The coat bomb (½ of coat) is placed under the seat and pushed up toward the back of the seat. It should be as close as possible to seat supports or brackets. Second bomb (½ of coat) is placed on other side of stadium in the same manner among seats purchased.

STADIUM SEAT ticketing

All tickets will be purchased with cash after ME6-7-8 return to US. It's preferable that ME6-7-8 purchase tickets. ME6-7-8 will each meet individually with their two US attack team members to brief them on actual attack. Stadium seating charts would have already been viewed online in the Middle East. Seating layout should be checked again at stadium ticket window and/or while attending an earlier game for familiarity.

An earlier game at target stadium, one to three weeks before November 21, should be attended by either or both men (ME6-7 or 8 and/or US-ATs) to identify seat sections and general design of stadium. No photos. No notes. No measuring. Purchase tickets for "folding seats" in any section available before aluminum bench seats but always prefer seats at the 25-30 yard line. Prefer Row 25-30. Prefer end of row. Purchase four seats. Two seats in tandem. Such as end of Row 30, end seat #40 and adjoining seat #41. Also, purchase Row 29, end seat #40 and seat #41. These seats will be fairly close to end of stadium. On another day or at a different ticket window, buy four seats on the other side of the stadium. Same seating preferences. Most important are folding seats and end of row seats so US-AT bomber can come and go without rubbing against people. All tickets kept in pants pocket, not coat pocket.

If no tickets available at ticket window, then improvise. Ask whether a block of tickets is always "released" for sale at the last moment. Find out best way to obtain them. Last resort is to arrive at stadium early and buy one to four tickets off the street. Have plenty of cash. Prefer three or four tickets together rather than one. Inside stadium and just before detonation time, there may be preferable empty seats to use. Improvise.

ME6-7-8 TRAVEL to US for second time on or about October 15, 2015

Travel arrangements are similar to those four months earlier. ME to Europe. Europe to US. Only change is that each ME member departs from different European city than first trip but arrives same US city.

ME6-7-8 PREPARE US-AT1 through US-AT6 for November 21, 2015 attack

ME6-7-8 have only five weeks to disclose attack plan and train all US-AT1 through US-AT6 members. There is nothing in writing. Person-to-person, verbal instruction only concerning time table, target, entering target, after-attack escape, explosive use, method of detonation, clothes, transportation, behavior at target, seating requirements, and what to expect during any part of the attack plan.

Please note for clarification:

ME6 arrives Salt Lake City (SLC) and meets with US-AT1.

ME6 then flies to Minneapolis (MSP) and meets with US-AT2.

During this five-week briefing period, it is expected ME6 will fly back and forth several times between SLC and MSP as needed in order to get both bombers, US-AT1 and US-AT2, to full readiness to complete mission. This task is difficult because of distance but very workable since both SLC and MSP are hubs for Delta Airlines. This means there are many flights between the hubs all day long. ME6 would simply drive to the airport and buy a full-fare ticket with credit card at the ticket counter for the next flight. If flight is full, ask to be put on the "revenue standby" list. If you don't get on the flight, you'll be automatically "rolled over" to the next flight, which might be an hour or two wait. This "rollover" gives some added seat priority for the next flight.

ME7 arrives New York City (JFK) and drives to meet US-AT3.

ME7 then drives short distance to meet US-AT4.

ME7 follows SAME ROUTINE as ME6 to train and bring US-AT3 and US-AT4 to full readiness. ME7 drives back and forth as needed.

ME8 arrives Chicago (ORD) and drives to meet US-AT5.

ME8 then drives short distance to meet US-AT6.

SAME ROUTINE as ME7.

Two days before attack date, all training should be completed with US-AT1 through US-AT6 team. Individual US-AT members should each still think he is sole bomber. ME6-7-8 depart US.

ENTRANCE TO STADIUM on November 21, 2015

Vehicle checked and ready. Arrive at Stadium area 1½ hours before game time. Park about ¾ mile from stadium near main exit street. Clothes as required. Home team color baseball hat. Binoculars hanging around neck. Belt with metal buckle on pants. Plastic bottle of water in hand ½ full. Accessories in pockets: Two cell phones, six safety pins, two very light rain ponchos to keep coat dry, two small plastic box cutters, (one hanging on car-key chain, the other flat about 1½ inch sq. in pocket with coins) Walk with crowd to main entrance. Casually observe security routine at gate. Do not stare at anyone. Do not question anyone. One ticket in hand. Keep other tickets in pants pocket. Water bottle in other hand. Discard water bottle when told. No comments. Keep moving forward.

Note: Binoculars and belt buckle serve secondary purpose in case of metal detector use for any reason.

INSIDE STADIUM on November 21, 2015

Note restroom location. Locate seats. Sit in higher seat with two empty seats in front. Watch game and cheer when crowd cheers. Do not keep checking watch. If someone sits down in your empty seats, immediately tell them seats are for elderly parents due shortly. Show them the tickets if necessary.

Approximately forty minutes before detonation time, leave seat and walk to restroom. Enter the *corner* stall. Hang coat on the door hook or improvise. Use box cutter to split vertical back of coat. Use six safety pins to fold under and secure jagged cut area. Return to seat carrying both coat halves with one arm. It will appear as one coat. Watch game for a few minutes. While a game-play is being cheered, stuff half-coat under and between seats. Next cheered play, vacate seat and walk to your seats on other side of stadium. If seats are occupied, show tickets and say your group is here now. Next cheered play, stuff other half of coat under/behind seat. Check time because it will be close to target time of 3:11 p.m. EST.

FINAL MOMENTS *before and* FIRST MOMENTS *after detonation*

Both coat halves in place. Leave seat. Walk immediately to end of stadium near ground level. Stand in an exit way shielded by a wall. Use cell phone to call first number. First bomb should explode. Immediately call second number. Second blast should be about 15-20 seconds after first blast. Immediately vacate stadium.

People will be stunned after first blast. Many will be moving and many will be screaming. Many will stand there taking pictures with their phones. Everything will change dramatically after second blast. Everybody will then be rushing for the exits. Be ahead of the stampede or get trampled. Don't be first to the exit gate. Be part of the early-out crowd. Imitate the fear of the crowd. Make your way to vehicle. Drive normally, leaving area. Arrive back into your regular environment.

ANNOUNCEMENT *from Middle East*

Within an hour, a claim of responsibility will be issued from the Middle East. The six attack locations will be mentioned and that the suicide-bombers have now become martyrs for their cause.

EXPECTED RESULTS *from the twelve blasts at six sites across the US*

1. High number of casualties from twelve explosions.
2. Very high number of injuries from explosions.
3. A number of casualties during panic-exiting stadiums.
4. Very high number of injuries during panic-exiting stadiums.
5. Over 400,000 Americans witness in-person a terrorist attack.
6. Many millions of Americans see terrorist attack live on TV.
7. About 250 million Americans see terrorist attacks on TV within twenty-four hours.
8. Over a billion people around world see attack on US on TV within forty-eight hours.
9. More than 12,000 camera photos at stadiums. Many will go viral.
10. Immediate panic and fear will spread across the US.
11. Many games and events will be interrupted or canceled across the US.
12. Sporting event attendance will fall and frustrations will rise in the US.

13. Another layer of ongoing security cost will take place in the US.

14. Other economic cost will increase for the US going forward.

15. Further realization that America cannot fully protect its Homeland.

STIPULATIONS WITHIN THIS PAPER

The writer attempted to put himself in the shoes of terrorists concerning the planning and execution of a successful attack.

Some speculation replaced actual knowledge of certain detail. Such as: Existence of terrorist cells in or around any particular area is unknown. Another speculation: Ability of any terrorist cell, single terrorist, or any individual to possess or obtain C-4 or Semtex or any type of explosive is unknown.

Many details within this paper are accurate. Such as: game date, team and location, temperature average, time zone, stadium, seat data, city data, bomb/explosive data, flight data, etc.

Some information presented is from "personal observation" of security at football games; football stadiums; basketball, baseball, hockey and soccer games; and domestic/international travel experience.

Personal note related to our general protection and security: Five or six times, out of many, in the last several months when asked to show ID for different reasons, including ... entrance, return a purchase, or small financial transaction, I varied from the usual. Almost as a test, I pulled out my University ID or my Concealed Carry ID. The person checking my ID would take a ½ second look and hand it back saying thanks. Thereby, fulfilling their duty to check ID. Questionable security?

END OF PAPER

A number of previous readers voiced several general comments and conclusions after the Terrorist Attack Paper was originally presented.

1. A similar attack would be quite feasible in the United States.

2. A similar attack will take place. It's a question of when and where, not if.

3. If the overall attack plot as presented would not be 100 percent successful, it's probable partial success would be attained. Such as: six IEDs detonate, instead of twelve, at three separate locations in three different states.

4. Such an attack would be interpreted as 100 percent successful in

each individual stadium if one or two bombs detonate, causing casualties and panic in that stadium and chaos in the region.

5. Such an attack may be the first substantial attack seen live on TV.

6. Such an attack would indeed be immediately televised around the world, including the sight of Americans screaming and running for their lives in unimaginable panic.

7. The Saturday ritual of celebrating or attending college football games would be tarnished forever and serve as a reminder of our vulnerability.

8. Entering sporting events would now mimic entering an airport.

9. Preventing 100 percent of attacks is impossible.

10. Such an attack would cause a high degree of negative emotions and a last a long time … for all Americans.

Numbers 1 and 2 above are most troubling. There are so many events across the country every week it would be impossible to prevent determined terrorists from executing serious attacks. An extra-big sporting event has plenty of advance noise and extra security on site. Everybody is aware. What about that other game across town? There's only 20,000 fans there and security is minimal. A successful terrorist attack in any crowded arena is devastating. Visual security is always beneficial, but security needs to go well beyond what citizens see at events. Authorities understand effective prevention is necessary and the key to prevention is early detection.

As you might conclude from the paper describing a terrorist attack at football stadiums, it would be difficult for a military force to prevent all soft-target problems. There are just too many people involved, and any military presence would have an unsettling effect on some citizens. In that same manner, it's quite different around hard-targets, which are often secluded or semi-secluded from the public. Military personnel on duty around critical infrastructure would not be readily noticed by regular citizens, but they may well be noticed by anyone surveilling the area. That circumstance is a preventative measure in itself. Unfortunately, it may cause terrorists to consider an easier objective.

The military should have a role to play with 24/7 perimeter protection of critical infrastructure, namely the type of sites and facilities which may be some distance from densely populated areas.

Areas around nuclear reactors, dams, water plants, some communication stations, some transportation facilities, energy production facilities, such as oil fields, refineries, and important power grid stations or other related equipment, should utilize military guards wherever feasible. An old but simple phrase explains why: **"It is better to be safe than sorry."**

Chapter Three

Border ... Super-Wall or Super-Military?

DOES THE UNITED States need to build a "Wall" along its Mexican border? No. How about a fence? Yes. Signs? Yes. Sensors? Yes. Illumination? Yes. Drones? Yes. Troops? Yes.

Approaching the border from the south, there should be many directional, warning, and threatening signs in Spanish and other foreign languages. But, from the north, or from the American citizens directly to the American government, there should be a single directional sign in plain English: Seal The Border.

The federal government's first priority is to protect American citizens from all adversaries. Adversaries secretly enter our country by crossing the border from Mexico. It has been happening for some time. Adversaries crossing the border are not North Korean uniformed soldiers, but they may be Middle Eastern terrorists or want-to-be terrorists. They may be South or Central American drug smugglers or Mexican gang members. These criminals cross the border by land, sea, and air, and it becomes a huge problem well beyond the border. They contribute to the widespread use of drugs, which has the potential to end American life as we know it just like serious terrorist attacks could at strategic locations.

Others, who are not so dangerous to society but have an adverse effect on it, cross the border to collect government benefits. Government benefits are often known as "earned money," which is taken from hardworking US taxpayers and changed into "unearned money" given to others for their increased comfort.

More serious than the generous US welfare system, giving away money to foreigners is a risk to each citizen's life, liberty, and happiness. People crossing the border illegally are not a benefit to citizens. Illegals are a cost to citizens.

Adversaries crossing the border include those vicious criminals and gang members who now rule the streets in big cities. Today, many Hispanic gangs exist throughout the United States. One of the biggest is MS-13 (Mara Salvatrucha), which may have 100,000 members. It deals in theft, drugs, and death. City, state, and federal law enforcement agencies work the gang problem 24/7, but they're falling behind because more illegals arrive all the time. What if those illegals could not get across the border? Would citizens be safer in the border area, in small towns, in large cities, and all across the country? Would law enforcement and social costs decrease?

Keep those questions in mind as you read and digest the following extensive information. It's the kind of detailed information that is rarely disseminated to a wide audience of American citizens. All matters mentioned should be more than important to you and everyone living in our free country. Many other sources could have been used since they quoted similar information … much of which comes from the FBI. It should be read and understood by all Americans. After all, it's our country … as of right now. Dire information follows:

ARTICLE FOUND AT: endoftheamericandream.com/archives/1-4-million-gang-members-and-more-pour-into-the-united-states-every-single-day
ARTICLE WRITTEN BY: Michael Snyder
DATE: JANUARY 12, 2012
TITLE: THERE ARE 1.4 Million Gang Members in the United States and More Pour into the Country Every Single Day

> A vast army of heavily armed criminals has embedded itself in every major city in the United States. In fact, nearly every community in America is now affected by these thugs. Drugs, theft and brutal violence are all part of the everyday lifestyle of the members of this army. They aggressively recruit our young people and floods of illegal immigrants are joining their ranks. Once civil unrest erupts in America, they will go on a crime spree that will be absolutely unprecedented and they will burn large areas of some U.S. cities to the ground. So who am I talking about? I am talking about the rapidly growing gangs that are terrorizing cities all over the nation. The FBI tells us that there are now **1.4 million** gang members involved in the 33,000 different gangs that are active inside the United States. The number of gang members in the U.S. has increased by 40 percent since 2009. Just think about that. That is absolutely astounding. Just since 2009, the number of gang members has increased by **40 percent**. The FBI says that 48 percent of all violent crime in this country can be directly traced to gangs and that this is a national crisis that is progressively getting worse. Unfortunately, the

federal government refuses to secure our borders and is allowing new waves of illegal immigrants to enter the United States every single day. A substantial number of those illegal immigrants end up involved in these gangs. Yet the federal government just stands by and allows it to keep happening. One day, the foolishness of this policy will be evident to all.

In many areas of America today, families live behind windows that have bars on them and they won't ever go out at night because it is just too dangerous. There are some communities that have pretty much been entirely taken over by the gangs, but instead of addressing the problem the federal government continues to spend a massive amount of resources checking out what might be in our underwear at U.S. airports.

Meanwhile, criminal gangs are thriving. They are becoming incredibly powerful and increasingly sophisticated. The following is from an FBI press release....

> *Gangs are increasingly engaging in non-traditional gang-related crime such as alien smuggling, human trafficking, and prostitution. Gangs are also engaging in white-collar crime such as counterfeiting, identity theft, and mortgage fraud....*
>
> *You have probably heard of some of the largest of these gangs.*
>
> *For example, the 18th Street Gang is the largest gang in the state of California. It is said that they have 15,000 members in California alone, and that on average they are responsible for at least one major crime in Los Angeles County every single day.*
>
> *It has been reported that police in Los Angeles are extremely hesitant to ever venture into the areas most heavily controlled by the 18th Street gang. They are absolutely brutal and they do not back down to anyone.*

The following is what Wikipedia has to say about the 18th Street Gang....

> *A US Justice Department report from 2009 estimates that the 18th Street gang has a membership of some 30,000 to 50,000 with 80% of them being illegal aliens from Mexico and Central America and is active in 44 cities in 20 states. Its main source of income is street-level distribution of cocaine and marijuana and, to a lesser extent, heroin and methamphetamine. Gang members also commit assault, auto theft, carjacking, drive-by shootings, extortion, homicide, identification fraud, and robbery.*

Another very prominent gang that you may have heard of is the Latin Kings. It is reported that they have 18,000 members in the city of

Chicago alone. They are believed to be the largest Hispanic gang in the entire nation.

One of the gangs that has law enforcement authorities the most concerned is MS-13. There are chapters of MS-13 in 42 states now, and if you cross a member of MS-13 there is a good chance that you will lose a limb or be hacked to death with a machete....

During 2011, we saw a large increase in "group crime" behavior. Some of the incidents have been absolutely horrific. For example, the following is how one local ABC News affiliate described the "flash mob" attacks that took place at the Wisconsin state fair earlier this year....

> Milwaukee police said that around 11:10 p.m., squads were sent to the area for reports of battery, fighting and property damage being caused by an unruly crowd of "hundreds" of people. One officer described it as a "mob beating."
>
> Police said the group of young people attacked fair goers who were leaving the fair grounds. Police said that some victims were attacked while walking. They said others were pulled out of cars and off of motorcycles before being beaten.

Can you imagine taking your kids to the state fair and having them witness that?

But this is just the beginning.

These gangs are becoming very organized and they are becoming very heavily armed.

The FBI says that rifles, machine guns, grenades and even artillery rounds are being found in the possession of gangs more frequently than ever....

Those that want to steal guns are becoming increasingly bold. For example, 21 machine guns were stolen a while back right out of an LAPD training facility.

Down in Miami, thieves have become so bold that they have actually been breaking into parked police cruisers and stealing guns and ammo out of them.

When people are stealing guns directly from the police that is a sign that it is very late in the game.

Our politicians spend so much time talking about the violence in Afghanistan and Iraq, but the truth is that the area right along the U.S./Mexico border is far more dangerous.

Just check out the following information from CNSNews.com....

According to the Mexican government, from January through September 2011 2,276 deaths were recorded in the Mexican state of Chihuahua, which borders Texas and New Mexico.

A Nov. 2011 Congressional Research Service (CRS) report states that over nearly the same period—January through October 2011—2,177 civilians were killed in Afghanistan, where a U.S.-led war against the Taliban is underway. It did not provide a breakdown of responsibility for that period, but said that in 2010, 75 percent of civilian deaths were attributed to the Taliban and other "anti-government elements."

Per capita, a person was at least nine times more likely to be murdered in Chihuahua last year than in Afghanistan.

Many of the areas along our border with Mexico are open war zones.

But do we hear about this much in the mainstream media?

Of course not.

Just across the U.S. border lies the city of Juarez, Mexico. Juarez is considered to be one of the most dangerous cities on the entire planet because of the brutal drug war being waged there. In fact, Juarez is the murder capital of the western hemisphere.

But most Americans have never even heard of Juarez.

Complete and total chaos reigns in vast areas of northern Mexico, and yet most Americans don't even realize that there is a problem.

Overall, more than 35,000 people have been killed since the Mexican government declared war on the drug cartels back in 2006.

You would think that would warrant some significant news coverage.

But no, the mainstream media can't talk much about that because then the people might actually start demanding that we secure our borders.

Amazingly, instead of securing our borders the Obama administration has been busy sending guns down to the drug cartels in Mexico.

That is what this whole "Fast and Furious" scandal is all about. As I have written about previously, ATF agents purposely allowed thousands of guns to be sold to individuals that they believed would get them into the hands of Mexican drug cartels.

But so far, nobody in the Obama administration has been held accountable for this.

During 2009 and 2010, 70 percent of the 30,000 guns that were recovered by authorities in Mexico were determined to have come from inside the United States.

That is a major problem.

These Mexican drug cartels and the gangs that work with them have become very heavily armed and they have become very bold.

It has been reported that Mexican drug cartels are now openly conducting military operations inside the United States. Scouts for the cartels maintain strategic lookout bases in the hills of southern Arizona, and the federal government has even put up signs that warn tourists to say out of certain areas. The cartels very much try to avoid any confrontations with our border patrol or with our local police, but once they are approached they are not afraid to open fire....

The chaotic drug war that is going on in northern Mexico has spread into many areas of Texas, New Mexico, Arizona and California. With each passing day, the gangs that are embedded in all of our major cities are getting stronger. They are a ticking time bomb that eventually will go off.

One day, when mass civil unrest erupts in the United States, the gangs will have a field day. Given the opportunity, most gangs will gleefully indulge in brutal violence, looting, arson, rape and mindless property destruction.

Sadly, this all could have been avoided.

Instead of strip-searching old women at airports, this is what we should have been dedicating our law enforcement resources to.

Instead of spending billions of dollars spying on the American people, the federal government should have spent billions of dollars on securing our borders.

Unfortunately, we made the wrong choices as a nation and so now we are going to pay the price.

If you're enraged ... you must be a normal American citizen. Apparently, politicians are different. Unfortunately, they are in charge of "gang" removal.

Many of the largest gangs, some mentioned above, are Hispanic. Some of those gang members were born to Hispanic parents in the United States. But many, probably most, crossed the border illegally. It should be understood that sealing the border doesn't directly remove gang members from city streets, but it does cut off or reduce the supply of new Hispanic members from the south. But more than that, sealing the border can drastically reduce the amount of drugs reaching the gangs for distribution.

The National Gang Center (NGC) provides some additional comments about gangs in the United States. The figures it reports were compiled between 1996 and 2011 and published sometime later.

INFORMATION FOUND AT: https://www.nationalgangcenter.gov/survey-analysis/demographics

TITLE: NATIONAL YOUTH Gang Survey Analysis

> *In virtually every survey year, law enforcement agencies report a greater percentage of adult (18 and over) gang members compared with juvenile (under 18) gang members.*

> *The most recent figures provided by law enforcement indicate that more than three out of every five gang members are adults.*

Although the NGC did not provide a reason for the increase in adult gang members, data suggest juveniles are not renouncing the gang-culture after their wild teenage years. Not a good sign for any effort to reduce gang violence.

Other comments from NGC suggest gangs and gang violence are spreading beyond large cities:

> *Conversely, smaller cities and rural counties, whose gang problems are more recent, are more likely to report equal proportions of juvenile and adult gang members....*

> *The most recent figures provided by law enforcement are 46 percent Hispanic/Latino gang members, 35 percent African-American/black gang members, more than 11 percent white gang members, and 7 percent other race/ethnicity of gang members.*

A chart from NGC showing what factors influence local gang violence indicated "drug-related factors" were most influential. Another reason the border must be secure.

It should be obvious why so many people, many carrying drugs, cross the border illegally. It's just too easy. The US government doesn't do enough to stop the flow, and the repercussions for those caught are weak and limited. When and if the border is firmly secured, it's doubtful many people would still attempt to cross it. You would think the politicians and other authorities would readily recognize that a secure border brings immediate relief to local, state, and federal agencies. For a long time, our southern border's been notorious as an "easy cross." Change "easy" to "difficult," and in a short time, the overall task of guarding the gateway to prosperity would dissipate. So would crime.

As it is now, our border isn't much of a border when compared to other civilized countries. US government authorities don't have a firm handle on how many people have entered, who they are, where they are, what they want, or whether any of them are a great danger to the citizens of this country.

Of course, plenty of boisterous recommendations and flimsy excuses have come from plenty of people about anything and everything concerning our porous border. But the fact remains ... the US government doesn't have a firm handle on anything concerning the southern border. What should be done?

The military should be used immediately. Just as the military can and should fulfill an important role in protecting critical infrastructure, it should do the same along the border.

The usual outcry over military cost will be loud and clear. Some will declare the military is already spread too thin. It's needed elsewhere to prevent another war. Or to serve in a current war in any one of several foreign countries. All valid points except our cost can actually be quite low to protect the border and there's already an ugly war taking place all around the border, so it needs our attention right now. The problem is associated with the Mexican government, the Mexican police, and the huge Mexican drug cartels. Making matters worse, within those three organizations it's sometimes difficult to tell who's who. As mentioned in the previous article about gang members, the Mexican drug war is spilling over our southern border, and its cost in money, lives, and containment is spreading deeper into the United States.

Other costs are also connected to the porous border. Providing welfare for many illegal immigrants, extra law enforcement work, and the usual prolonged legal proceedings are all very costly. Secure the border and costs go down. Way down.

Focusing only on the movement of drugs across the border, then across the country, and then into every big city in the nation, it should be easy to imagine the overall cost-savings ... if drugs stop at the border.

The very first paragraph in this chapter explained what has to be done to secure the border. Notice that an expensive super-wall does not need to be built. To begin with, it would probably take ten years to complete. Considering all the legal arguing about property rights, eminent-domain proceedings, and obtaining building permits, it would end up being the most expensive wall in the world. All of that can be avoided.

The Military Plan (MP) was discussed at the beginning of Part Two, Chapter One. Under the MP, all men and women would be required to serve their country a minimum of one year starting sometime between age eighteen and thirty. Admittedly, the "requirement" to serve would be a big noisy change from the all-volunteer military of the last forty years.

As mentioned earlier, the military service for all makes it pertinent our young people understand that "even one year of service will yield long-lasting personal benefits" to them. And that fact can also be very important to the entire nation going forward.

Today, it's probable that most young people would choose to serve a single year domestically rather than longer enlistments. And that could work out very well for security within US borders.

A large number of military members serving a limited service period is the perfect scenario for protecting our borders as well as our infrastructure.

Three basic or underlying reasons exist to secure the border and protect critical infrastructure. The reasons have been discussed and should be known to all but will be restated here.

1. Bad people carrying drugs cross our border illegally. Drugs have the potential to wreck the United States.

2. Bad people, notably terrorists, cross our border. They know destroying critical infrastructure has the potential to wreck our country.

3. Youth discipline. Protecting the border and critical infrastructure is a very important job. Using the military to do so is also very important. Time spent in the military delivers certain intangible benefits to our nation's youth and, therefore, to the nation itself. That may be just as important as the actual asset protection.

For too many youngsters, the trend of the last several decades has been more television and less exercise, more computer games and less study, more rebellion and less obedience, more obscenity and less decency, more drugs and less good sense. The military can change this overall lack of discipline.

How can the Military Plan (MP) secure the border inexpensively? How would the military operate at the border?

Under the MP there would be plenty of service members to work at the border. They're being paid whether they work at the border in Texas or Ramstein Air Base in Germany or Fort Richardson in Alaska. Actually, the border assignment would be even less expensive. Housing for military personnel assigned to protect the border would be provided at a nearby military base or a nearby reserve armory. One of these locations would be their permanent duty station, even though much of their time would be spent in the field at the border. Permanent, for most members is actually about nine months after basic and security training.

The majority of military border patrol members would come from draftees or enlistees who prefer one-year service commitments. They would also have volunteered for and then selected for Special-Duty Assignment (SDA). SDA means members would be assigned to guarding critical infrastructure or border patrol. They will also have completed several weeks of instruction including on-the-job training in the field. This SDA schooling would be the exception for those fulfilling one-year commitments. Many would school or train about a week for menial jobs around a base.

Military border patrol members would be assigned to a particular group that would work together similar to an Army rifle platoon. Call them Border Patrol Platoon (BPP). Approximately forty-five members would be in each BPP, consisting of one leader and four squads totaling forty-four members, including four squad leaders. Some members would be cross-trained, but all would work on patrol duty. Patrol duty means working in the field along the border. Time in the field would be approximately a week (or TBD) before rotating back to base for a week. Another BPP unit would rotate into the field. Time of the year and weather may determine time in the field. A large tent would serve as a sleeping shelter since the BPP unit would function 24/7 in the field, as is typical for service members. A second large tent would serve as an electronics station, which would also function 24/7. Work in the electronics tent is more specialized and will use some regular service members skilled in the operation of cameras, drones, and sensors, and will provide constant communications with all foot or motorized patrol members. If the last sentence sounds like border overkill, it's not … it's border-sealed.

The regular military reserves should be mentioned in reference to border and infrastructure security. The reserves generally train initially for six months, including a particular job training. After that initial period, they update training two or two-and-a-half days per month and fifteen days per year. These part-time duty days could be allocated in such a way that reserve members could assist with border security.

Military leaders, initially along with US Customs and Border Protection (CBP), would determine the number of people needed in one area versus another in order to assure safe operations and sufficient security to prevent all intruders. A model might be the same security routine used when protecting the perimeter of a large military base in a hostile area. Bases generally utilize a fence, as would the border. It could be a double-fence or whatever configuration works best for a particular topography. The fence must be effective in preventing intruders at all times of the day or night, whether it's hot or cold, wet or dry. The fence should assist patrol members in doing their job. Sensors would be used in conjunction with the physical fence to provide early detection of an attempted intrusion. Cameras, drones, lighting, and other means would be used as needed to support the mission.

That mission: Stop all illegal movement across the border.

Successfully completing the mission protects American citizens, secures the country, disciplines our youth, and reduces all operating costs of law enforcement and other related matters in every state. Related matters might be difficult to calculate, but they are real. Examples might be: reducing the ... drug culture, gang violence, merchandise theft, criminals medically treated, and court proceedings. All very costly. Who pays? Society. Who saves with a sealed border? Society.

Sealing the border is indirectly very cost-efficient.

The military will supply the personnel and technique to secure the border tightly and directly at the border. It will not operate beyond the border, nor is it supplanting other CBP responsibility functions. Some of those functions and other related information is found below.

INFORMATION FOUND AT: https://en.wikipedia.org/wiki/U.S._Customs_and_Border_ Protection

TITLE: U.S. CUSTOMS and Border Protection

> *... inspect and examine passengers and cargo at over 300 ports of entry.... curtail the spread of harmful pests and plant and animal diseases that may harm America's farms and food supply or cause bio- and agro-terrorism.... prevent people, weapons, narcotics, and conveyances from illegal entry by air and water.... collect over $30 billion annually in entry duties and taxes through the enforcement of trade and tariff laws.... fulfill the agency's trade mission by appraising and classifying imported merchandise.... conduct the largest number of working dogs of any U.S. federal law enforcement agency....*
>
> *There are 327 officially designated ports of entry and an additional 14 pre-clearance locations in Canada, Ireland and the Caribbean. CBP is also in charge of the "Container Security Initiative," which identifies and inspects foreign cargo in its mother country before it is to be imported into the United States.*

What does all the above CBP information mean to average citizens relative to the border being protected by US military forces?

It demonstrates the many, many areas that will have improved security after military personnel assume guard control of the immediate border area. It will allow the CBP to concentrate on other very critical areas such as cargo screening at 300 ports of entry and thorough inspections.

The military primarily functions as a strong visible presence directly at the border. The United States Border Patrol will initially provide leadership and guidance at the border since it's been there a long time. Leadership, command and management details should be worked out and agreed upon early with effective, tight security being the objective and overall end result.

If the border is sealed tight, it should be expected other entry points such as small or large ports will become more critical for smugglers. Ongoing intrusion threats won't end with a secure border but merely shift to these other areas. But smugglers, especially of drugs, will find ports quite narrow compared to a wide-open southern border. The additional CBP strength available because of less border responsibility will allow more thorough inspection of people at all border crossings and improve detection of banned or counterfeit merchandise in more containers at all ports.

The military taking responsibility for sealing the border will have a domino effect on improving CBP effectiveness in all areas. Ports are important, but so are less descript areas that are quite vast.

By sealing the southern border, it should be expected that some increase in incursion of undesirable people and drugs would occur via coastal areas and our northern border. The CBP should reinforce these areas as needed.

The Coast Guard will continue its job of inspection, interdiction, and protection of coastal areas and inland waterways. Its workload will increase, but under the MP, it will have more members available to reinforce its mission.

Canada would be expected to assist at the US border to a greater extent than presently. Mexico should play a larger role as well. The added security will benefit citizens in all three countries because more security personnel on either side of the border will mean more apprehensions of the criminal element.

Actions of hostile countries and desperate people should demonstrate to the United States ... secure the border or forever suffer the consequences.

Chapter Four

US Drug Culture

Is THERE ANOTHER fierce adversary in American life lurking in the shadows? Yes, there is ... and that enemy is inside our gate. That enemy is lethal. That enemy may be unstoppable.

Chapter Three covered the importance of sealing the border, thereby stopping most drugs before they enter the United States. This chapter speaks to the drugs already here.

Drugs in this country are an enemy of the people. That enemy is winning.

Drug use is dangerous. It lies to people. It steals their money. It takes their jobs. It takes their children. It kills their children. If it does not stop ... it will take everything we know and love.

What can be done to curb drug use in the United States? No, that question is much too weak. What can and must be done immediately to end all illegal drug use in the United States? Most people would say it can't be done. People don't care. There are no easy answers. Drugs are not a big deal. Drug use is not a violent crime. Drug use should not be a crime. And now, slowly but surely ... drug use is not even a crime. Problem solved, suggest the politicians. The crime is now legal. It's even better than that as the politicians can now tax drug use, apparently easing their conscience even more.

Today, marijuana is legal in some states. Tomorrow, it will be decriminalized in more states. Medical marijuana is legal in many states, and it appears the number of people needing, no wanting, medical marijuana is growing fast. What exactly does that mean?

As time goes by, additional states will focus on the additional tax flow from drug sales. Instead of making hard choices to reduce spending, politicians will give in to loud screams from the drug culture. "Collect more taxes from drug sales and everybody wins" will be the new mantra. Is that what politicians think? They must be smoking dope, and that, in itself, contributes to their effort to decriminalize.

There's not enough understanding as to the broad negative aspects of drug use. It affects all citizens. Hear that again … widespread illegal drug use affects all American citizens. Why is that so difficult for so many to understand?

What part of life is improved for individuals who abuse drugs? Improved disposition? Physical condition? Thinking? Dependability? Productivity? Wages? Anything? Anything at all?

All individuals have personal failings, but it doesn't stop there with the drug culture. Living within the drug culture is dying in life.

If individuals have failings, shouldn't they be charged with remedying those failings? Taking responsibility for their own actions is a good trait if drug abusers can find it. On the surface, it appears they often do pay a price. But it's rarely the financial price. Others pay much of that cost. The entire society pays, and the cost is higher than most realize. The extra cost to society is not sustainable.

The drug culture brings added cost at every level of law enforcement. It's not just the number of police officers on the street. It's the court system, which is often backed up for months. Criminal defendants are entitled under law to be represented in court. Representation is often appointed by the court. Free attorney for the defendant. Court cases are delayed, continued, and sometimes dismissed. Drug defense attorneys argue a drug law offender's innocence, and if the offender is found guilty, an appeal is sometimes filed. The guilty go to jail. Some go to rehab. Others laugh as they go back to the street. Who pays the cost? Society pays the cost, and that means the American citizen.

The argument here is not against gratuitous legal representation for criminals at trial. It's against illegal drug use being accepted as nearly normal in our society.

Stop the drugs … stop drug abuse … save our society.

The drug culture brings added costs to the entire medical system. The added costs start with a free ride to the emergency room, often extend to a stay in the hospital or rehab, and sometimes end in the mortuary before burial. Who pays these costs? Usually, it's society via higher taxes, higher medical bills, and higher insurance rates.

There's another cost on society that's rarely considered. It might be easier to understand if it's referred to as an economic cost on the overall country.

The United States competes economically with others around the world. China is the easy example. When cost to produce any product increases for any reason, the sales for that product decrease as sale price increases. If that product is produced in the United States, then fewer sales means fewer workers are needed in the United States.

Is this country more productive or less productive when some employees use drugs? The answer to that question affects everything we produce for sale to anyone, anytime, and anywhere.

Employees using drugs at work or suffering the after-effects of using drugs could be dangerous to themselves or coworkers. Even in a desk job, it's probable employees using drugs are less efficient and less reliable. Less quality work, more sick days, and job loss are all costly for any employer.

Poor employees with drug abuse problems get fired. When this happens, it's likely society's costs increase. Problem employees can't get a job. Society costs increase again. People can't make house payments or pay rent without work. The family suffers. Society costs increase again. This pattern can go on for a long time. Drug abuse can lead to the end of a job, a house, a family, a life, and eventually, to the end of prosperous society all under the weight of an out-of-control drug culture.

Most of us know of or have heard of an alcohol-related accident where a drunk driver killed another person. It's a common happening. It's a tragedy, but it's common.

Does our society really want to add to that statement? It's a tragedy, but it's common … and the driver was high on drugs. Increasing drug use means increasing dangerous drivers on the road. It's bad enough that drinking establishments provide parking lots for the convenience of drinkers. But drinking is legal, and responsible drinking is always recommended. Some drinkers set their limit at two drinks, which works for them. But does marijuana work the same way? Would that be two puffs on a joint? Or two marijuana cigarettes? Responsible bartenders sometimes refuse additional drinks, but it won't work that way with individuals smoking dope. As more states legalize marijuana, society can expect more innocent lives shattered by drug-drunk drivers. That's much worse than reading about celebrity overdoses. Celebrities are not so innocent.

It's rare for anybody to understand in full what illegal drugs cost our society. "Our society" … that's all of us together. Most citizens don't recognize the drug-damage-cost in family life. They don't know the amount of money being spent on illegal drugs. That same illegal drug money could have been used to purchase merchandise in local stores. That would suggest additional jobs and the circulation of more money throughout the area. More people would prosper.

The following article from *Frontline's* "Drug Wars" series delivers some ugly information about drug money.

ARTICLE FOUND AT: www.pbs.org/wgbh/pages/frontline/shows/drugs/special/math.html

ARTICLE WRITTEN BY: Oriana Zill, producer, and Lowell Bergman, reporter

TITLE: DO THE Math: Why the Illegal Drug Business Is Thriving

> *Globalization hit organized crime over the last decade and now is integral to its most profitable business—the international narcotics business. Once a regional problem involving a customer base of a few million, and barely a billion dollars in sales, the illegal drug industry is now a worldwide enterprise with tens of millions of hard core consumers spending hundreds of billions on opiates, cocaine and amphetamines and marijuana, as well as other drugs....*
>
> *The single largest marketplace for illegal drugs continues to be the United States.*

It may be important for the United States to be a world leader, but not in illegal drug use. That, in fact, hampers our leadership abilities in any area.

Continuing with excerpts from *Frontline*'s "Drug Wars" series:

> *All those drug sales mean that large amounts of cash accumulate in stash houses and collection points around the country. For the multi-billion dollar narcotics business—like any commodities business—it is essential that the suppliers and transporters be paid. That means the money must make its way south, and the traffickers, aided by specialists in money laundering, have devised myriad methods to insure efficient and safe delivery of their profits.*
>
> *Estimates on how much money is sent south each year range from 10 to 30 billion. For Mexican traffickers along the southwest border, the money is literally driven across the border in bulk amounts and then deposited into Mexican banks....*
>
> *When the drug money ultimately makes its way into the foreign economy, it is used to pay salaries of shippers and processors, as well as the bribes that supplement the incomes of government officials on both sides of the border. Whole regions of Mexico, Colombia and points in between have become dependent on the demand for drugs in the United States....*
>
> *While the US drug user may not intend to invest in this international drug economy, every dollar spent is ultimately fueling a mammoth and destructive system that depends on our drug dollars to survive.*

The above information gives an idea of the magnitude of the US drug problem. There are many estimates about the amount of money spent or wasted on illegal drugs. Some estimates are low. Some may be high. The actual figure is difficult to ascertain because people involved rarely incriminate themselves by discussing illegal drug matters. That alone suggests reported figures may be and probably are ... on the very low side. Some eye-popping information can be found below:

INFORMATION FOUND AT: www.zerohedge.com/news/2013-10-30/top-10-facts-about-us-illegal-drug-market
ARTICLE WRITTEN BY: Tyler Durden
DATE: OCTOBER 30, 2013
TITLE: TOP 10 Facts About the U.S. Illegal Drug Market

> *Recent surveys and research studies by sources from the UN to street-Rx.com put the size of the illegal drug market in the U.S. at anywhere from $200 to $750 billion. The market is notoriously hard to track by design, and it is constantly evolving as prices and usage fluctuates....*

> *Say what you want about the 1960s and 1970s, but the current decade has logged the heaviest drug use per person in the history of the United States. 23.9 million Americans aged 12 or older—9.2 percent of the entire population—were "current users" (i.e. had used in the past month) of an illicit drug in 2012, the latest data available from the CDC shows....*

> *While the drug market might generate large amounts of cash for suppliers, its cost to the state is astronomical.*

"Astronomical" is a big word. But it's a suitable word when talking about the financial aspects of the illegal drug culture. Unfortunately, it describes very well the cost to society, the illegal drug sales revenue, and the profits for criminals.

This "astronomical" reference in the above article refers to the government cost to deal with illegal drugs. It's probably not possible to arrive at an accurate dollar cost for the so-called "war on drugs." It's just too intertwined with law enforcement, social work, medical care, and many other ways. We just know the cost is ... astronomical.

The $750 billion figure for illegal drug sales is also astronomical. In fact, the largest corporations in the world would willingly stand-on-their-heads if they could generate sales revenue of even a third of $750 billion each year. Corporations sell products around the world. The dollar figure cited above was for illegal drug sales in the United States alone. Quite impressive ... albeit in a sick way.

To demonstrate what it takes for a business to reach a sales figure matching the drug figure of $750 billion, you would have to add together all sales revenue from these five global corporations: Ford + Boeing + General Electric + Exxon-Mobile + General Motors. Added together, their sales equal $750 billion.

There's another way to think of illegal drug money, and it's quite ugly. You could say it's astronomically ugly. If illegal drug sales in the US reach $750 billion or even $200 billion … just where does that money go?

All American citizens know illegal drugs are a problem, but many suggest it doesn't concern them. They often feel other people can waste their money on drugs if that's their choice. But what does that attitude do for the average man, his family, or our country?

American citizens should pause and think about who ends up with most of the money from drug sales. The astronomical sum of $750 billion paid out by American citizens for illegal drugs ends up in the pockets of bad people. Some extremely bad. It starts with those who control the growing fields for opiates or coca in foreign countries none of which are true friends of the United States. But they do love taking our money. Our money also goes to drug transporters, border smugglers, and dealers selling dope to our kids on the street. The end result is the poisoning of American citizens on their way to becoming addicts.

On average, nearly 50,000 people die from drug overdoses annually. And there may be thousands more not reported as drug overdoses for whatever reason. That 50,000 number is considerably higher than deaths caused by automobile accidents.

Another sad reality is the fast-growing number of young kids smoking marijuana. Is this not a wakeup call about the future?

Criminals receive billions of dollars. Violent drug cartels receive billions in profits and drugs are a fast-growing business. An "astronomical" problem.

Those regular citizens and politicians who ignore the American drug problem because it's distasteful should focus on its financial ramifications that hurt everybody. **If citizens viewed the drug problem financially, they might feel some urgency about bringing an end to it before it brings an end to them.**

Most people have heard about the violence in Chicago with deadly gang shootings every week. Much of that is drug-related. It's costly to Chicago residents, the city of Chicago, the state of Illinois, and the federal government. That means it's costly to the average working citizen. Violence, most associated with drug crimes, is now spreading into small towns and rural areas. Why wait until violence becomes nearly unstoppable as it is now in most big cities?

Few citizens realize a violent drug war is happening just across our southern border. It has already started to spill over into the US. Mexican drug violence has killed more than 100,000 people. More than a hundred journalists have been kidnapped and killed. And American citizens in the hundreds have been kidnapped and murdered.

The death figures should frighten all Americans. American politicians should take a firm stand. Or, at least, stand up and be recognized. This is not the distant Middle East. It's our neighbor's yard, and our kids sometimes play in it. More information follows:

ARTICLE FOUND AT: www.pbs.org/wgbh/frontline/article/the-staggering-death-toll-of-mexicos-drug-war/

ARTICLE WRITTEN BY: Jason M. Breslow

DATE: JULY 27, 2015

TITLE: THE STAGGERING Death Toll of Mexico's Drug War

> Over the course of wars in Afghanistan and Iraq, the number of civilian deaths has been staggering. In Afghanistan, more than 26,000 civilians are estimated to have died since the war began in 2001. In Iraq, conservative tallies place the number of civilians killed at roughly 160,500 since the U.S. invasion in 2003....
>
> But as U.S. involvement in each nation has dropped off in recent years, killings much closer to home, in Mexico, have steadily, if quietly, outpaced the number of civilian deaths in Afghanistan and Iraq combined.
>
> Last week, the Mexican government released new data showing that between 2007 and 2014—a period that accounts for some of the bloodiest years of the nation's war against the drug cartels—more than 164,000 people were victims of homicide....
>
> Over the same seven-year period, slightly more than 103,000 died in Afghanistan and Iraq, according to data from the United Nations and the website Iraq Body Count.

Over the years, the US media has had plenty to say about distant wars and related brutalities. That's understandable. But regular citizens hear very little about death and brutality in Mexico. That is not understandable.

Groups such as ISIS or al-Qaeda seek notoriety, and they get it with the decapitation and mutilation of innocent civilians. The exact same brutality takes place in Mexico. More decapitations may actually occur in Mexico than in the Middle East. That's not widely reported, but it should be since Americans vacation in Mexico and often cross the border for business or socializing.

American citizens may think they're immune from violence in Mexico, but that's not the case. Many have been directly affected by drug-related criminal activity while in Mexico. Visitors seeking "beginner" drugs or ordinary culture enrichment can find trouble. Fun weekends can end in death. Mexican violence continues to worsen, and authorities are often not helpful. It's quite common for visitors to be on their own when trouble arises.

Travel warnings exist, but they're hardly front page news. Most Americans are unaware of recent statistics. Information follows:

ARTICLE FOUND AT: www.breitbart.com/texas/2015/04/18/us-state-department-181-americans-murdered-in-mexico-since-2013/
ARTICLE WRITTEN BY: Ildefonso Ortiz
DATE: APRIL 18, 2015
TITLE: US STATE Department: 181 Americans Murdered In Mexico Since 2013

> *Nearly two hundred U.S. citizens have been murdered in Mexico since 2013. Fierce gunfights, kidnappings, bus hijackings, car-jackings and extortion by Mexican cartels are all possibilities that could be faced by U.S. citizens travelling into Mexico. These have resulted in the murder of 181 Americans in the past two years.*
>
> *In the most recent version of the travel advisory issued by the U.S. Department of State American citizens are warned to "avoid non-essential travel" to the Mexican border due to the continued violence.*

That warning to US citizens refers to the border area of our sunny neighbor to the south. That's our border area, too. Americans are warned to stay away. But others continue to come in our direction, and they do so by the millions. Generally, regular visitors to the United States are safe. If they need help, it's always available. That same attitude often applies to those who cross illegally.

The Breitbart article continues with some unwelcome figures that reinforce the State Department warning:

> *According to the Department of State, in 2014 one hundred Americans were murdered in Mexico. In 2013, 81 Americans had a similar fate throughout the country. The number of murdered Americans added to the nearly 199 Americans who were kidnapped last year. Breitbart Texas reports paint a grim picture about the true security conditions in that country in comparison to the image painted by Mexican officials.*

It's difficult to understand why there's not a revolt in the US over illegal border crossings and drug problems surrounding the border area. Americans die on the streets here at home and in neighboring Mexico because of drugs. American taxpayers pay a fortune in taxes to support efforts to reduce illegal drugs. Many others pay a fortune to buy drugs. Those American drug dollars flow to bad people here and abroad. Our youth suffer. Our future suffers. Mexico and Mexican drug cartels prosper. Isn't it time for all of that to reverse?

Much of Mexican drug production comes from an area known as the Golden Triangle of Mexico. This drug-growing area includes parts of the states of Sinaloa, Durango, and Chihuahua. The area lies about 400 miles due south from the New Mexico-Mexico border west toward the Pacific coast. It's the home base for the Sinaloa Cartel. Many intelligence authorities say the Sinaloa Cartel is the most powerful drug trafficking organization in the world. It has a hierarchy similar to an organized crime syndicate with large distribution cells in major US cities. It has hit-squads, a paramilitary force, and contracts with huge gangs in the US such as MS-13. It's part of the war that rages in Mexico. That war is spilling across the border area and leapfrogging into every big city in America. It must stop or it will end America-the-beautiful.

Illegal drugs may end up in US cities, but most actually originate well beyond Mexico. They're grown in distant lands, shipped to the Americas, processed, smuggled across the US border, and sold for the high dollars cities offer. Mexico does produce drugs in its own Golden Triangle area, but mostly, Mexico provides a 2,000-mile open-door to the money. Drugs flow into the United States. Money flows into Mexico.

Some American drug dollars go to the very people who wish to destroy us. We hear their chants of hatred on the news. "Death to America" is popular.

One of two very large opium poppy-growing areas in the Middle East is known as the Golden Crescent. It occupies parts of Afghanistan, Pakistan, and Iran. Do we really want to send American dollars to these places? American men and women have died and are still dying in Afghanistan. Weren't they there fighting for the Afghans' freedom from the Taliban?

We chose not to bomb or set fire to their poppy fields. Why was that? Was it politics or money? Is there a difference?

Those Afghanistan poppy fields may be off-limits for some reason, but their harvests end up killing Americans in America, and it continues today.

The United States has sent Pakistan several billion dollars in foreign aid every year for years. During those same years, Pakistan helped hide Osama bin Laden in a well-fortified compound. Meanwhile, Pakistan continues to grow opiates that end up as dope on our streets. Dope that kills Americans. Something doesn't add up. It's as if its "dope" rules our world.

Iran is another special case. Its arms kill and maim American soldiers. Its people chant "death to the great Satan." That would be America. We oblige the chanters by buying dope grown in their country. That dope causes death. Oddly enough … fulfilling the chanters wish.

Still another poppy-growing area that's collecting profitable dope dollars from America is the Golden Triangle. It covers parts of Viet Nam, Laos, Myanmar (Burma), and Thailand. It's a similar story here. We've spent billions in the area, literally died for nothing, and now end up with its dope on our streets. The Viet Nam War is over … but they're still killing us. Their dope, our dopes, and they get the profits. No wonder these areas are referred to as golden.

The Andean countries of Colombia, Peru, and Bolivia share a large growing area and have become major producers of illegal drugs, especially those drugs made from coca leaves. No doubt, they're the next "golden" area.

Colombia has been heavily involved in cocaine trade for many years, and it has been home to some of the most violent organizations in the world such as FARC (Revolutionary Armed Forces of Colombia), ELN (National Liberation Army), AUC (United Self-Defenders of Colombia), and others. These military guerrilla-type groups are both left wing and right wing in their ideology. They're all involved in violent crime, but especially illegal drugs. Illegal drug money from the United States pays for everything they need to continue and grow international crime. Although, recently, it appears the Colombian government has been doing a fair job at combating crime.

It's typical for illegal drugs from South America to be transported into Central America and Mexico before pausing for a minute at the US border. From there, they make their way into every US city. An amazing "two-way" journey. Bad people bring us illegal drugs, and we hand them a growing stack of billion-dollar bills to take home. We end up with a growing stack of ruined lives.

Venezuela, a communist-leaning country, is now a major exporting country for illegal drugs destined for the United States, Canada, and Europe. The drugs going to the United States are transported through the Caribbean countries and usually into Florida. Other drugs move from Venezuela to Central America by boat, north through Mexico, across our border, and into our neighborhoods and schools. Regardless of their origination, it appears the majority of drugs still cross into the United States from Mexico. That will continue until the United States stops it.

It should be obvious to US authorities that much illegal drug money supports major Mexican drug cartels. These drug cartels are some of the most murderous gangs in the world. Their brutality equals or surpasses Middle East terrorist groups such as ISIS and al-Qaeda. That should set off alarm bells for everyone.

Middle East terrorist groups may be based in distant lands, but their reach is worldwide. They spread their ideology with bombs and murder. Their names are familiar to most Americans since terrorist groups are visually boisterous and desire worldwide notoriety.

Drug cartels are different. They do not seek notoriety beyond their immediate areas of operation. American citizens living some distance from border areas have rarely heard of such names as Sinaloa Cartel, La Familia Cartel,

Knights Templar, Gulf Cartel, Los Zetas, Tijuana Cartel, Beltran-Leyva Cartel, or Juarez Cartel. All of these cartel names are well-known in Mexico and the illegal drug world. Although, in more recent years, some of these cartels have splintered into smaller groups so different names constantly emerge. The different cartels control different areas, and they're violent competitors. They kill each other.

Collectively, these cartels directly employ about 500,000 people. Indirectly 3 or 4 million. Most workers are in Mexico, but some operate in Central America and the United States. Today, their areas of operation are spreading fast, and that is very bad for the United States. These cartels mainly produce, transport, and sell illegal drugs, and that will continue because it generates the easy money.

Unfortunately, other "violent money crimes" are increasingly a problem. Crimes such as kidnapping, gun-running, extortion, robbery, forced labor, prostitution, and human smuggling are all increasing. They may be separate crimes, but most often they're related to Mexican drug cartels.

Much of this crime involves American victims. Tourists and other Americans in Mexico are robbed, murdered, and kidnapped for ransom. We hear about and worry about the other side of the world, but, as mentioned above, we have a violent war in our own backyard. Drug-related war is being waged between different drug cartels, the Mexican police, and the Mexican federal army. People are caught in the crossfire and end up trusting no one. Many flee north. The same can be said for the drug cartels. They're mainly south of the border, but they are now pushing north. Already drug cartels have members or associates in every big US city, including the far northern cities of Seattle, Minneapolis, Chicago, New York, and Boston. Drug cartels work with Hispanic gangs everywhere, but especially in the west and southwest where cartel members blend in easiest.

There are areas in Mexico where Americans can't go. Soon there'll be areas in America where Americans can't go. It's already happening.

There's another problem at the border that American citizens should be very fearful about and highly suspect. Authorities are hesitant to talk about it.

Terrorist organizations are working with or paying drug cartels to help smuggle individuals into the United States. It's difficult—no, it's impossible to know how many bad people have already entered and where they're located now. These suspected terrorist-type individuals have friends and can be maintained out-of-sight for long periods. These smuggled-in people could be more dangerous than the drugs. Politicians running for office rarely mention the problem, and it appears little deterrent action is taken to eliminate what is a huge threat.

A small part of that threat, mentioned in a *Washington Free Beacon* article, should be frightening to all Americans.

ARTICLE FOUND AT: freebeacon.com/national-security/investigation-collusion-between-terrorists-and-mexican-cartels-is-a-threat-to-u-s'

ARTICLE WRITTEN BY: Ali Meyer

DATE: AUGUST 17, 2015

TITLE: INVESTIGATION: COLLUSION Between Terrorists and Mexican Cartels is a Threat to US

> *Muslim terrorists are using Mexican drug cartels to infiltrate the U.S. southern border to plan attacks on the United States from within, according to Sun City Cell, a documentary produced in collaboration between Judicial Watch and TheBlaze TV.*
>
> *Mexican drug cartels are smuggling foreigners from countries with terrorist links into a small Texas rural town near El Paso and they're using remote farm roads—rather than interstates—to elude the Border Patrol and other law enforcement barriers....*
>
> *If people were disturbed or concerned about what they saw in this portion of the story, it is a fraction of the overall story.*

These quiet invasions across our border will continue until the border is sealed. It's not just poor people looking for the Promised Land. It's enough drugs to destroy our country, along with potential terrorists who wish to rain carnage onto a free people.

Another article also demonstrates what is happening at our border. The unsettling news follows:

ARTICLE FOUND AT: www.ibtimes.com/isis-entering-us -through-mexico-amid-islamic-state-fears-border-patrol-captures-2192635

ARTICLE PUBLISHED IN: *International Business Times*

ARTICLE WRITTEN BY: Aaron Morrison

DATE: NOVEMBER 19, 2015

TITLE: Is ISIS Entering US Through Mexico? Amid Islamic State Fears, Border Patrol Captures Afghan, Pakistani Men Being Smuggled Into Country

> *Six men from Afghanistan and Pakistan were captured in Arizona as part of a group of Mexicans attempting to smuggle them-selves into the United States and were detained by the U.S. border Patrol in Sonoita, Arizona, KNXV-TV, Phoenix, reported. The news stoked fears of Islamic State terrorism in the U.S. amid a debate over whether to admit Syrian and Iraqi refugees in the wake of terror at-tacks in Paris....*

> *The detainment follows a report Thursday by Breitbart, the right-leaning news outlet, about Border Patrol capture of eight Syrians attempting to enter Texas from Mexico in the Laredo sector....*

If the capture rate of potential terrorists at the border is similar to the capture rate of rapists in the United States ... the end result could be another 9/11 disaster waiting to happen.

Information about unusual people caught when crossing the border may be available, but it is not widely disseminated, especially to regular citizens. It should be. Citizens are voters. They can often force authorities to take action sooner rather than later. Politicians and other authorities too often prefer to start a series of studies ending with an island conference. Too slow. We're out of time.

If people from the Middle East have been captured crossing our border, it behooves authorities to determine immediately where they came from and exactly how they ended up crossing our border. If the authorities have them in custody they need to ask them. Ask them until they answer. Start with the easy questions. Did they fly into Mexico City? Who arranged travel from city to border? Why didn't they seek entry at a regular border crossing? End the questioning only when full answers are received. Then ... feed them.

Remember that capture rate? If one is apprehended at the border, could there be nine more who succeeded and are now making their way across the country? Middle Eastern people illegally crossing our border are not playing games. There's some evidence they seek and receive help from Mexican drug cartels. Drug cartels want money. Terrorists have money. Neither care about the welfare of the United States.

The following information is public. It may be relatively unknown, but still, it should be enough to alert all authorities of what's happening on the border today. And it may become far worse in the future. It's not the first warning for authorities. They're too often too slow until it's too late. Another red-flag article follows:

ARTICLE FOUND AT: www.judicialwatch.org/blog/2013/10/mexican-cartels-help-hezbollah-infiltrate-u-s/

ARTICLE PUBLISHED IN: *Judicial Watch*

DATE: OCTOBER 18, 2013

TITLE: MEXICAN CARTELS Help Hezbollah Infiltrate U.S.

> *In a shocking revelation made by a veteran U.S. counterterrorism expert, Hezbollah has infiltrated the Southwest United States by joining forces with Mexican drug cartels that have long operated in the region.*

> *Judicial Watch has for years reported on the chilling connection between Islamic extremists and Mexican drug cartels. In fact, as far back as 2007 JW wrote about an astounding Drug Enforcement Agency (DEA) report that lays out how Islamic terrorists and Mexican drug gangs have teamed up to successfully penetrate the U.S. as well as finance terror networks in the Middle East.*
>
> *In Hezbollah's case, a growing "business relationship" with cartels has allowed the Shia Islamic militant group to have a growing presence in the U.S., says Matthew Levitt, an esteemed terrorism expert with an impressive resume. Levitt is a former counterterrorism intelligence analyst at the Federal Bureau of Investigation (FBI) and State Department counterterrorism advisor. He also served as the No. 2 intelligence official at the U.S. Treasury where he operated the agency's terrorism and financial intelligence branch.*

If potential terrorists are secretly able to cross our border, doesn't that mean unsuspecting citizens are in danger? It's even worse if these potential terrorists are being assisted by drug cartels. Cartels and their associates can effectively transport and then hide drugs in every city. That means they could do the same for a group of terrorists.

Perhaps it's more difficult to smuggle in terrorists than drugs, but it appears cartels do successfully bring terrorists into the United States. Some are caught. How many are not?

Far more sinister results can happen when dealing with terrorists smuggled into the United States than with a cartel's drug delivery. Anybody who doesn't believe that should check daily worldwide headlines. They're written in blood.

Cartels assist terrorists for money because cartels will do just about anything for money. Money allows cartel bosses to live like kings and expand their crime empires. Terrorists want money too, but they will do just about anything for blood. Money allows terrorists to spread their ideologies, but killing infidels puts blood in the headlines. Terrorists want that notoriety.

What can happen if a drug cartel helps smuggle terrorists into the United States and then from the border to any large city? Almost anything.

Terrorists, nearly invisible in a big city, could prepare an ugly attack. An ugly attack such as a "hostage-ransom" situation with terrorists taking over a school and demanding 10 billion dollars or they'll kill 1,000 kids. Most of that money would go to a Middle East terrorist bank account and perhaps some to a Mexican cartel bank account. Or, much more probable, the cartel that assisted in smuggling terrorists across border and into a city gets paid and then vanishes.

Would the American government pay the $10 billion ransom? No need to wonder. The answer is … yes.

The following "three-day terrorist event" suggests where we're headed if we don't get a firm grip on suicidal foreign fanatics. You're not going to like this and it's going to hurt.

Day One is simple. Terrorists enter and secure school. Students forced to third floor. Multiple IEDs in place. Ransom demand of $10 billion. Meaningless negotiations follow. Endless television cameras watch. Recordings of hysterical kids broadcast. Parents' frantic demands and cries broadcast. Negotiations mum. A standoff? No, not even close.

Day Two. Second demand of $10 billion. Noon deadline. Stalled negotiations. Two kids are shown IEDs inside school. At 11:00 a.m., the same two kids walk from school to authorities. Kids, authorities talk. At 12:00 noon, "final demand" issued for $10 billion. Authorities hesitate. At 12:05 p.m., another two kids walk from school. At twenty-five paces, they're head-shot dead. Cameras jolt. Parents' knees buckle. At 1:00 p.m., $10 billion is paid. Terrorists inside school verify payment transfer to foreign bank. At 2:00 p.m., as an anxious nation watches live on TV … the school and all occupants are disintegrated.

Day Three. With trembling hands and sobbing sounds … America records the prior day as its worst day in history.

Who shares responsibility for this ugly example of a deliberate, unrepairable, unbearable tragedy? Everybody. In no particular order: Drug cartels, they who bring drugs, crime, and killers into our country and neighborhoods. Terrorists, they who have a mindset below that of a rabid dog. Drug abusers, who blindly pay out billions to keep cartels in business. Politicians, who will not tackle the drug problem that operates under their noses. Politicians, who mind their manners when speaking about or dealing with Muslim terrorists. Banks, that launder billions in dirty money, enabling drug trade, torture, and terrorism. American citizens, who have yet to say, "Enough is enough."

It appears the United States has a very big, very expensive, and very ugly problem with Mexican drug cartels. The cartels are winning the battle with drugs. It gets worse every day when another kid dies of an overdose. It gets worse every day when another billion dollars leaves the country for Mexico and beyond. It gets worse every day when men and women fighting the drug culture recognize it's nearly a hopeless situation.

The "war on drugs" is not working. The so-called war is against criminals, and the criminals are multiplying in numbers faster than those being jailed. That doesn't even include those drug dealers who were freed from prison during the last Democratic administration (2009-2017) due to a belief that incarceration periods were too long. That may or may not be true, but those drug dealers sitting in prison are not standing on the corner selling illegal drugs. Sadly, those serving time in jail are being replaced by others on the streets, including more and more regular Americans. Why would that be? Because the money is big and easy. You've heard the terms … big money - easy money. Sometimes it's true.

Recently, an American citizen and female flight attendant exited her plane with $3 million of illegal drugs stuffed in her luggage. Flight crews usually breeze through TSA security checks, but she was stopped for some reason. Probably by a dog with brains.

Flight attendants earn about $50,000 a year. That income requires a lot of work-days compared to $3 million in one day. It's unknown how many times she brought that much dope into our neighborhoods. It's also unknown exactly how many regular Americans would choose to grab a $3 million payday. That may be unknown, but it's probable the number of grabbers would be high. Big money. Easy money.

Flight attendants are in a favorable position to become mules or couriers for drugs. They're in a trustworthy job, travel out of town, spend time on the ground in foreign countries, and know airport security very well. That makes them desirable accomplices for drug dealers moving drugs across borders.

Many occupations present easy methods for smuggling drugs. But it's not the occupation that's necessarily the connection. It could be an American vacationer in Mexico who sees a fair chance of success smuggling drugs into the country. Combine that possible success with big dollars and it easily sounds very American. That's a shame.

The unpleasant question that needs to be asked and then addressed by authorities concerns the amount of money available in the drug world. For "big money" money, how many American citizens would choose to carry drugs into the United States if their circumstances were similar to the flight attendant mentioned above? An accurate answer will always be unknown. Guesses may be unconscionable.

When money amounts are temptingly large, as with illegal drugs, it's amazing and bewildering at the same time what people will do to reach their idea of financial success. Some will even build submarines in hopes of transporting drugs through ocean waters. Some are successful. Others await rescue in their fiberglass coffins.

As illegal-drug abusers pour billions into illegal-drug purchase, surely they're aware of or have read about peers who lose their lives of promise. Drugs are literally killing us at an increasing rate. And people involved with pushing drugs are increasing at an even faster rate. Big money. Easy money.

It appears banks are attracted to the same big and easy money. That's what makes the previous statement in "Day Two" possible: "Terrorists inside school verify payment transfer to foreign bank." There may be some indirect twists and turns with the money, but the transfer-deposit-withdrawal transaction gets done.

Apparently, many banks, knowingly or unknowingly, participate in the illegal drug business. That doesn't necessarily mean they have blood on their hands. But it does appear their hands are dirty. Sometimes filthy.

Banks are happy to promote openly regular customer and community business, but they rarely discuss their possible involvement with moving money around for the drug trade operators.

Below, parts of several articles paint a morally bankrupt picture of US banks' "financial-drug habit." Who's involved? What's involved? And, why?
ARTICLE FOUND AT: www.businessinsider.com/how-mexican-cartels-launder-their-money-2015-2
ARTICLE WRITTEN BY: Christina Sterbenz
DATE: FEBRUARY 20, 2015
TITLE: THESE ARE the 2 classic ways Mexican cartels launder money

> *Mexico is home to several drug trafficking organizations (DTOs): the Sinaloa cartel, La Familia cartel, Knights Templar cartel, Juarez cartel, and others.*

> *Generally, these organizations buy cocaine processed in South America and smuggle it into the United States to sell. After that, however, they need a way to get the money back to Mexico—and secretly....*

> *While many cartels take the risk of smuggling profits back to Mexico in bulk, more sophisticated groups launder money to avoid seizures by border patrol. To do that, they use two basic methods: through financial institutions and trade-based money laundering.*

Both methods briefly mentioned above can be quite sophisticated. Drug cartels can deposit profits into a bank, which are then transferred between different accounts in different countries. Certain variances take place, making transactions "less noticeable" to authorities. Dirty money in ... clean money out.

The second method involves what appears to be "regular commerce" between businesses. The difference is the drug organization may own the businesses being used, and the product being bought and sold may be drastically mismarked. A far-out example might be selling a hunk of lead painted the color of gold for a million dollars. The sale price is about a million dollars out of proportion, but the million dollars is received as a bank wire transfer and can then be withdrawn as clean money. It happens every day.

The following article is intriguing because the bank involved admitted some wrongdoing. Usually, banks pay a fine and suggest mistakes were made. This information says a lot about crime in the United States.

ARTICLE FOUND AT: www.bloomberg.com/news/articles/2010-06-29/banks-financing-mexico-s-drug-cartels-admitted-in-wells-fargo-s-u-s-deal

ARTICLE WRITTEN BY: Michael Smith

DATE: JUNE 29, 2010

TITLE: BANKS FINANCING Mexico Drug Gangs Admitted in Wells Fargo Deal

> *Just before sunset on April 10, 2006, a DC-9 jet landed at the International airport in the port city of Ciudad del Carmen, 500 miles east of Mexico City. As soldiers on the ground approached the plane, the crew tried to shoo them away, saying there was a dangerous oil leak. So the troops grew suspicious and searched the jet.*
>
> *They found 128 black suitcases, packed with 5.7 tons of cocaine, valued at $100 million. The stash was supposed to have been delivered from Caracas to drug traffickers in Toluca, near Mexico City, Mexican prosecutors later found. Law enforcement officials also discovered something else.*
>
> *The smugglers had bought the DC-9 with laundered funds they transferred through two of the biggest banks in the U.S.: Wachovia Corp. and Bank of America Corp., Bloomberg Markets magazine reports in its August 2010 issue.*
>
> *This was no isolated incident. Wachovia, it turns out, had made a habit of helping move money for Mexican drug smugglers. Wells Fargo & Co., which bought Wachovia in 2008, has admitted in court that its unit failed to monitor and report suspected money laundering by narcotics traffickers—including the cash used to buy four planes that shipped a total of 22 tons of cocaine....*
>
> *Wachovia admitted it didn't do enough to spot illicit funds in handling $378.4 billion for Mexican-currency-exchange houses from 2004 to 2007.*

More shocking information:

INFORMATION FOUND AT: rense.com/general28/money.htm,'

WRITTEN BY: JAMES Petras, Professor of Sociology, Binghamton University

DATE: SEPTEMBER 1, 2012

TITLE: US BANK Money Laundering—Enormous By Any Measure

> *There is a consensus among U.S. Congressional Investigators, former bankers and international banking experts that the U.S. and European banks launder between $500 billion and $1 trillion of dirty money each year, half of which is laundered by U.S. banks alone....*
>
> *Washington and the mass media have portrayed the U.S. as being in the forefront of the struggle against narco trafficking, drug laundering and political corruption: the image is of clean white hands fighting dirty money. The truth is exactly the opposite. U.S. banks have developed a highly elaborate set of policies for transferring illicit funds to the U.S., investing those funds in legitimate businesses or U.S. government bonds and legitimizing them.... Citibank, the biggest money launderer, is the biggest bank in the U.S....*

What can be said? What can be done? Does anybody care? Not much.

The next bank laundering story is mentioned only because of the substantial fine the bank paid to the government. Interestingly, the title tells most of the story.

REPORT FOUND AT: https://www.prisonlegalnews.org/news/2015/aug/31/british-banking-giant-fined-laundering-mexican-drug-money-through-us-banks/

PUBLISHED BY: PRISON Legal News

WRITTEN BY: MATTHEW Clarke

DATE: AUGUST 31, 2015

TITLE: BRITISH BANKING Giant Fined for Laundering Mexican Drug Money Through U.S. Banks

> *In December 2012, the U.S. Department of Justice (DOJ) fined major British bank HSHC almost $2 billion following an investigation that found HSBC was being used by Mexican cartels to launder drug money by transferring billions of dollars from its Mexican affiliates into U.S. banks.*

If you'd like to be "taken for a ride" on a very, very expensive luxury train, just board the following train-of-thought: Banks pay enormous fines when caught laundering drug money. But the bank executives are not criminally charged or sent to jail. The banking company subtracts the dollar fine expense from its profits. The banking company then raises fees for regular customers to cover "any" of its expenses, to increase profits or to spend "as it sees fit." Executives may or may not get their yearly bonus, but if so, they spend it "as they see fit." The enormous fines go to the government. The government spends the money "as it sees fit." At some point, the criminal drug cartel withdraws the laundered money from the bank. We don't exactly know what it does with the money because criminals, as do bank executives, operate under a blanket of secrecy, but we can assume, cartels spend it "as they see fit."

Any questions? Questions about drug-money in our country? If you're looking for straight answers, if there are any, who would you ask?

Former President of the United States, Barack Obama? No, you wouldn't ask him … he's apparently been higher-than-a-kite 100 times so his answers might be tainted. Other past presidents? No, recent past presidents, apparently, also smoked dope. How about the president of the biggest bank in the world? No, he wouldn't know anything about drugs. And if he did know anything about drugs, he wouldn't say much. Bank privacy laws. Nor would he want to incriminate himself. There's always the police. They know plenty about illegal drugs. But they don't have time to answer questions because they're too busy chasing around problems caused by illegal drugs. So there you have it. Nobody can answer your questions about illegal drugs. So don't ask questions. Act.

If the rich and famous and powerful care little about drugs, then individual families need to take action to curb illegal drug use within their own families.

Regrettably, regular American citizens with families, usually working hard to make ends meet, are the same souls who quietly suffer the indirect consequences of all drug abuse. They worry about drug use at local schools and in their neighborhoods. They fear peer pressure and movies have a strong influence on their children. At the same time, they pay the high public cost of trying to control drug abuse. They also pay for the aftermath of drug abuse.

Citizens have questions and need answers that calm their fears. As usual, those questions seem to have few answers. Satisfying answers are fewer yet.

These American citizens need a spokesperson. One who can speak to all citizens, and in return, all citizens would listen and understand. A spokesperson who can educate the country about the ill effects of drugs on so many of us and in so many ways. Someone who can find and deliver those magic words that immediately change drug abusers into drug renouncers and accomplish it almost overnight. A tall order for any one person.

Wondering about this until the "supreme-orator" emerges may take time … astronomer's time. Astronomers have their own measuring system since the time and distance they measure is so great it's incomprehensible for most of us.

Is there such a person?

There are historical figures. Several could convince anybody of anything, but they're historical for a reason.

Our presidents obviously have little credibility, nor are they ever heard by all.

What citizen could speak with such authority as to convey to all drug abusers that we, the citizens of the United States, wish for them to end illegal drug use because it threatens our way of life and our country itself?

If there is any one citizen with complete command and credibility who can effectively speak to all for all, it appears that angel is unknown. Instead of one … maybe all, maybe the country could speak to the country. The country should ask all citizens to stop illegal drug use. The drug abusers, all drug abusers, are killing the country. Ask them to stop. Ask them to stop taking drugs immediately. Ask them to save the country. Ask. And it shall be given. Hasn't that worked in the past?

All citizens together can't speak at once, but all citizens do elect representatives, and those representatives are supposed to speak for the people by carrying forth the people's wishes. All senior elected officials should be assigned the task of asking all drug abusers to stop taking drugs. It would actually be quite simple.

All senior elected officials would include the 50 governors, 435 representatives, 100 senators, the vice-president and the president. A total of 587 wise men. Obviously … some few are women. And, some fewer are wise.

The following five-point plan should be put in place immediately. The plan could be referred to as … "Ask."

1. Set date to announce Ask such as the Saturday or Sunday before the Fourth of July.

2. All elected officials would be required to publicly sign a pledge of "no drug use."

3. That pledge would include agreement to accept random drug testing. Accept immediate removal from office upon positive test. Accept loss of pension upon positive test. This public pledge would demonstrate the seriousness of the Ask plan to all citizens.

4. Distribute and broadcast information to all citizens about the benefits to them after eliminating illegal drug use. Benefits such as:

- Saving lives of tens of thousands of youngsters.
- Eliminating ruining lives of hundreds of thousands of youngsters.
- Improving lives of over 30 million drug abusers. Maybe many more.
- Increasing take-home pay of all workers as less taxes needed.
- Improving economic output, thus economic condition of the country.

- Eliminating giving hundreds of billions of dollars to criminals who mean us harm.
- Improving law enforcement coverage in all areas.
- Eliminating millions of costly drug-associated crimes a year.
- Improving health care in all ways. Cost. Timeliness. Quality.
- Reducing drunk-on-dope drivers on road.
- Lessening incarceration costs.
- Lessening rehab costs.
- Improving school performance and lessening school disturbances.
- Improving all aspects of court system operation.
- Receiving more respect from other countries.
- Reducing possibility of another country gaining "some" control of the United States.

5. Day of Ask announcement would require all elected officials be in attendance and display a solemn atmosphere. The officials, in unison, "ask" all Americans to stop using illegal drugs. Stop for themselves and stop for the country. Officials should remind Americans that stopping illegal drug use "for the country" is as patriotic as is going to war to defend the country. All American citizens are thanked for their patriotism. Short, solemn, and meaningful presentation. Officials depart without any interviews or speeches. No additional words from politicians that would surely dilute the event.

Many other benefits would exist beyond the short list in number four above. Many on the list could use further explanation, and the last one seems a bit far-fetched. But is it really?

Not according to the authors of *The Opium Wars*, as quoted below.

Source: Hanes, W. Travis and Frank Sanello. *The Opium Wars: The Addiction of One Empire and the Corruption of Another*. Naperville, IL: Sourcebooks, 2002.

> *Imagine this scenario: the Medellin cocaine cartel of Columbia mounts a successful military offensive against the United States, then forces the U.S. to legalize cocaine and allow the cartel to import the drug into five major American cites, unsupervised and untaxed by the U.S. The American government also agrees to let the drug lords govern all Columbian citizens who operate in these cities, plus the U.S. has to pay*

war reparations of $100 billion – the Columbians' cost of waging the war to import cocaine into America. That scenario is of course preposterous and beyond the feverish imagination of the most out-there writers of science fiction. However, a similar situation occurred not once, but twice in China during the nineteenth century. In both cases, however, instead of thuggish Columbian drug dealers, it was the most technologically advanced nation on Earth, Great Britain, that forced similar conditions on China.

The above scenario may sound impossible, but look a little closer. Note the individual phrases the authors used in the first two sentences. All of those circumstances have or are happening right now with subtle variations. Parts of US cities are like war zones. If we don't stop drugs coming into cities, it's the same as allowing it. Drugs are untaxed. And it appears in some areas that Hispanic gangs rule the streets, thus foreign-born drug lords are governing parts of our cities. Today, there are indeed parts of large cities where Americans never go. In some cases, that includes law enforcement. It's too dangerous. The attitude may be … it's a waste of time and life to enter certain city areas. And what about that $100-billion figure mentioned above as war reparations? Since the 1970s, the nation's war-on-drugs has cost about $1 trillion.

Thus, the last benefit cited in number four above appears valid.

Illegal drug use in the United States threatens our security, our economy, our way of life, and the lives of our families. It must stop. Immediately. Remember the four S's:

Stop drugs. Save lives. Save money. Save society.

It's not a theory. It's a fact.

PART THREE: ECONOMY
Saving the United States Economy

Chapter One

Manufacturing, Oil, Gas, and Grain

ARE WE FIGHTING an economic war?

The United States needs to remember an old phrase: *To the victor go the spoils.*

It seems as if there was a time when the United States manufactured almost everything and sold it to almost everybody in the world. Wasn't that a fairly good position to occupy? Can the United States climb back up?

In the early 1950s, the US share of the world's exports was about 17 percent of the total world output for goods. That 17 percent was nearly triple the combined percentages of Germany, Japan, and China.

The above percentage information was gleaned from a graph on the website listed below:

INFORMATION FOUND AT: https://people.hofstra.edu/geotrans/eng/ch5en/conc5en/ shareworldexports.html

TITLE: SHARE OF World Goods Exports, Leading Exporters, 1950-2014

THE GRAPH AT the site shows the world export percentages for the four leading exporters from 1950 to 2014. One remark, which should serve as a warning to working American citizens, states:

> *The relative decline of American exports has been an enduring trend, losing its status of the world's largest exporter in 2003 to Germany and to China in 2009. Japan's share substantially improved....*

Through 2014, China, Germany, Japan, and the United States were still the world's leading exporters. However, the United States has steadily lost share since the 1950s while the others have all gained share, especially Germany and China.

That unfortunate trend will continue until America figures out that some definite changes are necessary at all levels. The changes do not have to be dramatic initially but change must start immediately. American workers can start their "change" by understanding the ramifications of the last sentence in the last paragraph. **Steadily losing share, if not reversed, indicates the end is coming.**

Many Americans balk at any kind of change, but American workers need to recognize they're being out-produced by others around the world. And they need to be openly challenged as to what they're going to do about it. If certain work attitudes continue, American jobs will continue to slip away. It should be simple for our workers … their attitudes or their jobs. Easy choice?

American manufacturing will continue to be difficult because most often the product can be produced anywhere. Something in our manufacturing process must be adjusted to our advantage. That may be difficult, but that advantage must be found soon. Doors are shutting faster than opening.

Workers in some foreign countries have a much lower cost of living and much less expectation in life. They don't need two of everything. They earn far less than Americans, even when adjusted for cost-of-living standards. Their employers have fewer costly government regulations and offer fewer benefits to workers. Workers take fewer breaks and work diligently. The end result … foreign product is most often less expensive and its quality is often equal or better. Most of the world buys price. Much of the world buys quality. Either way, America has to meet or beat the world's preferences.

In some ways, the article below sums up what most Americans already know from daily use of products they purchased. Those daily use products are sitting in their driveways. Those products were purchased for different reasons, but one of the reasons is usually the buyer's judgment of quality and value. Vehicle quality and value often equate with longevity on the road. An embarrassing article follows:

ARTICLE FOUND AT: www.usatoday.com/story/money/cars/2015/05/07/consumer-reports-cars-over-200000-miles/70956532/

ARTICLE WRITTEN BY: Chris Woodyard, *USA Today*

DATE: MAY 7, 2015

SOURCE: CONSUMER REPORTS

TITLE: CONSUMER REPORTS: 10 Cars That Will Go 200,000 Miles

> With the average amount paid for a new car now firmly above $30,000, it makes sense to hold on to a vehicle as long as possible in order to squeeze every usable mile out of it before it needs to be traded in.
>
> But when it come to the long-mileage derby, the car you choose can make a big difference on whether you'll hit the magic 200,000-mile mark.

> *In its June issue, Consumer Reports looked at the models that hold the greatest likelihood of turning over 200,000 miles. Five are Toyotas. Five are Hondas. No other cars or brands make the list.*

What happened? Other countries and manufacturers, around the world, used to copy the United States. Should we now copy them? Should we copy Japan's technology, management, workers' skills, or workers' physical and mental commitment for doing a good job? Or is it an extra-good job?

Can America rise to the occasion and meet the challenge of lower-priced product while at the same time delivering a better quality product to the world? No, probably not. At least not in the short run. But over ten years may suffice. Change the trend ... and the future will again look hopeful for most citizens.

If America really can't compete and win the cost and quality battle in most manufacturing areas, then we are doomed to be the service sector providers. But to whom do we provide service? Mostly each other. Much service work is local rather than international, which means we're not bringing in enough dollars from our foreign product providers. Service is fine, but manufacturing is better.

Another problem is the wage scale. Most manufacturing jobs pay very good wages compared to service. Today, we see vote-seeking politicians grandstanding for $15 per hour for flipping burgers. What does that do? It increases the price of burgers and decreases the number of jobs. Many unions are screaming for the same thing. Higher wages bring higher prices and the spiral continues. We need to sell product to the world. That's what the world does to us.

Many would say we are doing all right in some manufacturing areas. That may be correct. We are doing all right in some areas, but we need to do better in all areas. Is that possible? Yes. But any improvement requires effort, not luck.

It's difficult to be the leading manufacturer with competitors like China. We all know the story there. But there's a particular problem that needs to be mentioned, and it concerns China and our manufacturing base. It's something you hear little about from politicians, unions, or corporations. It's another challenge to American industry that's coming soon, and it may change everything when it happens.

Today, the United States is a major exporter of aircraft, vehicles, and military equipment. Those big ticket items are areas in which we're still fairly strong in sales to other countries. If that export strength changes, the United States will find itself in a much worse trade deficit position.

That is about to happen. Right now, we are holding our own with sales of aircraft, vehicles, and military equipment both domestically and internationally.

The competition is fierce from Germany and Japan in autos; Europe, Canada, and Brazil in aircraft; and many countries in military equipment.

What happens if China strongly enters those markets? If China can inexpensively manufacture high-quality doorknobs, computers, and almost anything else Americans purchase every single day ... then they can inexpensively manufacture aircraft, automobiles, and military equipment.

Here's the bad news. China is already producing those items. Mostly for domestic use. But now they're ramping up vehicles and airliners for export to countries such as the United States. It appears quality may not yet be fully perfected for export grade vehicles or airliners, but it won't be long. Often, that final quality test comes after foreign buyers provide complaint-feedback to the manufacturer. That's happening now with cars and will take place before long with airliners. Americans might remember when Japanese cars first arrived in the United States. They were too small, sounded like cheap motorbikes, and people thought the quality was not up to our standards. People laughed.

It wasn't long before people focused on the price of Japanese cars, which was less than most American models. Price sells. Owners started bragging about great gas mileage. Quality kept improving until they were the most reliable cars on the road. Instead of being junked out at a typical 75,000 miles, owners found their Japanese cars pleasantly surprised them on the high side for mileage.

It's difficult to believe, but starting in the early 2000s and for the next ten or so years, about 16 million Japanese vehicles sold in the United States compared to about 200,000 American vehicles sold in Japan. Who's in charge of that equation? Japan. Who needs to "go the extra mile in effort" to change that lopsided import-export imbalance? American workers. American vehicle manufacturers. American government. American buyers.

The next ten or twenty years could find a similar imbalance emerge with Chinese vehicles sold in the United States. The current overall trade deficit with China is bad enough. Add cars and trucks into that mix and US manufacturing jobs will take another big hit. America, waiting until after the fact to take action won't work very well. We already did that with Japan.

It's true that some Japanese vehicles are now made in the United States. That's good, but it is not good enough. That limited local production is also offset by the fact that many US vehicles or their parts are manufactured on foreign soil.

Already, vehicle manufacturing in China far surpasses all other countries. Current production is nearing 20 million units per year. Nearly all sales are domestic. There's also quite a few American cars sold in China, but those cars are produced in China by Chinese companies that partnered with American companies.

Generally, in today's US automobile market, most vehicle names are split among three countries. When Chinese cars arrive in sizable numbers, it'll be a four-way split. One of the four may well fade. That's scary because the trend points to fewer American cars. More Chinese cars equates with fewer American jobs. Any laughter at Chinese cars on the street will be short-lived.

It should be remembered that most Japanese and German vehicles manufactured in the United States are sold here, not exported. Other countries, such as Korea, do some manufacturing here as well. Both Canada and Mexico manufacture vehicles and parts, which all contribute to vehicles sold in the United States. It's almost like a jigsaw puzzle of parts coming together.

It should be expected airliners being imported from China will find slower acceptance in American markets. That happened with European builder Airbus years ago, but now if you fly several flights within the United States, you'll be flying on at least one Airbus plane. Boeing has competed very well internationally with Airbus over the years. Most of those years experienced strong worldwide growth, which benefited both companies everywhere. Boeing and many American aviation suppliers did well with aircraft sales in the Far East. That could change in the near future. If Comac, the Chinese commercial aircraft manufacturer, produces a quality airliner at lower cost to airlines, you can expect heavy pressure on US and European sales. As always … lower sales equal fewer jobs.

It's important to remember manufacturers of automobiles and aircraft each have numerous suppliers of parts. When sales slow, it has a ripple effect that spreads rapidly down the chain of suppliers. Job losses mount.

Without substantial changes, manufacturing in the United States will have a difficult time rising from the ashes anytime soon. That's sad, but business owners, government, and workers all had a hand in transferring our manufacturing to offshore facilities.

For business, it was the almighty buck and, in some cases, survival. The government had to save mankind so it piled on costly regulations. In some cases, short-sighted unions thought they knew best. Higher pay and wasteful work rules or we'll shut you down. Short-sighted demands. Many companies did partially shut-down as they subbed work out to foreign-based operations or foreign companies striving to reach the top of the economic ladder with quality work, lower costs, and expedient production.

Politicians, when running for reelection, insist they'll bring all the jobs back. After the election, they're busy with other matters. Perhaps they need to figure out that many Americans can afford a foreign-made $10 quality doorknob but not an American made $16 quality doorknob. If somebody wants to fix the doorknob situation, he needs to work on the $16 knob, not the $10 knob. It does little overall good for the average citizen if the government maneuvers the $10 knob up to $12 in order to sell a few more $16 knobs made in the United States.

Is there a way to protect American manufacturing jobs? Yes, there is, but some Americans may need to be pink-slipped before they'll accept the necessary changes. **The workers who should accept change are the same workers who already have strong manufacturing jobs.** Many are the same workers who say … "Pay us more money or we'll shut you down." Little economic sense. The same can be said for government. The government strangles manufacturers with costly regulations. Bureaucrats seem to enjoy their job of antagonizing US business first and helping US business last. More of … too little economic sense.

If the country wants to compete against the world in manufacturing, the following six steps or changes should be adopted. None are exceptional, and most will be very difficult to implement completely. None are a cure, but all would be a big step in the right direction. US manufacturing improvement must be found in order to counter foreign competition. There is no other way.

Costs fall first. Sales increase second. Jobs added third.

Over time, the following changes would become more beneficial to all:

1. Somebody must educate manufacturing workers, especially automobile and aircraft union workers, about basic economic principles such as supply, demand, and cost factors. Explain, with vivid display, what has happened to other American workers and will happen to them if they can't produce "quality product at lower cost" relative to China.

2. Demonstrate to workers that they're in an economic war and America is losing that war. Patriots will step up.

3. Some union workers may be paid $50 per hour with high benefits and extremely favorable work rules. If those figures are far out of line with the average worker, they should be narrowed down. Not big changes, but little "changes that benefit the country" relative to foreign competition. Workers can still be at the top of the pay ladder compared to the average worker. Would workers make these economic changes? Ask them. Are workers tough enough and patriotic enough to make changes? Ask them.

4. Public companies are owned by shareholders. All workers or employees should be shareholders. Limited part-owners. All public companies or employers should provide a Dividend Reinvestment Plan (DRIP) for all employees. Employees could select an amount deducted from their paychecks and deposited into their DRIPs. Another program similar to a DRIP and perhaps incorporated into a DRIP would be one in which employees and company arrange for some employee compensation to be paid in company treasury stock instead of money. Most workers are uninformed about this type of transaction. Educate them. Reduce production costs by reducing employee dollar pay and providing some of their earned income in the form of company shares to be held long-term. Example: If employee is paid $500 per week, change figure to $475 per week plus $25 per week paid in company treasury stock. This would be arranged differently than a deduction from regular paycheck. The employee's pay would be lowered by 5 percent to $475 per week. Employer's labor cost factor would be lowered by 5 percent. Employees are able to increase or decrease dollar amounts in a regular DRIP, but they would be unable to be that flexible with treasury shares as part of income. There would be a long-term holding period for treasury shares. **Such a plan obviously needs legal work.** Many employees own DRIPs or similar plans in the companies they work for now. All employees should participate. DRIPs can benefit them, the company, and the country. Notice: Two different type of plans were briefly mentioned above concerning worker pay.

5. The government bureaucrats should remove or adjust most regulations that add costs to business and few benefits to regular citizens. The regulators and management should work together with a single goal in mind. That goal being to improve vastly the country's competitive position. It's as simple as that.

6. Business owners and executives should be strongly reminded ... their overall compensation often influences general worker attitudes. Better attitude equals much better work production. Patriotism should be evident on all levels.

All six suggestions are meant to reduce company cost to produce product. The idea is basic and simple. Reduce product cost and more product sells. More product sales means more workers needed. More workers means more jobs and money in the community. More money in the community means more spending in the community, leading to more jobs. Many other factors are involved, but the end result is expansion, which means more prosperity for all. This scenario is basic and almost automatic. Naturally, many things can interrupt the end result. If management uses any cost savings generated to shift money only into their pockets, the desired end result will be altered. The idea is to lower product costs so as to sell more product nationally and internationally, which benefits the country. More sales of American-made doorknobs and more export of knobs means less import of foreign-made knobs, all of which benefits our workers, our companies, and our country. The current trend must be reversed.

Is all of this necessary today? Yes, it is if the country is to improve its manufacturing base, which is mandatory for long-term survival. It's especially true as China increases its dominance in all areas, shortly to include automobile and airliner manufacturing for export.

American workers and American government should each contemplate how the country would change economically if China became the export leader to the US and the world in both automobiles and aircraft. That thought should shake you because that reality may be just around the corner.

Briefly, one area not covered in this book is robotics. Robots are now used in much industry. Soon, that will be so in storefront shops such as restaurants and small merchandise. Part-time type jobs will be lost. It is mandatory the US specialize in building robot-type systems. Displaced workers will need to flip from turning-over burgers to turning-out robots. Won't be easy. Must be done.

Just before the 1-6 list above, the following question was asked: Is there a way to protect American manufacturing jobs?

Another, but slightly different question: **Is there a *better* way to protect American jobs?** Yes, there is a better way, and America needs to move in that direction immediately. The first question referred mostly to manufacturing jobs but "better" refers to jobs producing commodities. **Specifically oil, gas, and grain.**

Oil, gas, and grain production is much different from manufacturing transportation vehicles, doorknobs, electronics, shoes, or screws. China now has the upper hand in trade with the United States. If we can make it ... they can make it better, faster, and cheaper. Try shopping "American" sometime. You'll be out all day reading labels. By the time you get home, you'll be able to speak Mandarin. Changing that experience will be frustrating, but it needs to start immediately.

China manufactures goods. We drill for oil. We drill for natural gas. We grow grain like nobody else. China ... manufactures goods. Get the picture?

If the United States designs and builds widgets or gizmos or just about anything else, the Chinese can copy it and build it tomorrow. They are very good at that.

The article below is a scary example of apparent Chinese capability. It should make you highly concerned.

America's newest and most advanced fighter jet, Lockheed Martin's F-35 Joint Strike Fighter (JSF) has recently entered service. It's probably the best in the world. That's good news.

Not-so-good news follows.

ARTICLE FOUND AT: nationalinterest.org/blog/the-buzz/Americas-f-35-stealth-fighter-vs-chinas-new-j-31-who-wins-13938

ARTICLE WRITTEN BY: Dave Majumdar, defense editor

DATE: SEPTEMBER 25, 2015

TITLE: AMERICA'S F-35 Stealth Fighter vs. China's New J-31: Who Wins?

> *Recently revealed details concerning China's Shenyang J-31 fighter suggest that the aircraft not only looks like the Pentagon's Lockheed Martin F-35 Joint Strike Fighter (JCF), but it offers comparable aerodynamic performance. But the real question is how far along Beijing has come in the development of subsystems like radars and engines....*
>
> *On the surface, the J-31 looks very much like a twin-engine F-35 clone—and there are plenty of reasons to believe that the Chinese jet was based on stolen JSF technology—and could eventually be more or less a match for the American jet.*

The above article is worrisome because ... if China can obtain secret plans for our newest jet fighter, it can probably get plans for any US project, whether it's military, commercial, or even personal.

Another similar but short article follows.

ARTICLE FOUND AT: www.defenseone.com/threats/2015/09/more-questions-f-35-after-new-specs-chinas-copycat/121859/

ARTICLE WRITTEN BY: Marcus Weisgerber

DATE: SEPTEMBER 25, 2015

TITLE: CHINA'S COPYCAT Jet Raises Questions About F-35

> *Did the Chinese theft of data on the US fighter jet and other weapon systems shrink the Pentagon's technical superiority? ...*
>
> *China's twin-engine design bears a striking resemblance to the single-jet F-35. Still, the Joint Strike Fighter is expected to fly slightly farther and carry a heavier load of weapons, according to the data, which was first reported by Jane's.*

Should the United States be worried about competition from foreign countries and especially China? Yes, and definitely yes.

As stated above, it'll take a super-effort by US manufacturing companies to compete favorably with China and the rest of the world. It will also take some period of time to catch up. What happens if time becomes short? What happens if China or any nation is the prime or only producer of a product dearly needed by the United States? This is not an unheard of problem. Rare metals are needed for specialized parts in aircraft and electronics. What happens if China is the sole producer or source of a rare product and it decides to withhold sale to the US?

Recently a uranium mine was approved by the US government for sale to a Canadian connection. Maybe that should not have happened. The mine was an important supplier of special material to the United States. Canada's friendly. But now it appears Canadian control has passed to Russia. Russia is less friendly. What happens if Russia and the United States have serious political squabbles? That US, Canadian, and Russian mine transaction that took place between 2009 and 2013 could prove to be a big mistake. A big political mistake.

The United States needs to maintain control of strategic material and maintain the ability to manufacture or obtain any product at any time. Depending on the product, if China supplies the US with 100 percent of some "necessity," there could be a supply problem at any time. Why not have China supply 99 percent and America produce 1 percent? The 1 percent being an obvious extreme minimum. If our relationship with China deteriorates, at least the United States can start ramping up production. Not a perfect scenario but a start.

What about those areas that may be "better" than manufacturing? Namely, oil, gas, and grain.

Oil and gas production is something our government has indirectly curtailed from 2009 through 2016. What's wrong with the United States being the world export leader in oil and gas? And you can add grain to that wise formula as well.

Does anybody see a difference in competing with China in manufacturing versus competing in production of oil, gas, and grain for export?

Generally, whatever the United States can manufacture, the Chinese can also manufacture. It's not only China. Other countries strive to be low-cost producers as well. China is just the obvious example.

What about commodities? China needs oil, gas, and grain.

Every day we buy and use Chinese low-cost products, which is evident when shopping at Walmart. Every day, China needs oil and gas for commercial manufacturing operations. It needs grain to supplement its food supply. For years, we've heard how the Chinese waste nothing when harvesting an animal for food. That's hungry.

The United States can and must become China's main supplier of oil, gas, and grain.

We've allowed ourselves to end up in the position of buying everything we need from China. We're its biggest customer … an importer of everything Chinese. It's prudent for the United States to at least try to balance the export-import deficit with China, and the only way to do that now is exporting oil, gas, and grain. Almost everything else it can produce itself.

The United States does export certain big ticket items such as vehicles and airliners to the world, including China. However, most American vehicles sold in China are produced in China. This limited American export success is about to decrease. As China ramps up its own airliner production, it will be importing fewer Boeing aircraft. When it starts selling inexpensive airliners and vehicles around the world, Boeing … and America will suffer economically.

It's mandatory the United States act now to exploit this window of opportunity for exporting oil, gas, and grain to the world. The opportunity won't last forever. Even now the US government and many foolish Americans fail to recognize what is happening. America must take these six actions immediately:

1. Explore, drill, and extract more natural gas and more crude oil from America's vast reserves. Sell and export petroleum product around the world especially to China.

2. Change the current regulation that bans the United States exporting crude oil and only exporting refined product. At the same time, prefer to sell refined oil because it's higher priced. Do not assist other countries in building refineries.

3. Build large new refineries strategically located on the East, West, and Gulf Coasts to expedite refining and shipping. Start now since large refineries take a minimum of five years to build.

4. Build appropriate pipelines, including Keystone. Canada is our major trading partner, including in the oil trade. Without Keystone, Canada may build its own pipeline to the Pacific Coast and lock up oil export to China.

5. Build the appropriate number of oil and liquefied natural gas (LNG) facilities to accommodate substantial exporting. This would include shipping, storage, and port facilities.

6. Grow more grain. Use quality soil, quality seeds, quality fertilizer, quality equipment, quality research, and quality know-how. The world needs food. Feed the world. Convince the world it needs the United States.

Now is the optimum time for action. A window of opportunity is open before foolish US politicians and smart Chinese businessmen slam it shut.

Chinese businesses are starting to export vehicles, and soon airliners, to the United States and the world. That'll be a crushing blow to America's export business and to its domestic economy as it's forced to absorb another familiar brand of imports.

Many US politicians running for office, some taxpayer-funded start-up businesses, and the vocal global-warming crowd are all clamoring for power generated by anything except fossil fuels. In other words … stop drilling American oil and buy more Chinese-made power equipment.

If the modern-day clamoring class succeeds in wrecking our great petroleum industry by ushering in alternative fuel at the speed of light, it's in for a surprise. Alternative, or renewable, fuel sounds like a can't-miss improvement for the United States; once it's perfected, the cost will fall below fossil fuels. That's probably not true. Today, America needs to be cautious how fast it's pushing alternative-fuel. Speed kills when it comes to cost. Many installations are government subsidized, and that makes it sound less expensive, but it's the opposite. Government involvement raises the cost for all.

Private industry should lead the way with its funds in perfecting alternative power. The critical measure would be a lower cost than fossil fuel with domestic-made equipment. Is twenty years too long to wait for those benefits? No.

Related problems are not being factored into the cost debate. What happens when millions of vehicles are powered with batteries, millions of homes with solar power, and many businesses with wind power? The government will say lower costs are right-around-the-corner, plus we're saving the environment. But what about the petroleum industry? Using less oil fuel means more direct and indirect jobs will be gone. The people who think they know everything about this matter will say not to worry because new jobs are being created with alternative fuel. Yes, that's true, but where will those jobs be located? Who will be making the alternative-fuel equipment? It'll be the low-bidder. Who will that be?

It's really not that confusing. Most fossil fuels can be drilled, shipped, and refined into gas right here in the United States. Isn't it better to drill more and create more jobs here? Compare that with all those added jobs being promised in the alternative fuel industry. It won't take long before batteries, solar panels, windmill parts, and electronic gizmos are all being produced in China. In fact, it's already happening. If oil and gas production workers must switch their jobs to the alternative-fuel industry, they'll have to move a long distance.

Fewer jobs in the US petroleum industry. More jobs in the Chinese alternative fuel system industry. Who wants that? China.

If China is expanding its export of vehicles and airliners, that means the United States will be producing fewer of each. Fewer workers needed in the United States. More workers needed in China. Alternative fuel equipment? More workers needed in China. Government assistance handout? More social workers needed in the United States.

Unless we change our thinking, the US trade deficit will continue to be lopsided in favor of the world, and especially China. Isn't there a better way to approach the future that favors the United States?

In order for the United States to improve its trade deficit, create many more high paying jobs, strengthen its economic security, become the world leader in certain critical exports, and give a boost to American attitudes, it must immediately put the following five-point plan into action:

1. Change the US Tax Code and business regulations to favor US business.

2. Change the US Tax Code to favor a company's production in the United States versus the same company's foreign production unit.

3. Adopt rules that allow US businesses operating in a foreign country to return financial assets to the United States without penalty.

4. Ask companies increasing production to do so in the United States, not abroad.

5. Adopt the above listed "six actions" that will facilitate the United States being the world export leader in oil, gas, and grain.

A first draft blueprint of this plan could be completed in thirty days. Put the first draft in newspapers and on the Internet. Let it serve as a wakeup call. Demonstrate to all citizens that American workers, business leaders, and the US government are serious about reversing the slide in US production. We need our manufacturing base back. Ask for comment on the blueprint, but continually move ahead and do what is best for the country. The comments are not for ideas but to gauge the temperament of citizens. The immediate result of publication may be deafening, but what you should be looking for is interest from companies willing and able to increase production locally. Many companies produce product domestically and overseas. For years, increased purchase orders meant increased work orders, but they ended up in the company's Chinese or Mexican manufacturing facility because it's cost was lower and often faster. Reverse that. Pressure the company's US unit to hold down cost, cut cost, and expedite order time, start to finish. Who has to bear down and get it done? All workers from the floor sweeper to the biggest chair in the office. Will this strategy work? Yes, it will immediately improve that unit's performance, which should mean more future orders. It doesn't mean a parent company's US-based manufacturing unit will out-produce its Chinese supplier. It means the cost gap is narrowed.

Any positive job news about companies adding US production versus foreign production should be announced. Make a public show of it. Maybe bringing jobs home to America will become fashionable. It might not matter if the plan has bugs to work out. All plans do. Keep moving ahead. The manufacturing competition the US faces has the strong upper hand. That competition is as close as Mexico and as far away as China. A foreign competitor's cost to produce is much lower, and each competitor is striving to continue that trend in one product after another. And their product quality is good and improving. Americans used to laugh at foreign junk. Now we wonder whether the laughter is directed at us. Laughter or not, this is a serious matter to the extent that it should be labeled an "economic war."

Today, it seems many American citizens live well and enjoy what might be called a calm lifestyle. Few feel they're in an economic war. These same citizens may think it's a waste of time and effort to bust their butts just for a small improvement in export manufacturing. Perhaps they prefer waiting for some general American business revival. That sounds fine for a slow dance contest, but the United States is in an economic war, and its economic adversaries are winning. They play hard and fast and not always by the rules. The rules? There are no rules in global economic competition.

Americans purchase numerous Chinese goods every day. Maybe they should stop. The reasons are many, including what's found in the following report, which has been read by very few citizens and understood by fewer: ARTICLE FOUND AT: 'www.foxnews.com/politics/2015/07/25/fbi-china-most-predominant-economic-espionage-threat-to-us-.html'
ARTICLE WRITTEN BY: Matt Dean
DATE: JULY 25, 2015
TITLE: FBI: CHINA the Most Predominant Espionage Threat to US

> Spies, largely of Chinese origin, are going to dramatic lengths to steal critical information from U.S. companies, officials within the intelligence community say.

The Federal Bureau of Investigation on Thursday detailed a sharp spike in the number of economic espionage investigations undertaken by the agency over the last year, with a 53 percent increase in caseloads....

A recent FBI survey of 165 U.S. companies found that China was the perpetrator in 95 percent of economic-espionage cases.

Officials say that theft of trade secrets and intellectual property has resulted in the loss of hundreds of billions of dollars from the U.S. economy over the last year alone.

It appears the FBI is quite busy, but does anybody believe all instances of espionage are being investigated? Corporate espionage may be similar to rape reporting, and most rapes aren't reported at all. The rape victim may feel the crime is too embarrassing or the damage is done, so what's the use. Could it be similar with some espionage cases? It would seem so.

It's not just industrial spying. The threats are everywhere, including from those seeking to take advantage of US military abilities and even tamer areas such as agriculture technology.

Some will find the following agriculture espionage case quite surprising. Unfortunately, it's one of many. Details just below:

INFORMATION FOUND AT: 'https://faculty.ist.psu.edu./bagby/432Spring08/T10/cases.html

PSU SOURCE: HTTP://SANFRANSICO.FBI.GOV/DOJPRESSREL/2006/SF121406.HTM

TITLE: UNITED STATES v. Xiaodong Sheldon Meng

This cybercrime case received national attention because of the severity of the criminal's actions. Systems engineer, computer systems analysts, and 3D graphics application senior engineer, Xiaodong Sheldon Meng, threatened American security when he was caught and indicted on 36 felonies counts for stealing military application trade secrets. Meng illegally took the data in order to sell them to the People's Republic of China....

Not all espionage cases are as scary as those involving military applications, but others may prove just as damaging. That includes corn. We have corn. They want corn. We buy Chinese products, but the Chinese prefer to steal our corn.

Grain is something the United States could export in larger quantities to help offset the huge trade imbalance it has with China and others. The following article speaks to that aspect of the economic war being waged against the United States.

ARTICLE FOUND AT: https://newrepublic.com/article/122441/corn-wars

ARTICLE WRITTEN BY: Ted Genoways

DATE: AUGUST 16, 2015
TITLE: CORN WARS

> *On September 30, 2012, agents from the FBI contacted U.S. Customs and Border Protection at O'Hare International Airport in Chicago with an urgent request. They wanted bags from two passengers on an outbound flight to Beijing pulled for immediate inspection. The passengers didn't track as dangerous criminals: Li Shaoming, president of Beijing Kings Nower Seed Science and Technology, a large Chinese agricultural company that develops corn, rice, cotton, and canola seeds, and Ye Jian, the company's crop research manager.*

> *In Li's luggage, agents found two large Pop Weaver microwave popcorn boxes. Buried under the bags of unpopped snack kernels were roughly 300 tiny manila envelopes, all cryptically numbered—2155, 2403, 20362. Inside each envelope was a single corn seed....*

> *Meanwhile, at a different gate, Wang Hongwei, another Chinese national believed to be in the employ of Kings Nower ... boarded a separate flight for Burlington, Vermont, where he had a car waiting for him to drive to Canada.... Border patrol officers were waiting when Wang pulled up to the Highgate Springs port of entry along the U.S.-Canadian border. He was selected out for a search, which turned up 44 bags of corn seeds under his seat and in his suitcases, as well as a notebook filled with GPS coordinates and a digital camera containing hundreds of pictures of cornfields. Questioned by agents, Wang would say only that he had purchased the seeds from a man named Mo Hailong, the director of international business at the Beijing Dabeinong Technology Group (DBN Group), the parent company of Kings Nower Seed.*

> *Not wanting to alert Mo, agents allowed all three men to leave the country, but their corn seeds were confiscated.... Eventually, their genetic sequencing was matched to seeds under development by Monsanto, DuPont Pioneer, and LG Seeds, which, including LG's parent company, Groupe Limagrain, comprise three of the four largest seed companies in the world. The GPS coordinates were found to correspond with farms in Iowa and Illinois, where those companies were testing the performance of new hybrids....*

> *The Department of Justice maintains that China is quietly permitting and even encouraging companies to steal American agricultural secrets right out of the ground.*

Is there any doubt there's an economic war taking place? Is there any doubt it's pointed directly at the United States? No doubt.

At least 1,000 criminal cases of economic espionage are under investigation or have already been prosecuted. Many other, perhaps most, instances of espionage remain unknown. That old warning-phrase of "Trust but verify" needs to be changed to "Trust but verify and watch like a hawk."

Is there much chance Americans are working in high-level technical jobs in China and stealing secret information for the United States? Little chance. The Chinese are not as trusting as Americans. Some might use the word foolish in lieu of trusting.

We educate many foreigners in science programs at our prestigious universities. Anyone who doubts that needs to do nothing more than pick up any major university graduation ceremony program and check the names of doctorate candidates in mathematics, physics, chemistry, and engineering. Good luck with name pronunciation. Those graduating students become scientists. They obtain work in US high tech companies but many maintain strict allegiance to their home countries. Does that happen often? Yes, it may be the norm, not the exception, and many of those students are from China. Is any of that against the law? No, but espionage is against the law and highly dangerous … for America.

America is a free and open society. Many nations are just the opposite. And America competes with those nations economically. Again, China is the easy example. Open and free may be an advantage for us at home, but it's also an advantage for our competitors who freely mix in our society. Compare that atmosphere with an American trying to live and work in China. China's closed secretive society may serve China well, but it yields no benefit to America. It's as simple as … they speak English, we do not speak Chinese. That language deficiency handicaps the United States when competing with China or any nation. The language problem is our responsibility. Much of the world speaks English, and it's not for our benefit. It's for their benefit.

We are in an economic war, and the world has come ready to compete. More than compete. China leads that fight, and it will continue to do so unless America makes aggressive changes.

Increasing US exports of oil, liquefied natural gas (LNG), and most grains benefits our entire country immediately. It starts with realizing we're in an economic war and initiating a plan for winning that war. That'll involve a painful but patriotic combination consisting of a super extra-work effort performed along with an energized attitude that it's being done for the country. It's a worthwhile combination. Perhaps similar to women in factories and the purchase of war bonds during the early 1940s.

Becoming energy independent at home and at the same time being the largest exporter of oil product in the world will not be easy to accomplish. But if you step back and look at the big picture, the end result should be evident to any observer. More high-paying American jobs. Millions of additional down-line jobs. A rebalancing of import/export trade. An overall thriving economy. Home happiness. All great reasons to move full speed ahead regardless of difficulty.

A fairly recent development for oil-field workers deserves a brief mentioning: Oil-field workers, called Roughnecks, are starting to see job competition. Some Roughnecks are being replaced by Iron Roughnecks. Automation in the oil field is very slowly taking the place of some manual labor. The remedy for this oil-field job loss is simple. Roughnecks build Iron Roughnecks in America.

The United States should never be dependent on power solely from another country. Or, countries. But, contrarily, the world would be in steady hands being dependent on energy from the United States.

Imagine a scenario where America must have certain power equipment and it is primarily available only from China. That could lead to uneasy if not difficult times for America. Energy independence for the United States should be job-one. Job two, without doubt, should be the United States exporting energy to the world. Especially China.

The global warming crowd would say alternative power supply brings energy independence. But not if China is the manufacturer of batteries, solar equipment, and other electronic necessities. If China provides most of our power equipment, then it has some power authority over us. Chinese manufacturing provides jobs for its people while enjoying profit from us. Meanwhile, America waits for the next shipment of solar panels.

The benefit for America supplying energy to the world is good jobs across the United States. It's not just drilling oil wells but maintaining an adequate supply chain from well to refineries to port facilities to destination. The chain is already in place; it just needs to be minimally expanded for increased export. Along the way, America's petroleum industry should maintain adequate supply to meet demand needs here. The industry can be trusted more than any foreign country. It's doubtful a fixed price at the pump is possible, so as with most other commodities, oil prices would fluctuate, but less so than when affected by foreign behavior.

There'll be plenty of argument against any large project that increases the size of our petroleum industry. There may even be some validity to what is argued, but the national need to survive, and survive as a prosperous country, is more important than ever.

One aspect of the growing petroleum industry should be further developed and perfected for general transportation: the efficient use of natural gas in vehicles. Currently, it is used in a very small percentage of commercial vehicles in the United States. There's already wider use in other countries. It appears there's little cost savings at this time, but it's a cleaner burning fuel, which many prefer. Natural gas filling locations are few and far-between compared to gasoline stations, and there are other concerns that need a remedy before wider-spread use occurs. With renewed interest in the financial benefits that could be derived from the petroleum industry, this may be the perfect time to exploit natural gas for maximum benefit to American consumers. Approximately 60 million US homes are heated by natural gas. Once safe and easily functioning equipment is developed, a family vehicle could be replenished overnight in its own garage.

It is true that future batteries will work very well in average-size vehicles, but who will manufacture those batteries? Sooner or later ... China.

The United States has large reserves of natural gas in the ground similar to crude oil. Crude is used domestically. As previously indicated, there's a drastic need for the United States to lead the world in exporting energy. That energy, or petroleum product, should include crude, refined crude, and liquefied natural gas.

Some will say exporting oil will dry up supply in the United States, causing much higher costs for gasoline. There are ways to control that circumstance. Greatly increasing the oil-exporting business necessitates the building of some additional refineries and storage facilities. More storage capacity will allow domestic supply to be adjusted as needed. An adequate lead-time schedule for delivery would be needed, which is no different than usual. Oil and gas supply would be used for US consumption first and foreign needs second. Continuous drilling and adequate storage should satisfy both domestic and foreign demand. Exporting increases all operations, and that is what we, as a nation, need now. Canadian oil would also be shipped south to refineries and ports for export.

Reasonable cost and supply of petroleum product at home would be a primary requirement to ensure overall success for the whole project. That project being improved petroleum infrastructure to handle major exporting and adequate supply in the United States while maintaining normal price fluctuation. All of which benefits the balance of trade problem and the $20,000,000,000,000 debt the United States skates with on very thin financial ice.

Citizens should remember ... becoming the largest petroleum exporter in the world is about a ten-year project with many issues to work through, but the end result will be substantial economic improvement for the United States.

Continuing skeptics should check the following list of strong benefits for America, its citizens, and even the anti-fossil fuel enthusiasts. Regular citizen concerns usually focus on gasoline costs. Other benefits, beyond fuel costs, also center around motor vehicle use but not exclusively. Some may be surprising.

- Lower transportation costs than today
- Lower gasoline use than today
- Lower overall auto emissions from driving
- Lower number of road accidents and deaths
- Lower vehicle insurance costs
- Lower cost fluctuation at the pump
- Lower costs for transportation departments
- Lower trade deficit with China and others
- Higher revenue for city, county, state governments
- Higher number of jobs across the petroleum industry
- Higher number of jobs in related fields

Additional jobs created bring additional benefits to society in general. More money is spent. The economy improves. Society operates more smoothly.

The country must get on track to reverse the sliding economic trend of the last several decades. Our nation is passing $20,000,000,000,000 in debt. That mark should be avoided, and petroleum's another answer.

Some may be curious about the above-mentioned benefits that include less gasoline used, fewer auto emissions, less cost of insurance, fewer accidents and deaths, along with higher revenue for government transportation associated departments. Fair questions. Those benefits are all related to each other. How?

They're all connected to speed.

All vehicles on the road should travel at lower average speed. It's that easy. Slower speed means less gasoline used, which means less emissions into the atmosphere. Less speed means fewer accidents, which leads to lower insurance rates. Those drivers who refuse to slow down will be ticketed.

Most drivers driving at the signed speed limit see others roar past. It happens in all speed zones, but it's most noticeable on expressways. Expressways may be marked 70 mph, but average speed is probably 75-plus. Many fly past at 79. The presumed thinking must be ticketing starts at 80. And much of the time that's about right. Therein lies the key to many of the benefits mentioned, including higher revenue for government departments. More speeding ticket revenue means less citizen-taxes needed for government operations.

The "save gas, save lives, save money" initiative would start with multiple announcements broadcast for thirty days. Make it quite simple: all vehicles traveling faster than the posted speed limit will be ticketed without exception. That should do it. If it doesn't, then it should be read again but a little slower.

An early directive would be sent to any governing body that has the ability to set speed limits. A similar order would go to all transportation departments instructing that no road signs would be changed to a higher limit. Those directives would prevent ambitious souls from proposing a speed-limit increase or a sign department changing signs from 70 to 80 mph, trying to outsmart a sensible regulation that offers many benefits as stated.

No new speed-limit adjustment and no speed-limit sign changes means the speed limit actually remains exactly the same. There is no need for the government sign departments to change millions of signs to a lower speed number. That would cost taxpayers $100 million and it's not necessary. Law enforcement just needs to enforce the speed limit as marked. If the speed-limit sign says 35 mph, then tickets are handed out at 36 mph. That effectively lowers speed and generates the benefits as suggested. Simple.

This program may sound trivial considering the main objective is saving the American economy, but it connects with citizens on an everyday personal level. And it brings favorable local results. It saves gas, lives, and insurance costs, and it will curb raising local taxes to pay for city and county services. Local government treasuries will swell with speeding ticket receipts. Courts won't get bogged down because speeding tickets can be paid by mail or electronically.

In some locations, ticketing can be accomplished using a camera. This is controversial now and will continue to be, but its use will probably expand.

Regardless of initiatives such as limiting speed or limiting theft of seeds … the US economy must improve. The economic trend of the last several decades must be reversed relative to our debt and trade with the world. Going much beyond $20,000,000,000,000 in debt is not a manageable situation. The best time to fix the economy is well past. What is left in time is … today. If the United States and its citizens do not reverse the trend immediately, the country will awake to find out tomorrow is too late to fix anything.

Chapter Two

Past Water Infrastructure Neglect Equals American Jobs Now

IN ORDER FOR the American economy to survive, we need to sell oil to the world. In order for the American citizen to survive, we need to sell water to ourselves. Clean water.

Many will say oil and water don't mix, but ... today they do. Today, we need both to survive as a prosperous nation.

Oil should be a top priority in the United States. It will bring good jobs to citizens across the country. The time for oil production and export must be right now.

Water should be a top priority in the United States. It will bring good jobs to citizens across the country. The time for clean and plentiful water must be right now.

The big difference between oil and water production in the United States is economic. Oil will put money into our country's treasury and water will take it out. The flow in both directions is necessary ... right now.

The country's water infrastructure involves many different operations, including pipes, pumps, processing equipment, and storage facilities in every city. These operations usually concern drinking water, wastewater, or storm water. All are vitally important, and all have their own set of problems.

Safe and adequate drinking water is mandatory, and it's a daily need for all citizens. Our drinking water, being a necessity, is relatively safe and plentiful in the United States today. Compare that luxury to many other countries. But that luxury is starting to fade at an accelerating rate.

Regulations for treatment of wastewater are meant to improve living conditions for all, but the cost to implement those regulations is often prohibitive.

For non-city dwellers, it was not long ago when individual waste-handling systems in the backyard were sufficient and cost $2,500 to install. Required equipment is now over $25,000 in many suburbs. Larger neighborhood treatment plants have been allowed in some locations, but they're also costly and often unsightly.

Citizens who live with city sewers are fortunate, but many water drainage lines as well as supply lines are becoming inadequate, and maintenance costs are increasing every year.

Over the years, storm water has been directed in such a way as to avoid flooding, but floods still happen, and they're increasing, as this headline states:

ARTICLE FOUND AT: www.usatoday.com/story/weather/2017/01/04-floods-natural-disasters-2016/96120150/

ARTICLE WRITTEN BY: Doyle Rice

DATE: JANUARY 4, 2017

TITLE: U.S. HAD More floods in 2016 Than Any Other Year on Record

That headline alone should serve as a warning for the future.

New development, perhaps more so than in the past, calls for more drainage work to alleviate flooding possibilities, and new development is constant.

Questions arise every day with every leak in every water system. It's time for authorities to begin seriously worrying about water across the country. The underground water pipes may be out-of-sight, but they shouldn't be out-of-mind. Politicians need to face the ugly possibility that safe and plentiful water could become a widespread problem. Prevention should be a forethought, not an afterthought.

Our future water infrastructure problems have already arrived, and replacement work is already past due. Our politicians are out sailing.

The American Society of Civil Engineers (ASCE) released an extensive report on America's infrastructure, which includes water infrastructure. The report suggests serious problems that need attention now.

REPORT FOUND AT: www.infrastructurereportcard.org/water-infrastructure/

DATE: 2013

TITLE: REPORT CARD for America's Infrastructure

> At the dawn of the 21st century, much of our drinking water infrastructure is nearing the end of its useful life. There are an estimated 240,000 water main breaks per year in the United States. Assuming every pipe would need to be replaced, the cost over the coming decades could reach more than $1 trillion, according to the American Water Works

Association (AWWA). The quality of drinking water in the United States remains universally high, however. Even though pipes and mains are frequently more than 100 years old and in need of replacement, outbreaks of disease attributable to drinking water are rare.

Water mainline breaks numbering 240,000 every year? That figure equates with more than 650 breaks every single day. Millions of citizens must be inconvenienced every week, and those frustrations have to be growing. Unless you've experienced a water interruption, most problems associated with water infrastructure will remain hidden from your thoughts.

Water mainlines run for miles in small towns and thousands of miles in big cities. That doesn't include small waterlines that branch off to all individual properties. When there's a break or serious leak, it's fixed in a day or several and everybody returns to happy. But what just happened? Nothing permanent.

When an old or very old pipeline springs a serious leak, it gets dug up and then patched. The same old pipeline is corroded for many miles under the city streets. It has many smaller leaks in many places, and those small leaks grow bigger, and soon, the waterline is a series of patches in a mismatch of piping. The problem continues to be a problem. People are inconvenienced, their utility costs increase, and precious water is lost. And, in a few days, it all happens again.

Most problems center on the age of pipelines, but the construction material used when waterlines were first installed also makes a difference. That material could be cast iron, PVC, copper, fired clay, concrete, steel, asbestos cement, or even hollowed-out wood. The wood would be hard to find today. Besides, some pipes being 150 years old all have their own unique drawbacks such as corrosion leading to rust, contraction, or expansion because of weather and other more mundane problems concerning friendly tree roots.

People still drink water today that passes through lead pipes if their old-house plumbing has never been updated. Years ago, lead was used in most plumbing systems. Today, it's taboo. Interestingly, the word plumbing is derived from the Latin word *plumbum*, which means lead.

The following article mentions the city of Flint, Michigan, which is experiencing the nation's most recent large scale water problem. It reiterates what has been said and suggests lead in drinking water is and will continue to be an ongoing problem.

ARTICLE FOUND AT: www.foxbusiness.com/features/2016/01/28/america-s-water-infrastructure-is-in-need-major-overhall.html

ARTICLE WRITTEN BY: Matthew Morrow

DATE: JANUARY 28, 2016

TITLE: AMERICA'S WATER Infrastructure Is in Need of a Major Overhaul

The current crisis in Flint, Mich., over potentially toxic levels of lead in the city's water could serve a larger purpose if it draws attention to the nation's aging water infrastructure. By some estimates, more than $1 trillion in upgrades are needed to the vast system of mostly underground pipes.

Most Americans are fortunate to be able to turn on the tap and get water they need each day with no issues. This is made possible by more than 156,000 public water systems that provide drinking water to about 320 million people through more than 700,000 miles of piping criss-crossing the U.S....

But experts say concerns over the U.S. water infrastructure can no longer be ignored. According to some estimates, about 1.7 trillion gallons of water are wasted every year due to lack of pipe replacement and broken and leaky pipes.

Flint has about 100,000 citizens and is not far from Detroit. If you include the metropolitan area around Flint, the population is over 400,000. Either number is a lot of people to experience toxic water problems. You can't just go next-door for water. Local suppliers will have empty shelves within hours.

Flint has notoriety because it's a sizable city, but Detroit has 4 million people in its metropolitan area—that would be a different kind of notoriety. How long will it be before a very large US city experiences a Flint disaster?

This is not a problem waiting-to-happen. It's happening now, and it is a problem, and it's getting worse. And it's a bigger problem than the political sleepers care to admit.

The following information is part of a report from the American Water Works Association. It indicates our drinking water problem goes well beyond drinking water. The association's comments follow:

REPORT FOUND AT: www.awwa.org/Portals/O/files/legreg/documents/ BuriedNoLonger.pdf

TITLE: BURIED NO LONGER: Confronting America's Water Infrastructure Challenge

Given its age, it comes as no surprise that a large proportion of US water infrastructure is approaching, or has already reached, the end of its useful life. The need to rebuild these pipe networks must come on top of other water investment needs, such as the need to replace water treatment plants and storage tanks, and investments needed to comply with standards for drinking water quality. They also come on top of wastewater and stormwater investment needs which—judging from the US Environmental Protection Agency's (USEPA) most recent "gap analysis"—are likely to be as large as drinking water needs over the coming decades. Moreover, both water and wastewater infrastructure needs come on top of the other vital community infrastructures, such as streets, schools, etc.

It appears many decades of pipe patchwork have run their course. Such patchwork may have been sufficient for a time, but it's no longer an efficient remedy. Old pipes now leak in between patches. Whether patching was cost-effective over time doesn't matter. And it's not just pipelines that need updating. New water infrastructure will mean updating pumping stations, storage tanks, and some reservoirs.

The replacement of existing water infrastructure will be an enormous and costly undertaking that will continue for decades. Numerous contractors and suppliers will be working with numerous city and private water companies. Every level of government…county, city, state, and federal will be involved in some way. That alone could add decades. Cumbersome governmental direction and meddlesome oversight will assure a long, drawn-out project that may end up being referred to as the "project of the century."

Hopefully, this very large-scale project taking place across the country will benefit American communities and their immediate citizens with steady work. Any other scenario, such as employing foreign companies and their employees, would be a disgrace, especially since American citizens will ultimately foot the bill.

Yet another concern needs to be mentioned. Terrorism in the United States is increasing. It's an ugly circumstance that must be considered when building or updating any important infrastructure. Water storage tanks, reservoirs, and some related operating facilities easily qualify as critical infrastructure. Because safe drinking water and proper waste removal are indispensable for everyday life in the United States, water infrastructure is a critical asset, and today, all critical assets must be secure.

There are reservoirs that serve the public with clean drinking water located literally a stone's throw away from public areas. Effective physical security is absolutely needed. In this age of terrorism, any new installation should be designed and located with maximum security in mind. It should be the same for facilities being updated. Other facilities, perhaps newer and needing no operational updating, should be evaluated for security purposes. If adding a barrier wall substantially improves security, then it should be added.

In the years after the 9/11 terrorist attacks, many water company personnel attended multiple meetings with security specialists and local government people to discuss "what if, how to, and who pays," concerning adequate protection of water supply. After discussions, studies, and proposals were finalized, it appears the usual results took place. Some water facilities became well-protected, some partially protected, and from there, it dropped off to no protection whatsoever. It's probable overall security has increased quite a bit, but terrorists usually look for and then attack the weakest link such as a relatively obscure water facility in a small town.

The Department of Homeland Security offers its current thinking regarding the general safety of water systems below.

INFORMATION FOUND AT: https://www.dhs.gov/water-and-wastewater-systems-sector

TITLE: WATER AND Wastewater Systems Sector

> *Safe drinking water is a prerequisite for protecting public health and all human activity. Properly treated wastewater is vital for preventing disease and protecting the environment. Thus, ensuring the supply of drinking water and wastewater treatment and service is essential to modern life and the Nation's economy.*
>
> *There are approximately 153,000 public drinking water systems and more than 16,000 publicly owned wastewater treatment systems in the United States. More than 80 percent of the U.S. population receives their potable water from these drinking water systems, and about 75 percent of the U.S. population has its sanitary sewerage treated by these wastewater systems.*
>
> *The Water and Wastewater Systems Sector is vulnerable to a variety of attacks, including contamination with deadly agents; physical attacks, such as the release of toxic gaseous chemicals; and cyberattacks. The result of any variety of attack could be large numbers of illnesses or casualties and/or a denial of service that would also impact public health and economic vitality. The sector is also vulnerable to natural disasters. Critical services, such as firefighting and healthcare (hospitals), and other dependent and interdependent sectors, such as Energy, Food, and Agriculture, and Transportation systems, would suffer negative impacts from a denial of service in the Water and Wastewater Systems Sector.*

It appears Homeland Security is well-aware of possibilities for an adversary to attack certain infrastructure, causing great harm either directly or indirectly to any citizen. Any citizen … could increase in number to include an entire city. Even if there are no deaths from a water-poisoning attempt, there would still be costly panic. Many Americans panic easily. They're not used to adverse utility problems, and when their water and children are threatened, the reaction will be swift and loud. Citizens trust authorities have made wise decisions that prevent such incidents. However, it doesn't always work out that way, and sometimes authorities panic, too.

An unusual report originating in Portland, Oregon, is just below:

REPORT FOUND AT: www.livescience.com/Portland-flush-drinking-water-peeing-teen.html

REPORT WRITTEN BY: Megan Gannon, news editor at *Live Science.*

DATE: APRIL 17, 2014.

TITLE: WHY PORTLAND Reservoir Was Flushed After Teen Peed in It

> *Officials in Portland, Ore., are flushing 38 million gallons of public drinking water after a 19-year-old was caught on camera urinating into an open reservoir on Wednesday (April 16).*
>
> *The water, which had already been treated, was tested for contamination after the incident. As expected, the sample came back clean, Jaymee Cuti, a spokeswoman for the Portland Water Bureau, told Live Science.*
>
> *Officials acknowledged there was little public health risk from a small amount of urine in an open reservoir that is presumably exposed to the droppings of wild animals all the time. So why dump the whole supply? Bureau officials say they won't stand for serving their customers "purposely tainted drinking water."*

Well, what can you say? Funny article? Interesting article? Or, does this article tell citizens something they're entitled to know while also serving as a warning?

What does this article, reported in many newspapers, tell us about our drinking water supply? The following will leave a bad taste in your mouth:

- Non-purposely tainted drinking water may be okay to serve customers.
- The water referred to in the article was "already" treated.
- The water was in an open container/reservoir.
- Anybody and everybody had direct access to treated drinking water.
- Authorities sometimes/often make poor decisions.
- Authorities are lax in protection of drinking water.
- Other information about the same incident:
- Exact same incident happened three years prior.
- Nude swimmers were caught in "treated water" at a prior time.
- Incident reports are from Oregon only.
- "Already treated" water goes directly to mainline for drinking.
- The cost attributed to peeing incident was about $175,000.

- The 38 million gallons lost equaled about 760,000 quite full bathtubs.
- There was a regular wrought iron fence at the "edge" of the water.
- There was a sidewalk along the iron fence.
- There was a warning sign put up by authorities that read as follows: *"This is your drinking water. Don't spit, throw, toss anything in it."*

It's doubtful such a weak and idiotic sign would stop anyone from mischief. A brat would find it invitational. A terrorist directional.

From time to time, or perhaps every day, taxpayers should ask themselves whether authorities, generally government authorities, are proactive enough in protecting citizens from harmful situations. Or, are they busy waiting around to see what develops so they can clean up the resulting mess and then stand front-and-center congratulating each other for a job well done?

Since 9/11, recommendations have been issued to "cover" open water storage tanks and protecting reservoirs. Covering may be impossible for some storage areas, but some type of alternative protection and security must be implemented. The added work or security measures are costly, but the turmoil that would follow a serious attack on our water resource is unthinkable. Today, the nation needs to be strongly proactive.

Other serious water issues plague certain regions of the country. Many of these problems are a result of weather patterns. California is an easy example.

California produces most of the nation's fruits, vegetables, and nuts. Agriculture needs more water. Citizens need more water. California needs more water.

It appears that seven of the ten years between 2007 and 2017, crop production in California was threatened by drought conditions. Drought causes food scarcity. Scarcity causes food prices to increase.

A bountiful crop harvest means lower cost for all citizens. It brings needed revenue into the state and assures farmers continued livelihood.

Under drought conditions, more water must be diverted to crops. The state partially solves this problem by taking water away from a large majority of citizens and directing it to a small minority of citizens associated with crops. Citizens are forced to stop watering their yards and refrain from washing their vehicles. Brown grass and dirty cars are a common sight. That's the political fix. Solve one problem by creating another.

Over the years, the state has diverted billions of gallons of water in order to save a mouthful of smelt. We eat fish. We don't save them. Forfeit smelt. Save people. Obviously, saving smelt is another politically correct fix.

Is there a better way? Maybe. Politicians can't change the weather, and citizens can't refuse to pay the state when fined for watering their grass. But citizens could solve part of the problem themselves and without political interference. They just need to change their personal and very personal water usage habits. That sounds like a simple fix because it is simple. That is … the theory is simple. And it's a long way from any mandatory or idiotic political fix.

All California citizens should simply turn off the water when brushing their teeth. Most people apply toothpaste, wet their toothbrush, and brush for a minute or two or three. The water runs. Other personal face care may take even more time. The water runs. Most often the open faucet is dumping unused water down the drain. The same thing can be said about washing dishes in the kitchen sink. Turn the water off. If you turn the bath and kitchen water off, you may save enough water for the farmers and your yard. The usage will equal out. Less wasted water in every bathroom and every kitchen and more useful water for every farmer and many private yards. Everybody should be happy and satisfied. That's a bit of a stretch but worth a try.

Everyone, referring to all residents of California, should be brushing their teeth two, three, or four times per day. A very good practice. When brushing … turn the water on, off, off, off, off, on, off. Mostly off. It should be off about 90 percent of the brushing time. The same for other facial care or similar everyday tasks such as washing dishes.

It's assumed all citizens would participate in this "personal conservation of water." That participation assumption is actually a … necessity.

All residents must fully participate in order to reach the objective. All refers to all.

Again, the objective is to save enough water to have a successful crop industry every year.

Thirty-nine million people live in California. All 39 million must turn the water off. The first task is to explain the benefits of doing so. Explain how the economic benefits of plentiful crops reach all citizens. Stress the importance of good citizenship, of being part of the "save water" team. Suggest citizens physically practice turning faucets off until it's a habit. Mental willpower will not suffice. Habit is better. Considerable practice will be needed before any turn-off-the-water habit is entrenched. Practice … and then more practice makes perfect.

The "personal conservation" plan is quite simple. The implementation and adherence to the plan will be quite difficult since most personal use of water is behind closed doors.

Once water-saving personal habits in the bathroom and kitchen are established, it should be easier to add other uses that accomplish conservation.

Washing a car is one example. People squirt their car with water, drop the gushing hose to the ground, hand-wipe a section of the car, and then pick up the still-gushing hose. This process might be repeated twenty times. A hose nozzle with automatic off/on squeeze handle should be used. The driveway doesn't need excess water. The squeeze handle could save 80 percent of car-washing water.

It's not just for California. All residents in all states should save water. It's a precious resource that is not guaranteed.

Solving national, but especially regional, water scarcity problems is important and will require considerable effort. Seven main points should be considered immediately:

1. The water problem, especially in California, does not require the government to establish another new, costly, and burgeoning department. Government compliance departments usually consist of a Monday–Friday, eight-hour-day operation, large buildings, excess employees, and a squadron of vehicles, each carrying two obnoxious people who enjoy running around the state handing out notices to citizens. The government water-policing personnel would be more inefficient than the water-wasters themselves. Government compliance enforcement is just too costly.

2. Remedy for any scarce water problem should start with water-use education for all citizens and then personal practice, ending with sufficient conservation. Personal remedy is free.

3. Increase reuse of water. Such as: Personal—rainwater off your roof. Commercial/Industrial—recycle water for reuse or secondary use.

4. Increase research, development, and use of desalination plants.

5. Increase research and development for recycling agricultural water.

6. Many citizens will need help saving water, and American manufacturers can provide that help. They've already started. All new showerheads, faucets, and toilets should be water-saving appliances. Such as: faucets automatically shut-off after 2-3 seconds, and toilets automatically flush a minimum of water after use. Water amount should "automatically" adjust relative to "time" on seat. Yes, toilets will know everything.

7. National "Goal of the Year" should be: Fix all leaks in all faucets.

Drinking water and water infrastructure are of critical importance.

Water is necessary for life. Water is necessary for commerce. Water infrastructure must be updated or replaced, and it must be secure. Not all of it, but enough of it that the cost will reach a trillion dollars over the next decade.

Chapter Three

Education for the Real World,
Not for Tomorrow ... for Today

ELECTION TIME IS education time ... again. Get ready to be educated ... again, about education. A through Z will be promised.

Politicians get an A for effort ... to get elected. An F for suggesting free education is ... free. And, a Z for the end result ... which is zip.

That about sums up the noisiest time of any effort to change education in such a way as to improve the working future of US youngsters. The noise and promises turn silent the day after election. Once the politicians have something else to do, it's easier for serious educators to get down to business. Regrettably, they usually discuss business first. Business is money. Education is work.

It should be obvious to teachers, school boards, community leaders, employers, parents, and students themselves that the final result after twelve years of schooling has not been very successful. The lack of success is not just in lower test scores. It's in social areas as well. Educators need to formulate a curriculum beyond regular academics to ensure proper social achievement. School boards may resist that notion, but it must be done. Kids need better preparation to effectively compete in life. Perhaps school boards can prove the following quote deserves a failing grade:

> *"In the first place, God made idiots. That was for practice.*
> *Then he made school boards."*
> — Mark Twain (1835-1910)

We should all hope the quote was valid a 150 years ago and not today. Many will debate that insatiably.

Today, early grade school and high school students need some additional instruction in areas that improve everyday life immediately and going forward.

That's especially true for those starting high school. Certainly, improving regular academics is important for everyone, but there should be additional instruction in high school that would prove to be very beneficial for average students. Actually for all students. High school is not just preparation for college. It's preparation for life, and for many, life starts the day after graduation and includes performing in a very competitive world.

A high school student should be looked upon in the following way: a young kid, barely a teenager, enters high school and is schooled and coached for four short years. After four years, the kid graduates and is immediately referred to as an adult. Old enough to vote, die for country, pay bills, get married, raise a family, and work. One of these is vital to sustain a normal life: work. Therefore, the four high school years should go a long way toward assuring a student can be successful at work.

Those graduating high school today and looking forward to a prosperous beginning need to check all recent headlines to be sure they're ready, willing, and able to succeed. Have all the basics-for-success been covered during grade school and high school?

Those basics start with the usual requirements, such as proficiency in reading, writing, arithmetic, and computers. Computers shouldn't be a problem. Neither should the others, but is today different? Yes, today is different.

Kids leaving high school may be proficient in using computers, but exactly what does that mean? Have they completed 5,000 hours playing computer games? Are they able to text their friends at lightning speed? Yes and yes, but what they really need is 1,000 or more hours of computer training that is directly suited for millions of jobs in almost all areas of work. Areas that do not need a college degree. Millions of jobs … for skilled workers using computers and other low-tech and high-tech machines. An extra year of technical high school or vocational school would go a long way in filling those jobs. This area of education is very important today. But it will not be explored beyond this paragraph.

A young person entering the job market today needs to understand what all those worldly headlines mean relative to landing a decent job.

What does it mean when you read that 95 million people in the United States aren't working? Many millions of these people would like to work if they could find and … qualify for a job. Some look, and some have stopped looking. Many of the 95 million may be retirees or in other non-working categories. But still millions would prefer to work. Those millions are no longer listed on monthly unemployment statistics because they've exhausted their weekly benefits. Add these silent job seekers back into the unemployment-rate and the percentage rate is much higher than indicated. All, or more accurately many, receiving unemployment assistance, a number in the millions, are seeking work daily. And then there are the legal and illegal immigrants who enter the country every day. The actual number living in the United States may be staggering. They seek work and most are very good workers. Many extremely so.

If graduating students, now job seekers, add up the categories of job seekers mentioned above, they will find they're in competition with many millions of "hungry for a job" citizens. Those are not only US citizens. They're also US residents who are not citizens. A growing category.

And after all of those tens of millions of job seekers in the United States, American workers are now facing the rest of the world bidding on much of the same work. Let's just say that's another 100 million workers around the world. They all seek a decent job for a decent wage. Who gets the work?

Americans need an advantage.

Are today's graduating students in the United States fully prepared for the task-at-hand? Doubtful.

American high schools must provide an advantage for graduating students. About 40 percent will be quickly known as graduating workers.

Often, those high school students going on to college are able and permitted to take advanced courses. That's beneficial in being accepted at the college of their choice. Those same students study more than average in high school. Those students are creating an advantage for themselves. An academic advantage that can be applied upon high school graduation.

Today, all graduating high school students, regardless of their future plans, need an "advantage." It doesn't matter whether they are college-bound or seeking work.

What they don't need is any kind of disadvantage. And certain behavior is always a detriment to success.

What about those high school graduates, assuming everyone knows they need at least a high school education, who got caught up in the drug culture? Or perhaps just light experimentation? Maybe they were arrested for some minor infraction that now shows up on their record. Maybe they weren't arrested but they, let's just say, smell like dope. Are they competitive in the job market or doomed? Is there a way to correct that possible scenario in school? Sure … early education about the dire effects of drug use is very important and steers kids toward avoidance. But is that stronger than peer pressure?

It's probable peer-pressure has a greater effect, increasing disadvantages for young people compared to increasing advantages.

Watching popular sports or going to a fitness center will give observers a glimpse of the current fashion trend with young people. Multiple tattoos.

Charming artwork to friends may appear a permanent desecration to others. Obvious shortsightedness rarely looks good on a resume. Some jobs suggest short sleeves. Then there's summer. Long sleeves to hide foolish choices could represent a deterrent to a job done well. Buyers judge sellers. They buy when they're comfortable with the seller, not when they're uncomfortable. This isn't all the time. Just most of the time.

Luckily for the United States, our youngsters are rounded up in the same place for most of their early lives. School.

Isn't that the perfect place and time to teach students everything they need to know to be successful in life?

Most educators would say, "We're already doing that." But is that true? Is it ever completely true?

Today we have 2 million people in jail. We have tens of millions taking drugs. We have tens of millions not working. We have tens of millions on public assistance. We have tens of millions who've lost hope. Hopeless … the actual number might be well-beyond any guess.

Can all this be cured in school? No. But school is the best place to start, and the best time is right now. And for the first eighteen years of a person's life, he or she is in the exact same place every day. Once again, that's school. A perfect setup for teaching everything one needs to know to go successfully forward in life. If that sounds silly or juvenile, then parents, educators, or employers should try to find another time and place when all youngsters are together … thereby making it easy to deliver necessary, and hopefully pleasant, indoctrination.

Following are some unusual but timely questions that should be asked of all school teachers and administrators.

What about "proper-behavior" that's needed in life but rarely learned in school? Some kids get it at home and some kids get just the opposite. Can the avoidance of peer pressure be taught? Is there a course in discipline? Is there a good course in good manners? Budgeting? Frugality? Self-determination? How about just plain common sense, common courtesy, and proper etiquette? All are important behaviors, all are important in life, and all are especially helpful in obtaining a job. All are advantages.

Americans are in global competition for decent jobs. That does not mean graduating students are moving to Ireland or Japan. Nor does it mean Chinese workers are applying for jobs at the local fire department. It means American high schools must improve their students. It means American students must improve themselves. They need to demonstrate excellence in every way possible. That includes superior knowledge, proper appearance, good manners, and strong determination.

The effects of global competition that all new job seekers face can be seen right down the street. Just look at that big empty building that use to be a booming factory. Those factory jobs and the accompanying office jobs in the same building are now located in a foreign country. America and American workers lost those jobs to global competition. It doesn't matter whose fault it was back then … it matters that we fix it now.

America needs an advantage.

America needs overall excellence, and that excellence starts in its schools. And it includes excellence in multiple areas. Not in multiple tattoos or graffiti.

America's "global competition" has read the following information. Most Americans have not. They should … today.

That information follows:

ARTICLE FOUND AT: www.businessinsider.com/pisa-rankings-2013-12

ARTICLE WRITTEN BY: Joe Weisenthal

DATE: DECEMBER 3, 2013

TITLE: HERE'S THE New Ranking of Top Countries in Reading, Science, and Math

> *The OECD is out with new global rankings of how students in various countries do in reading, science, and math. Results of the full survey can be found and delved into here.*
>
> *You can see below how Asian countries are obliterating everyone else in these categories.*
>
> *The United States, meanwhile, ranks below the OECD average in every category. And as the WSJ notes, the US has slipped in all the major categories in recent years:*
>
> *The results from the 2012 Program for International Student Assessment (PISA), which are being released on Tuesday, show that teenagers in the U.S. slipped from 25th to 31st in math since 2009: from 20th to 24th in science: and from 11th to 21st in reading, according to the National Center for Education Statistics, which gathers and analyzes the data in the U.S.*

OECD refers to "Organization for Economic Co-operation and Development."

WSJ refers to *"Wall Street Journal."*

PISA refers to "Program for International Student Assessment."

Other information gleaned from the article shows that students who score the very highest score in all three categories reside in Shanghai, China.

Those students with the second highest scores, also in all three categories, live in Singapore.

Those students scoring in third, fourth, and fifth place in each of all categories—including reading, science, and math—came from just five countries. Those locations: Korea, Japan, Finland, Taipei, Taiwan, and Hong Kong, China.

United States students, as indicated above, scored lower than many countries in one or more areas, including such countries as Estonia, Iceland, Vietnam, Poland, New Zealand, and the Slovak Republic.

The Slovak Republic spends the equivalent of $53,000 per student compared with about $115,000 per student in the United States. Other countries were not directly checked, but it appears the United States spends more money per student than nearly all other countries. Possible exceptions being Luxembourg, Norway, and Switzerland.

The dollars spent per-student comparison should raise questions everywhere in the United States. Any questions? Mostly silence from authorities?

The PISA report should be earth-shattering for students, parents, teachers, teacher unions, schools, school districts, employers, cities, states, and all citizens.

But if the scoring report was actually earth-shattering to any or all of these groups, wouldn't the situation be remedied by now? The low scoring by American students is not new. It's been happening for some time and appears to be worsening. Soon ∴ somebody has to pull the rip cord on this trend.

Who's in charge? It would appear nobody. But somebody must be in charge because every year, or certainly every election year, somebody prepares papers that propose a tax increase in order to fix the local schools. Or fix all schools in a city. Or all schools in a state. That "fix" equates with local, city, or state tax increases.

Are buttons related to education? The United States used to lead the world in manufacturing almost everything. At least it seemed that way to the many citizens who worked hard making shoes, cars, tires, steel, hammers, hats, and buttons.

If the United States wants to lead in anything in the future, then educators should strive to boost the dismal scores from high school students, which must improve substantially relative to world competition.

That will take time unless most other countries cut back on educating their future workers. And they won't do that because they want what we used to have as a society. The best of everything.

The United States government, or anyone who might be concerned about education, jobs, or the future prosperity of the country, should note some comments from BBC News, the world's largest broadcast news organization:

ARTICLE FOUND AT: www.bbc.com/news/business-32608772

ARTICLE WRITTEN BY: Sean Coughlan

DATE: MAY 13, 2015

TITLE: ASIA TOPS Biggest Global School Rankings

> *The biggest ever global school rankings have been published, with Asian countries in the top five places and African countries at the bottom.*
>
> *Singapore heads the table, followed by Hong Kong, with Ghana at the bottom.*
>
> *The UK is in 20ᵗʰ place, among higher achieving European countries, with the US in 28ᵗʰ.*
>
> *The OECD economic think tank says the comparisons—based on test scores in 76 countries—show the link between education and economic growth....*
>
> *It shows once again the poor performance of the United States, slipping behind successful European countries and being overtaken by Vietnam....*
>
> *The top five places are all taken by Asian countries – Singapore, Hong Kong, South Korea, Taiwan and Japan....*
>
> *If you go to an Asian classroom you'll find teachers who expect every student to succeed. There's a lot rigour, a lot of focus and coherence...."*

The following three comments from the report should serve as a warning:

> *the standard of education is a "powerful predictor of the wealth that countries will produce in the long run."...*
>
> *Poor education policies and practices leave many countries in what amounts to a permanent state of economic recession....*
>
> *Improving education would produce "long-term economic gains that are going to be phenomenal."*

Perhaps the United States, being made up of students, parents, teachers, teacher unions, schools, school districts, employers, cities, states and all American citizens, should just adopt the last three comments above. Rewrite them with fewer words and use them as a rough underlying foundation for improving general education. Then expand the time and scope of subject matter being presented in elementary and high school so it benefits future working students and, ultimately, the national economy. Students would immediately benefit in this manner: getting hired for good jobs, strengthening their abilities to do good jobs and, over time, helping the US economy expand.

The three comments from the Organisation for Economic Co-operation and Development (OECD) report are meaningful for the US economy, and they should be even more meaningful for US education policies. Those comments are slightly reworded and restated below:

1. A "high standard of education" predicts wealth for the country.

2. "Poor education policies and practices" leave a permanent recession.

3. "Improved education" produces phenomenal long-term economic gains.

Take the above three comments together and they form a great foundation for educating our students for the future. Collectively, the comments could be referred to as the Foundation for Financial Future (FFF).

The OECD's mission is to promote policies that will improve the economic and social wellbeing of people around the world. Education can do that.

Mission statement can found at: www.oecd.org

The reasons for educating our youth are many. But, for the good of our nation and for national economic purposes, the FFF for education, as stated above, should be the underlying reasons to promote a more commonsense curriculum. That being ... a slightly altered curriculum to assist our youth after high school graduation in their work lives and everyday social lives.

It's as easy to understand as the above "1, 2, 3." Broadly educated individuals, even without a college degree, have an easier time finding work and performing well at work. The entire nation then benefits as it becomes more competitive in the world. That change in trend, becoming more competitive, must take place.

A life track consisting of ... a thorough education, job, family, friends, promotion to better job, and a happy home is extremely basic and beneficial to the individual. And the entire nation benefits as well.

Compare that life track to today's reality. Unfortunately, many millions have squandered their early educations for one reason or another. They can't keep a job. Family is split. Happy-home nonexistent. They live-off taxpayer money. And their numbers are growing. Are they adding to the national prominence in any way? Or are they subtracting in every way?

There will always be unsuccessful citizens. Maybe their education wasn't broad or intense enough. Maybe their local education system failed to understand a thorough education leads to individual success as well as national economic success. "Maybes" will abound. But in today's competitive world, a broad-based education is a necessity. Especially for those limited to high school.

Today's high school curriculum should be altered in two ways. Altered referring to "additional instruction and observation." The first way, "additional" instruction, benefits students immediately and beyond in both their social and work lives. The second way, "observation," will assist students with their fast-approaching work lives.

Some minor change, cautiously presented, should also take place in elementary school. This change would be very early introduction to proper social behavior and exposure to several unbelievable scientific phenomena. The social behavior would be presented with some demonstrated practice. The unbelievable science presented very minimally with the goal of stimulating curiosity and imagination.

By far, the major changes, basically additional instruction and practice, would occur in early high school years. The additional instruction would concern highly important but very normal everyday behavior for all people ... certainly important for the nation's youth.

The additional areas to be taught and learned, at least for the high school students, will sound quite unusual to educators. Some areas of instruction may appear a waste of time because students already understand, or at least think they understand, what should or should not be practiced in daily life. But to clarify some ... everybody may know proper behavior, but there's always some percentage of people who really don't know much or just refuse to act responsibly. Maybe it's 10 percent. Maybe it's 25 percent or even more. Whatever the percentage, it appears to be increasing, which is costly to society. It's this same small percentage of people who are the largest cost factor on society. It may be only 10 percent of people who understand little about normal everyday proper behavior, but they're the same people who constantly have a difficult time with daily interactions, job performance, relationships, and any kind of responsibility. They're usually the same people who are well-known to the local police. They're a cost to society. A financial cost and a cost in time, effort, and tears. That may sound crude, but it has a direct bearing on what is being suggested here.

What if a change in schooling, adding in numerous skills needed in everyday life, could effect a positive change in students advancing from school to adult life? What if added schooling, over time, could cut the 10 percent problem-people figure in half to 5 percent? Or 20 percent to 10 percent. That difference, down the road, could be a huge savings to the local, city, state, and federal budget. Stretching that point a bit, or more, what if the "two million people in prison today" figure was cut in half as suggested in the above percentage? Prisoners would then number one million instead of two million. How much money would that alone save society?

There's a probable correlation between the percentages of troubled kids in school and the number of them who end up in adult trouble with the law.

Continuing with the example stipulating a large reduction in numbers of prisoners, some other benefits should be evident. Many more regular Americans, instead of sitting in prison, could be standing productive. A big difference … all from a small education change early in life. It's possible, maybe probable.

The added cost to better prepare youth in early school is minuscule compared to the savings of social costs throughout the life of an unsuccessful or troubled person. It wouldn't just be prison cost savings. That's at the extreme end. There's an endless stream of other costs associated with people who are having a difficult time in life. Even if only moderately so. If early additional-learning beyond "reading, writing, and arithmetic" can improve their chance for success, then it should be tried as soon as possible.

What should be learned in high school besides regular academics?

Group A: The A group is a partial list of those simple behaviors needed in life that seem to be missing for many:

- Good manners
- Good grooming
- Common courtesy
- Proper dress
- Proper etiquette

Group B: An early operational-understanding of the following words would greatly benefit students as they advance in life:

- Responsibility
- Perseverance
- Integrity
- Morality
- Discipline

Group C: All subject matter presented in high school is beneficial. Some right away, some increasingly so with time such as:

- Money
- Frugality
- Body language
- First aid
- Police encounters

Group D: Extra tools should always be available to improve learning and grades in reading, writing, arithmetic, and computers. Important keys follow that should be presented to students during their first weeks of high school:

- How to study ... and get an A.
- How to read graphs and tables and other various formats.
- How to use the library, plus all the knowledge you need is right there.
- How to use a "today" list. Careful, you must finish your list today.
- The Universe ... stimulate your imagination and open your mind.

Group E: Some challenges in school should be just plain fun. How about figuring out exactly what those old guys meant when they quietly snuck phrases into history that became "famous quotes." Quotes, famous or not, can be fun, interesting, beneficial, important, thought-provoking, and even life-changing. Included might be quotes from several wise men such as:

- Buddha (563-483 BC)
- Confucius (551-479 BC)
- Plato (428-348 BC)
- Thomas Edison (1847-1931)
- Winston Churchill (1874-1965)

As you can see, there are five different categories above listing a total of twenty-five short subjects. These subjects should be presented, discussed, and studied but not for a grade. No tests and no grades. They're free ... so students should take in all they can absorb. Some subjects should be touched upon in grade school. Some should be presented quite seriously and others not so much. The goal is to introduce all students to "beneficial-to-them behavior," stimulate their imagination, and provide some practical information that will absolutely improve their lives, especially those with little home direction.

Perhaps the following quote from Plato summarizes that goal:

"The direction in which education starts a man will determine his future in life."

Why discuss particular quotes with students? Because it might lead to a unique "learning moment." It's not a teacher teaching or parent preaching. It's an historic figure passing on words of wisdom from the past that may even be more helpful today. At the very least, quotes selected should be: intriguing for the average student, cause some excitement, and hopefully become memorable. Class discussion and debate may lead students to a more energetic outlook on education. Wouldn't that be great? More students who wish to learn more today and beyond.

Could the behaviors listed in Group A above improve a student's life today? What would parents say at home? What about a part-time job interview? Who gets the job? Shouldn't Group A be part of education?

Young people are always told to show respect for their elders. That's proper. Young people who master Group A will get plenty of respect in return … from their elders. That's proper as well, and it makes for a better atmosphere in all relationships. The benefits are so widespread it would be foolish not to expose youth to good behavior early and often. Early in grade school and, in some way, every year through high school graduation.

The Group B … could be a hundred other good traits, but in the classroom, time is always short. Whether these words represent character traits, personality, or one's qualities, if they could just be turned into water … how refreshing that would be. We could all drink a glass of "great-trait water" in the morning so our chances for a rewarding day would be vastly improved.

For some people, it's that easy. They know their actions speak louder than words. When they interact with others, their personality traits are revealed almost immediately. The result can be very positive or just the opposite. It's the just-the-opposite result that needs to be changed or eliminated. That can be remedied in school. Or, at the very least, "good personality traits" can be exposed to all students in school. As an example: everyone should be taught what it means to be a responsible person and then shown the probable outcome in life if one never takes responsibility for anything. Explain to students how good character can be a choice and it's theirs to make.

Perseverance may be a similar discussion as that with responsibility. Expose students to the meaning of perseverance. Compare two men swimming across a cold, swift river. Persevere or perish. Only one outcome makes sense. Yet in real life, either outcome is quite possible. Students may laugh and suggest the example is far-fetched. Yes, but how many times in their life might they hear, "It's time to sink or swim." Students will find that phrase all-too-common and very real at the time. Preparation for real life presented at an early age may prove just as important as reading, writing, and arithmetic. Many qualities, if not learned early in life, may never be learned at all. For many, it will take self-discipline to get started and self-discipline to stay with it. Some will think it's too demanding. A person is either responsible or not, and that may not change with age. Maybe it's just true that irresponsible people will always be irresponsible. That's hardly reason not to discuss it thoroughly in school and explain the benefits of being responsible or the ability to persevere in accomplishing any task.

The subjects listed in Group C are all of a practical nature. Who benefits from practicality? Everybody. That includes young people. Especially young people, because the earlier in life one establishes practical and wise everyday behavior, the smoother one's life progresses. That includes the wise use of money every single day.

Before discussing youth and money, one word should be mentioned. It's on the C list, and it's one of the most important words for young people to understand. If you don't understand it when young, you'll have to work longer hours to keep up with the Joneses. That word is "frugality." Frugality equals smart. Frugality leads to wealth. Learn to be frugal. That's all you need to know. A couple of unusual examples follow:

Being frugal with toothpaste? Maybe that sounds too frugal, but it'll serve as a good illustration to save money and even have fun. The habit of using enough but not too much toothpaste can be transferred to many other daily or weekly chores. It all adds up, especially over periods of time.

When you see an advertisement for toothpaste, it often shows a toothbrush with three-quarters of an inch or more of paste across the bristles. That's enough to foam-up your mouth all day. You only need one-third or less of that amount of paste.

For simplicity, let's say a tube of toothpaste cost $3 and lasts one person one month. That equals a cost of $36 each year. Use one-third as much paste and you'll save $24 each year. Ridiculous, eh? Try this: Family of four brushing their teeth and each saving $24 per year equals $96 saved per year. Do that for twenty years times $96 and you save $1,920. During that twenty years, the $1,920 savings are constantly being added to a DRIP (stock investment plan) in a major company that pays a dividend. Any company such as: GE, JNJ, PG, KO, or MCD. At the twenty-year mark the stock being held in the DRIP has doubled in value. The original savings of $1,920 is then worth $3,840. Dividends would have actually added a lot more value.

The two kids in the family have left home and the parents, having been frugal with toothpaste and average stock investors, now use the $3,840 for a Hawaii vacation. The vacation is sort of … free; everyone's teeth are fine and the kids have learned frugality can pay off with free vacations.

Too simple of an example? Yes. But could it work almost exactly as demonstrated? Yes. In fact, it's highly probable.

Don't forget … the lesson of "frugality" is being presented to young students. It has to be understood, and a colorful example may be the best teacher.

A much stronger example: a young couple; both have office jobs and both rush to work daily, but each stops at separate deluxe coffee shop for premium coffee and a fancy Danish roll. Cost is $6 each morning for each person five days a week. Total weekly cost for both equals $60.

The couple then decides to be frugal. Each brings coffee and two cookies from home. Cost equals $1 per day for each. Total weekly cost equals $10. Weekly savings by skipping the coffee shop equals $50 or $2,600 a year. Young couple decides to take a skiing trip some place in the West every winter until their legs give out. Cost of a skiing vacation is about $2,600. After being frugal with coffee and roll each morning, their cost to have a great time skiing … basically free.

Being "frugal" should be a way of life. It's most beneficial for the average citizen. Being frugal is best learned at an early age. School is the perfect learning place. Simple.

Vehicles are usually the hot topic in high school, and any related discussion should command attention. Perhaps this is the perfect time to explain asset appreciation or depreciation. The drain of money from a hopped-up, depreciating vehicle could be part of the money education process. Students need to learn the math of money.

As an example: Kids need to learn the difference between buying and owning an asset that appreciates in value over time compared to one that depreciates over time. One builds wealth, and over time, wealth facilitates a more fulfilling life. Surround yourself with depreciating assets and you'll find the first of every month is frustrating. None of this is guaranteed. Not even close. However, certain outcomes are … very probable.

A not-too-unusual story illustrates one of the money-themes young people should understand. It appears many, if not most, adults have failed to grasp the overall significance of this simple money-transaction example below:

Mickee buys a beautiful convertible vehicle for $30,000. His payments are $500 a month for six years or seventy-two months. The interest rate is higher for a vehicle compared to a house. After six years, Mickee paid about $36,000 total. After ten years, Mickee is forced to spend $2,000 for tires and replacing a worn-out convertible top before selling the vehicle for $3,000.

Minnee, far-sighted and money-wise sister of Mickee, buys a very small, extremely dirty one-bedroom house with two-foot high weeds in the yard. Minnee pays $30,000 for the house. Her payments are $500 a month for six years or seventy-two months. The interest rate is lower for a house compared to a vehicle. After six years, Minnee paid about $33,000 total. After ten years, Minnee sells the well-kept house for $45,000.

Important stipulations or criteria for the Mickee and Minnee money-machine example follow:

1. Wild estimations (but very possible) dollar figures used in example.

2. Mickee and Minnee both continue living in parents' house for the ten years.

3. Repairs cost $2,000 toward end of vehicle life.

4. Repairs and improvements cost $2,000 plus for house just after purchase.

5. Minnee rents house for $500 per month. Tenant pays utilities.

6. Mickee's budget is extremely tight every month.

7. Minnee's budget allows shopping, vacations, and savings.

8. Mickee makes seventy-two payments with his hard-earned income.

9. Minnee makes seventy-two payments with tenant's hard-earned income.

10. Minnee pockets $500 rent each month after seventy-second month.

11. Mickee and Minnee each have extra spending money after seventy-second month.

End result after ten years:

Mickee has $3,000 after vehicle sale. He may or may not buy another convertible vehicle. He will probably continue to live in parents' large house.

Minnee has $45,000 after house sale. She has $24,000 from rent collected after mortgage paid off. She has an extra $250 (minimally estimated) of earned income each month (seventy-two mouths) since her income was not used to make a $500 payment as was Mickee's. That extra savings equals $18,000. Minnee, after ten years, now has $45,000 + $24,000 + $18,000 or a total of $87,000. Minnee plans to buy a two-family house in up-town and move into one apartment. The second apartment will be rented in order to pay or help pay the mortgage payment on the two-family or for any other purpose Minnee desires.

One asset depreciated and one asset appreciated. Much difference?

If the above type of practical money-math thinking is taught, learned, and practiced by all high school students, then as they enter adult life, both they and the entire nation will benefit.

Often, learning about money at an early age improves one's financial decisions throughout life. Basic financial education should start small and simple in early grade school and continue stronger in high school.

Simple rule: Teach youth everything about money. It will benefit everything about the country.

Often related to a young person buying a vehicle is another item on Group C list. Police encounters. Unfortunately, people speed. Fortunately, police stop speeding vehicles. That police encounter leads to another simple rule to learn early in life: Do exactly what the police tell you to do. Simple.

There's another item in Group C that few people know thoroughly. They should because it can be used successfully every single day. It could mean the difference between success and failure.

Wouldn't it be a great advantage to know what or at least have a good idea of what is about to be written on a sheet of paper before anything's written on that paper? Is that possible? Not quite, but often people telegraph what they're going to say, do, or write before they do so. Knowing that would provide considerable advantage in many situations. Maybe all situations. Do you have to be a psychic? No, you just need to know body language. When dealing with others, the outcome of any interaction between people is often forecast by body language.

Psychology Today, a well-known magazine, entertainingly sums it up very well.

ARTICLE FOUND AT: https://www.psychologytoday.com/basics/body-language

DATE: NO DATE

TITLE: BODY LANGUAGE, Microexpressions

> *People are constantly throwing off a storm of signals. These signals may be silent (non-verbal) messages communicated through the sender's body movements, facial expressions, voice tone and loudness. Microexpressions, hand gestures, and posture register almost immediately, a silent orchestra that can have long-lasting repercussions.*

Body language is something we should all understand, observe, read, and practice. It can keep us out of trouble or get us in trouble. Quite beneficial.

It's generally thought speaking a second language is beneficial. That's particularly true depending on one's location or the person you're dealing with at the time. Such as … using your rusty French while vacationing in Paris. But if your second language is body-language, it can generally be used in any location and with almost all people.

Is the Group D list for honor-roll students? Yes, although they're probably familiar with everything on the list. The D list is extremely important for *all* students. The subjects covered in Group D will not only improve grades but also open up new worlds for all students.

Knowing how to maneuver through a library is like having your own key to the knowledge vault. And, where is that library? It's down the hall at school. It's down the street in town. It's on your desk at home. It's in your hand at all times. Use it.

Being lightly exposed to the basic wonders of the universe will stimulate the imagination of all. Hopefully, that includes kids entering high school who are, more than anything, looking forward to their first vehicle. Many think driving, especially driving really fast, will be the coolest thing on earth.

What's printed on that speedometer? Is that 100 mph? That's not cool. It's not even fast. Riding a light beam is cool … and fast. Demonstrate to kids the difference between 100 mph and the speed of light. Traveling to a distant star will take how long by motor vehicle? The blackboard can't even handle that written number. Now that's cool, especially if one's imagination is stimulated to the edge of … incomprehensible.

Would any of that far-out knowledge stimulate a wannabe race car driver into a wannabe astronaut? Unknown, but hopeful.

Maybe such far-out information will lead to an increased quest for knowledge. Maybe an increased membership in the science club. That's a club in need of more American members. Instead of ten kids staying after school for detention, why not ten kids staying after school for a science club meeting? **The country could use more gang activity—the science club gang.**

One of the most important subjects in Group D for the average student is about "study and grades." If a student masters an instruction class entitled "How to Study and get an A," he or she will no longer have to worry about grades. At least, that's the theory. Positive results in all classes, after completing a "How to Study" class, will thrill students and probably floor parents.

Numerous books, tapes, seminars, and courses are available to improve study habits and grades for new college freshmen. This material is made available so students have an easier time adjusting to a more rigorous study schedule. A few professors will utilize the first day of class to detail for students the exact way to get good grades in the class. That's great for those who listen or haven't missed the first class. But how to study or how to get an A is usually more involved than good tips from a sole professor. Specific instruction is best.

Incoming high school students are much different from those entering college. **High schoolers are a cross-section of students with varied pasts and a variety of different views about their immediate futures.** Most will lack good study habits and some will exhibit very bad attitudes. Others are anxious to learn as much as possible.

Do they all need instruction in how to study? Yes. Learning how to study more efficiently benefits students in high school, after high school, and well beyond. Having more efficient study habits usually means getting more knowledge out of English class and more know how out of woodworking shop. The idea is to digest as much learning as possible from any and all classes. All are beneficial, some much more than others, to a wide variety of students.

Presenting a new subject, in this case, how to study, to new students at a new school and a new time, will exhibit the usual problems but also some social-type problems like inconvenience. Students, parents, or teachers may object because of the timing. Timing such as … when is there an easy time slot for this new, unusual, and unnecessary study class that doesn't interfere with my precious time? That stance would be unfortunate since all parties involved should be seeking the same student success, and that same success will lead to overall education improvement for the entire nation.

At an extreme minimum … there should be a one-hour how to study class each day for five days. That five-day class should be presented either the very first week of high school or some part of the prior week.

Students starting college can always find how to study materials and other particular course aids available at the bookstore. Those starting high school need the same study help, and some need a lot of help. Those students who are not academically inclined or not interested in going to college may need extra social help as much as study help. Give it all to them in high school. Where else? When else? These are usually the same students teachers find difficult to teach, or they think they already know everything. Are there many of those guys in public schools? Ask any teacher.

The difficult students may need considerable assistance in finding their best study habits, and that may be a time-consuming task, considering what works best for one student may not work at all for another. And that's saying it politely.

It should be stressed … how to study instruction needs to be treated seriously.

The same attitude should be used for grade school as well. Teaching kids how to study and learn should be the number one subject presented and learned. That means learning how to study before actually having a class that requires concentrated study in order to get a passing grade such as an A. How to study is also a subject that changes from grade school to high school to college.

High school, being the last academic schooling for many, is the most important. It's a time to expose students to a double-dose of serious instruction for serious advancement in knowledge.

First, have a general how to study instruction class presented at the start of high school. The course would be basic instruction to optimize learning in all subjects.

Beyond that general or basic instruction, there is specific instruction. Specific instruction from a specific teacher for a specific subject. If Ms. Teacher is teaching freshman English, she should explain to her class during the first week of school exactly how each student could earn an A grade. It's her opinion, but it's her class and her favorite subject, and she teaches it her way. If she puts a high weight on detailed homework being turned in on time and complete, she can dictate that as a sure way to good grades. The point is … all teachers should inform their students early and exactly how to study and how to get an A. Many already do this, but the instruction needs to be clear and demonstrated the first week of school. High school should be the start of serious learning. Start fast and make sure all students understand what is expected of them. Allow no slackers. American students need to pick up the pace in academics and other beneficial instruction. Learning how to study is a necessary first step.

To reiterate what is needed to get an A: A general how to study class presented to freshmen when first starting high school and a course-specific how to study and get an A briefing at the start of each and every high school course by that particular class teacher. An "A" should equal "material learned."

The last group of recommended non-academic subjects is Group E. Group E has the potential to be a fun exercise, but also to stir the imagination of students. And that is the general intent.

The teacher or the school board should select several quotes from several famous and wise old folks who are generally thought to have left their mark on the world. They've left for us what are now known as intriguing, valuable, or curious "quotes." What did their words mean originally, and what do they mean today? Are they words to live by … or are they words to die for?

Here's one bit of free wisdom from Plato for high school students:

"Apply yourself both now and in the next life. Without effort, you cannot be prosperous. Though the land be good, you cannot have an abundant crop without cultivation."

What does this quote mean to the average student? Speculating … if you ask forty students in a public school, you'll be lucky to get twenty answers. And that's if you press them hard for an answer. You can expect ten of the twenty answers to be one word: Nothing. The quote means nothing. Is it possible the twenty not answering are deep thinkers? Perhaps they're thinking outside-the-box? Probably not. It's more likely they're thinking outside-the-school.

The Plato quote was singled out because it may suggest to students that education and effort, their education and effort, was thought of as being of utmost importance more than 2,000 years ago. Ancient thinking that benefits future life. If students put some effort into understanding the wisdom in Plato's quote, they may find it beneficial to them today … and tomorrow.

Another Plato quote might stir a little more curiosity:

> *"Human behavior flows from three main sources: desire, emotion and knowledge."*

Students pondering this quote may find enough interest for discussion or debate. That's better than nothing.

Quotes often represent wisdom from wise people to less-wise people. And it's generally free. If it's wisdom and it's free, isn't that the perfect combination for all of us to enjoy? We all need wisdom, and the price is right.

Students learning nonacademic subjects in high school will find all instruction, academic or social, benefits them and, at the same time, benefits the country. If this is so … how can it not be implemented as soon as possible?

If high school is supposed to prepare students to go into the world on their own, then, in all ways, prepare them to do that as well as possible.

Well beyond the five groups of nonacademic subjects listed above, another area needs to be addressed. It's a method of learning used in some universities but rarely in high school. And it would be no easy task to implement in high schools. But, again, it's something to help guide and prepare students going forward. It would give them an early taste of the real world, and they may even find their calling from having early access to it.

Some universities offer what is known as a co-op program. Most often, these programs are found in engineering colleges. Students attend regular classes but skip one, two, or more semesters. During these "no class time" semesters, the student works at an engineering job full-time and is paid. The work is related to the student's field of study and usually takes place at a local corporation.

The entire co-op program is a partnership between the university and the corporation. The university provides the required academic study and the corporation offers on-the-job training. An excellent combination for an industrious student.

A similar program available at the university level is an internship. These programs are usually during summer break. An internship is not as limited as a co-op program might be, meaning a wider selection of areas is available in which to work. Many internships are in the area of business. But those students majoring in one of the sciences as well as business have opportunities in different areas such as pharmaceuticals. Law or pre-law majors might find a summer internship in any company's legal department. There may or may not be wages with internships. For students, the main draw may be a foot in the door for future employment.

Co-op and internship programs at the college level provide many benefits for students and employers. Students gain advantage by furthering their education and finding employment in their field. Employers gain advanced knowledge of a prospective employee's work habits and abilities, which can lead to a future relationship if desired.

College students majoring in a particular field gain practical experience in the same field, which is great for their careers. You might say they're getting an early look at their futures.

What about high school students? These younger students could use some early direction concerning their future work choices. Why can't similar co-op or internship programs work for them?

Some differences must be considered, and they center on academic experience and age. College students have a set major area of study such as engineering. With co-op work, usually in the field of engineering, student workers are actually paid for doing basic engineering work.

High school student courses are not nearly as specialized as upper-class college courses, which would limit technical work. The second difference is age. An engineering or other specialized department may not be the best workplace for a fifteen or sixteen year old. A twenty-one-year-old college student is in a different position because he or she may be within a year or two of entering a work career.

Engineering was used as an example because it is quite specialized and not for the average student, nor a student that deplores math.

It is understandable why co-ops or internships are generally limited to college level students. But what if the programs were tweaked a bit, making them suitable for high schoolers? If an engineering firm is uncomfortable with a sixteen-year-old employee, perhaps a young student observer would be okay. A better example might be a student observer in a hospital. It's not on-the-job training, but a student might find medicine or helping people to be of strong interest. It could lead to a change of direction in high school, a new desire to attend college, or work in a medical specialty such as being an x-ray technician.

Why would the above scenario be good for a high school student?

Many students, usually not those already planning college, linger in high school without direction. Their general courses are ... general. If, through a limited co-op or internship program, a student is stimulated to be an x-ray technician, then that is a success. He might be interested enough to increase his science courses pointing toward a post-high school medical-technology certificate in order to land a job in a hospital's radiology department.

Questions from the above scenario remain. Are US high schools, teachers, and students ready for co-ops or internships? Probably not, but with a few changes, these programs may be the answer that would guide students in a productive direction. These programs work well in college, but they could work well in high school and, in fact, they do, but mostly in other countries such as our neighbor to the north. A list of Canadian co-op student benefits follow.

ARTICLE FOUND AT: https:/www.myblueprint.ca/benefits-of-co-op-and-work-experience-in-high-school/

ARTICLE PRODUCED BY: my Blueprint education planner

DATE: FEBRUARY 12, 2013

TITLE: THE BENEFITS of Co-op and Work Experience in High School

> *Work Experience programs, cooperative education programs or co-ops are common in most Canadian high schools. They are designed to increase learning for students while providing them with the opportunity to explore their career options. These programs let high school students spend part of the day in the classroom and part of the day in a workplace environment and allows high school students to gain realistic work experience while still in school....*

> *What are the benefits?*

> *You learn your strengths, interests, and special skills*

> *It provides you with career exploration and planning*

> *It can enhance and enrich your academic experiences*

> *It improves your employability skills*

> *It can help you develop knowledge and skills through hands-on experience*

> *It helps you develop maturity and self-confidence*

> *You gain valuable work experience*

> *You can develop networking opportunities*

> *You earn high school credit*

The benefits listed here appear to be exactly what many US high school students need when they graduate. Canadian students are gaining valuable experience while still in high school. That's great for Canada and good for the United States.

It's good for the United States because school boards, educators, or other interested parties need to go no farther than Canada to obtain answers about high school co-ops. If these Canadian programs help average students, then the United States should copy them with or without minor change and introduce them to American high school students. Copy Canada. Avoid five years of intermittent discussion-meetings at some fancy hotel.

American graduating students need every advantage they can get in today's world of extreme competitiveness. And that includes anything that might facilitate one getting in the door and staying there as an employee.

High school internships and co-ops are not unheard of in the United States. Several high-profile programs exist. Two will be briefly mentioned below.

ARTICLE FOUND AT: www.lanl.gov/careers/career-options/student-internships/high-school/

ARTICLE PRODUCED BY: Los Alamos National Laboratory

DATE: NO DATE

TITLE: HIGH SCHOOL Internship Program

> *Point your career towards Los Alamos Lab: work with the best minds on the planet in an inclusive environment that is rich in intellectual vitality and opportunities for growth....*

> *The High School Internship Program provides qualified Northern New Mexico high school seniors the opportunity to develop skills and gain work experience, while receiving exposure to a variety of career fields. This popular program provides employability skills and assists local area high school students with the school-to-work transition.*

Another similar high-profile program:

ARTICLE FOUND AT: www.sandia.gov/careers/students_postdocs/internships/

ARTICLE PRODUCED BY: Sandia National Laboratories

DATE: NO DATE

TITLE: INTERNSHIPS & Co-ops

> *Mentoring, training, and practical work experience in a world-class research environment.*

> *Intrigued by the possibility of applying classroom theory in a real-world work environment? Consider Sandia.*

> *Each year, Sandia welcomes students from around the country— from those in their final years of high school to researchers obtaining PhDs—to work in a variety of technical and business positions. Interns work on real-world, challenging projects to contribute to critical national goals.*

It's interesting that these two very high level technical laboratories utilize high school students in co-ops or internships. It's understandable if they've used these types of programs to obtain top talent from university engineering and science schools. But it appears they also need lower level prospective workers throughout the company, so they recruit through high school internships. Does that make sense? Absolutely. It's good for the student and company.

A good job is the outcome we want for all high school graduating students. Again, we're referring to those graduates not continuing into college or the military. All high schools and many companies should be involved with co-ops and internships because everybody benefits. It doesn't have to be a technical job in a technical company. It could be work in a business office or on a factory floor. It may not be physical work at all.

It's important to understand that physical work or a job does not necessarily have to be offered or included for the high school student program.

Observation of the workplace may suffice. It could serve as an introduction to life beyond school and as a way to create interest in a possible vocation. Something for the average student, soon-to-be worker, to look forward to in the very near future.

Maybe the reverse happens. Introduce young students to farm work and they may run in the other direction. But at least they'll have an appreciation for hard work and what it takes to complete necessary tasks, regardless of circumstances such as time, money, or weather.

The belief here is that many benefits from college level co-ops and internship programs can be utilized by younger students even without the work, pay, or job aspects. Students get exposure to work-life. They can also get exposure to real-life situations. The time spent in observation-training will not be a full-time semester but instead a part-time obligation for a few weeks. It should be noted that all or nearly all students would need to fulfill the observation-training, not just a few selected for a limited number of internships. Hence, the amount of time involved for each student is somewhat limited as is his or her choice of assignment. Students might voice a preference but without a guarantee.

Students could be immersed in a busy work atmosphere, which might be thought of as active-observation, or strictly stand off to the side in what might be observation-from-a-distance. Instead of this wide variety of description, a single more-inclusive heading should be designated. That would be an easier reference as details and requirements are worked out between school authorities and those establishments agreeing to assist educating students through internships in different types of work environments.

Perhaps the heading, "Observation-Internship," fits as well as any.

School boards should initially investigate the Canadian programs as well as the US programs mentioned earlier. The determining factor to implement any co-op or internship type program should be: Would it improve the average student's potential for success in life and workplace relative to obtaining a good job and performance on that job?

A limited and rough format of a high school student Observation-Internship program will be laid out for several possible tracks. Much tinkering will be needed before and during the initial phases of any program.

The following five areas are examples of specific types of work that could function well for high school students participating in an Observation-Internship program. Other types of work could be included. Several of these areas will be explored in order to demonstrate how an Observation-Internship program might operate with high school students.

- Law Enforcement
- Hospital
- Farming
- Airport
- Utilities

The following general criteria is stipulated for the examples presented. Different schools or locales may be quite different for a number of reasons such as city or rural location.

1. All non-honor roll high school students required to participate.

2. The time and grade level used for high school Observation-Internship is the last half of the sophomore or first half of junior year. The summer of same year could also be used.

3. Student to choose their first and second area choice, which is not guaranteed.

4. School authority to designate final internship assignment based on several criteria, including student choices.

5. Student hardship requests will be considered.

6. Student responsibility or requirement may vary with each internship.

7. Transportation will be provided if needed, depending on assignment.

8. Student may apply for two separate internships. One required.

9. Internships may or may not be within normal school hours.

10. All regular academic curriculum requirements remain current.

The first example is an Observation-Internship in "law enforcement." A partial description of the internship follows:

- Internship is strictly observational.
- Preferred start time correlates with police shift change when possible.
- Estimated time 5-8 p.m., M-T-W-TH or twelve hours per week for four weeks.
- Second time slot 5-9 p.m., F-S-Sun or twelve hours per week for four weeks.
- Primary - two students ride in backseat of two-person police patrol car.
- Students do not exit police car unless told to do so by police.
- Includes time spent observing procedure within police station.
- Includes visit to and observation in local jail and courthouse.
- Includes short briefing when possible.
- Student requirement: two-page report on policing.

How would the close-up observation of law enforcement benefit the average high school student?

When students are exposed several days in each of several weeks to a high profile type of work such as law enforcement, it should provide them a limited understanding of the work requirements and an interesting view of our society. Especially since police work has the following unusual characteristics:

- Blue-collar type physical job taking orders from superiors.
- White-collar type job giving orders to regular citizens as a manager.
- Knowledge of court procedure.
- Knowledge of city, county, and state law.
- Dealing with the public.
- Working rain or shine, night or day.
- Work that is important, sensitive, and sometimes dangerous.

Students exposed to police work will have a chance to see society at its best and its worst. They may become very interested in law enforcement or just the opposite. It could lead them to law school in hopes of being a prosecutor or a defense attorney.

The second example is an Observation-Internship in the medical field. More specifically, a hospital and any specific work department found in its operation. Some characteristics are similar to law enforcement work, but hospitals have a much wider variety of jobs and some very scientific. A partial description of what to expect in a hospital Observation-Internship follows:

- Internship is strictly observational.
- Small groups of students observe.
- Estimated timing 9-4 p.m., one day per week for eight weeks.
- Transportation provided by school bus.
- Observation and briefing in multiple major departments.
- Departments range from custodian to surgery.
- Some hospitals may provide overhead viewing room for surgery.
- Student requirement: two-page report on one high profile department.

Many students when thinking of hospital or medical work think of doctors and nurses. Their work is well-known. But by checking hospitals such as Seattle Children's Hospital (SCH), a bigger story can be found about possible medical employment possibilities. It's probably typical of all large hospitals.

The following information is general and not quoted but partially gleaned from the website listed below:

Information found at: www.seattlechildrens.org/clinics-programs/A-Z/

The number of hospital departments and services totaled about 166 at SCH and would be similar at most hospitals. Nearly all services were in the actual medical field. The remaining few were largely paperwork needs such as insurance and records, but both still within the medical field.

What does that mean for the average student? It means no matter what career field you pick, there's probably a job in a hospital that fits your field. Even a chef or a plumber.

It's important for all students to recognize that their work-life starts fairly soon and they could be working at a hospital in the basement maintenance department as an equipment repair person or in the top floor operating-room as a brain repair surgeon.

The difference in these jobs is obvious. But both jobs could be very good jobs. It all depends on the individual's level of satisfaction with her work and her previous effort as a student.

Is it possible the surgeon was deeply affected by the earlier Plato quote while the floor person ignored it?

That Plato quote again:

"The direction in which education starts a man will determine his future in life."

Another example of an Observation-Internship for high school students is a little different from either law enforcement or the medical field. It's farming.

Farming may be a little scary for some since it sounds like work instead of a job. That may be partially true, and it would be the same for a livestock ranch. Chores for farming or ranching are endless. The work needs to be completed regardless of weather conditions, and much of the work changes from season to season.

What can a student learn by observing on a farm or ranch? In certain ways, it is similar to both law enforcement and the medical field.

The work is important, it must be done right, on time, and people's lives depend on it. That may sound unusual, but if all American students graduated with that same understanding and determination about "work," it would be far easier for them going forward in life and quite beneficial to the entire nation.

An Observation-Internship is not performing a task or training for a job. It's trying to introduce the psychological part of and understanding of what it means to study, prepare, and completely ready yourself, all while in high school, to enter the work-world and be a success.

The following is a description of what an Observation-Internship might be like on a farm or ranch.

- Internship is mostly observational. Getting dirty is possible.
- Short explanations of timing for planting, harvesting, and feeding.
- Estimated timing 7-9 a.m., 6-8 p.m., one or two days per week.
- Continued timing, 4-5 weeks early season, 4-5 weeks late season.
- Transportation by school bus.
- Student requirement: two-page report on farming.

It should be noted that Observation-Internships will vary considerably depending on the region of the country. The immediate surrounding area makes quite a difference as well. Ranches are found in the West. Farms are common, but very large grain-farms are found in the Plains states. Numerous large hospitals are found in large cities. Not in the country. Some airports have facilities for everything aviation. Some operate two flights a day. There are always obstacles to overcome. Neil Armstrong grew up in a small rural town with 5,000 people. He went pretty far.

In any region, sensible cooperation between local businesses and the local school board is mandatory for successful internships. And travel and transportation availability for students will always be a determining factor.

It should be evident to students, parents, educators, and public authorities that a shake-up in high school curriculum, instruction, and method is needed immediately. A combination of three separate but related factors should signal a universal call to action. Those three factors:

1. OECD scores. American students ranked about twenty-fifth in the world.

2. Global competition for jobs. Americans are falling behind.

3. American youth culture. Improve exercise, morals, language, education, and work-ethic. Reduce electronic games, tattoos, drinking, and drugs.

There's little doubt these three factors demonstrate that some dramatic change is needed for many American youth, and that change is best accomplished before and during high school. Later is too late.

There should be an all-out-effort to equip high school graduates with a wide variety of tools for entering global competition and then becoming successful. A good place to start would be by implementing the following, which, at least around the teacher's lounge, would probably be known as the demoralizing-dozen.

1. School authorities investigate instruction methods of OECD's top five.

2. School authorities investigate Canadian high school co-op methods.

3. School authorities implement improved teaching methods.

4. Immediately increase classroom standards for all teachers.

5. Introduce limited practical social instruction in grade school.

6. Introduce substantial how to study instruction in high school.

7. Introduce substantial practical social instruction in high school.

8. Introduce Observation-Internships in sophomore and junior year.

9. High school freshman start one or two weeks early for practical instruction.

10. One week added end of each high school year mostly for review.

11. Low grade students assigned one week of summer subject catch-up.

12. Holiday breaks—one day only except December 20 - January 1.

These changes are designed to improve every student's future life in all ways. As always, some students will benefit more than others. It may be that average students benefit most. That's excellent because the average student often enters military, family, or work-life immediately after high school graduation. Other graduates enter a university, community college, or vocational school.

The earlier start date and the additional review week in high school is needed for added social instruction and added special preparation for success. Success in school, success at work, and success for life equals success for the country.

Chapter Four

Rebuilding Infrastructure—An Endless Task ... So Why Not Start?

QUICK. TAKE A wild guess. How much infrastructure in the United States needs upgrading, rebuilding, replacement, or strengthening for security?

If you answered, "All of it" ... you'd be fairly close to correct.

As with education ... infrastructure is a noisy election talking point. That doesn't mean infrastructure rebuilding isn't really needed. It just means, as usual, when the election is over, the noise is silenced for another four years. Four years is not that long, but if you go through the silly cycle ten times, you'll notice the bridges are starting to creak and crack. Ten election cycles equal forty years.

Bridges are a good "age" example. Many bridges being used today were built forty years before that ten-times election count. And some, forty years before that.

That means citizens, every day, are using bridges forty, eighty, and 120 years old.

Age doesn't tell the whole story. Structural condition does, and there's plenty to talk about there. The American Society of Civil Engineers (ASCE) reports every few years on the condition of all infrastructure and all should read it.

ASCE's report indicates the United States is slipping behind in bridge maintenance and replacement. That's not the fault of people using bridges. It's the fault of the noisy, smiling, handshaking crowd that rarely stays on top of matters such as bridge infrastructure. These politicians need to get their hands dirty once in a while.

INFORMATION FOUND AT: www.infrastructurereportcard.org/bridges/

INFORMATION FROM: ASCE American Society of Civil Engineers

DATE: 2013

TITLE: REPORT CARD for America's Infrastructure

> *Over two hundred million trips are taken daily across deficient bridges in the nation's 102 largest metropolitan regions. In total, one in nine of the nation's bridges are rated as structurally deficient, while the average age of the nation's 607,380 bridges is currently 42 years. The Federal Highway Administration (FHWA) estimates that to eliminate the nation's bridge deficient backlog by 2028, we would need to invest $20.5 billion annually, while only $12.8 billion is being spent currently. The challenge for federal, state, and local governments is to increase bridge infrastructure investments by $8 billion annually to address the identified $76 billion in needs for deficient bridges across the United States.*

Is that a lot of money? The answer is … no, no, no, and no.

No, because bridges are too important to ignore since they connect people, places, and things. Those "connections" are our daily life. Bridges must be safely usable every day of our lives all across the country.

No, because the government's overall waste of money, if curtailed, could easily exceed the cost of all needed bridge work. The $76 billion needs to be spent, but spent with some sensible rationale. Sensible rationale in the government is often more deficient than any bridge.

Is $76 billion a lot of money? No. ASCE has estimated the cost for "all required work" to upgrade, repair, and rebuild all of America's infrastructure between 2013 and 2020 to be $3.6 trillion. Now that's a lot of money. And strangely, it shows the $76 billion figure to be easily affordable.

No … being the fourth no, may be shockingly surprising to some citizens.

Some statistics explain how the figure of $76 billion is apparently just throw-away money to our government. Such as:

INFORMATION FOUND AT: www.cgdev.org/page/aid-pakistan-numbers

INFORMATION FROM: CENTER for Global Development

DATE: No Date

TITLE: AID TO Pakistan by the Numbers

"*In total, the United States obligated nearly $67 billion (in constant 2011 dollars) to Pakistan between 1951 and 2011.*"

Pakistan became a country in 1947, just several years before 1951. Therefore, it appears as if the United States has supported that country almost every year since its birth. In Pakistan, US must stand for that rich relative … Uncle Sam.

The big question for sane taxpayers to ask is this: If the United States government had used the $67 billion (Pakistan foreign aid) to instead maintain and update our bridges over the same time-frame, 1951 to 2011, would our bridges be in adequate condition today so $76 billion would not now have to be extracted from the sane taxpayers? The answer is yes. Finally, a yes after so many nos.

Another question for citizens: If Pakistan knew the location of Osama bin Laden for years, why didn't it bother to inform its favorite uncle, the United States, of that knowledge?

Another article about our bridge infrastructure problem follows below. Another opinion? No, it's about the same:

INFORMATION FOUND AT: https://www.nace.org/Corrosion-Central/ Industries/Highways-and-Bridges/

INFORMATION FROM: NACE international

DATE: NO DATE

TITLE: CORROSION RESOURCES for Highways and Bridges

> *The U.S. Federal Highway Administration (FHWA) has rated almost 200,000 bridges, or one of every three bridges in the U.S., as structurally deficient or functionally obsolete. Furthermore, more than one-fourth of all bridges are over 50 years old, the average design-life of a bridge....*

> *Corrosion is a leading factor in the degradation of bridges. NACE International, the corrosion society, has more than 30,000 members, many of whom specialize in corrosion control in highway bridges....*

Many highway bridges are a problem, and that needs to be corrected because all American citizens use them daily. American citizens can't fix the bridges. The government must make those arrangements.

In recent years, there have been major bridge collapses. Those shocking incidents always serve as a warning and a reminder that work needs to be done. But headlines fade after a week or so, and so does the energy that's needed to start major projects. It's usually a money thing. But today, citizens need more work and the country needs to rejuvenate itself in many ways. Infrastructure should be front and center.

Other bridges, such as those used by trains, also need attention. Mostly, that's a different situation because railroad companies are responsible for their own bridge work. They generally use the same bridge repair companies that contract with the government for public or roadway bridges. That means bridge work should be booming, which would mean jobs and income for many citizens.

Looking at the nearly $4 trillion in infrastructure projects that are needed, it's obvious the work will never run out, but the money has already evaporated. What's the current national debt figure? Passing $20,000,000,000,000 and that's a monster and it's on our back.

Part One of this book covered "saving money." Many of the financial adjustments mentioned there will cause pain, but what choice does the country have today? The country needs money for debt reduction, national security, education, and infrastructure. The country needs to save money somewhere because it needs to spend money everywhere.

Other limited information from ASCE:

INFORMATION FOUND AT: www.infrastructurereportcard.org

INFORMATION FROM: ASCE

DATE: 2013

TITLE: INLAND WATERWAYS

> *Our nation's inland waterways and rivers are the hidden backbone of our freight network—they carry the equivalent of about 51 million truck trips each year. In many cases, the inland waterways system has not been updated since the 1950s, and more than half of the locks are over fifty years old. Barges are stopped for hours each day with unscheduled delays, preventing goods from getting to market and driving costs up. There is an average of fifty-two service interruptions a day throughout the system. Projects to repair and replace aging locks and dredge channels take decades to approve and complete, exacerbating the problem further.*

Surprised? Most citizens think of trucks and trains as carrying freight over roads and tracks and usually not inland waterways. But these waterways are part of US infrastructure, and as with bridges, roads, airports, dams, and pipelines, our waterway infrastructure is deficient and obsolete. In other words ... the government, run by politicians, has failed to maintain properly and consistently, needed infrastructure for trusting citizens.

If there are breakdowns or slowdowns with freight because of poorly functioning infrastructure, that's a cost factor, and it's passed on to consumers who generally don't even know it. So there will be higher-cost no matter whether something is updated or not.

It's often wiser to pay the cost to replace or at least update infrastructure so it operates properly for the next fifty years than to continue to pay for minor and major repairs until there's a complete breakdown or stoppage. It may be a fine line in deciding to repair or replace, but considering the ASCE report, it seems the government has band-aided most infrastructure until its breaking point, which appears to be right about ... now.

Levees are another critical infrastructure. Many are in terrible condition since insufficient modernizing or updating has been done over many decades as we've all watched widespread flooding on television.

Like bridges, levees need help:

Information from: ASCE
Title: Levees

> *The nation's estimated 100,000 miles of levees can be found in all 50 states and the District of Columbia. Many of these levees were originally used to protect farmland, and now are increasingly protecting developed communities. The reliability of these levees is unknown in many cases, and the country has yet to establish a National Levee Safety Program. Public safety remains at risk from these aging structures, and the cost to repair or rehabilitate these levees is roughly estimated to be $100 billion by the National Committee on Levee Safety. However, the return on investment is clear—as levees helped in the prevention of more than $141 billion in flood damages in 2011.*

Is another Katrina-type disaster waiting to happen? How often do we hear of drastic flooding in some area? Weekly or monthly? Flood events appear to be increasing, and some areas that've flooded once often get swamped again and again. Flooding from heavy rain is a natural occurrence so it can't be eliminated, but it can be partially controlled. That means anti-flooding infrastructure must be up-to-date and operational.

Usually, taxpayer funds are used for any flood prevention work and for the necessary clean-up after a flood.

Levee failure can't be blamed for most floods, but there are many times when lesser remedies such as natural or manmade runoffs or even a maze of storm sewers can't handle extra heavy rain or prolonged rain. Constant improvement is needed for these systems, but nothing compares to a sudden levee break or even a levee pump failure.

Why was Hurricane Katrina so bad? Levees failed. Katrina is a prime example of what can happen and will probably happen again.

Levees are another vital infrastructure area where death and destruction has happened and will have to take place again before an adequate updating program will be implemented. Not just in New Orleans but across the country.

The estimated cost to rehabilitate levees is higher than the bridge work.

Levee liability should be looked at a little differently than bridges. The ASCE information spoke about slow-change over the years when old farmland changes to new community land. Levees used to protect farmland. When farmland floods, often the cost is lost crops. Very serious but not nearly as serious as when a housing development has sprung up on the same farmland. A community lost to flooding for whatever reason will not soon recover.

The presumption would be that the entire community knew before development and housing purchases that nearby levees helped stop water from flooding the area. Taking risks is fine, but the purchaser should understand there will be a cost factor if there's flooding. If a levee fails and it's because the levee, as infrastructure, was not adequately updated or reinforced by government authorities, then there's a question about how fault is distributed. It's usually that way. But doesn't it make sense that those citizens making the choice to live in an area of flood risk should bear some cost to maintain or repair levees that protect them? That's different than costs associated with levee failure.

It's also different from flood insurance, which covers property damage. Other special funds for living expenses may be allotted to homeowners after a disaster as well. The insurance, which is relatively inexpensive, is a necessity in any area designated as a flood zone. But there should be a special-fee paid by homeowners in any area that could be affected by levee failure or partial failure. Those fees, special fees, should be used solely for cost of specific repairs or maintenance of local levees. Not for flood damage repairs or cleanup, but for the flood-prevention levee system. Fees from homeowners and businesses in the threatened community would not be used for any and all levees but just their local levees that mostly protect them. The citizens who bought in a community protected by a levee system should be responsible for some extra cost. They chose to purchase there, knowing floods are possible; therefore, they should contribute more than other citizens.

Bridges, waterways, and levees are all associated with water. But, at a much higher level than water is another area of infrastructure needing attention.

Most citizens are not familiar with this infrastructure, but other citizens use it often. It has to work correctly at all times or there'd be serious disruptions across the country. A worst-case incident would make headlines immediately.

That infrastructure is America's Aircraft Traffic Control system. Better known as ATC. The system controls all aircraft, but especially commercial aircraft, including those entering the United States from around the world. The system works fairly well every day, but limited breakdowns, some serious, are not unusual. A number of similar systems around the world are far more up-to-date.

The overall ATC system currently in operation is over forty years old. For safety and for efficiency, America's ATC system needs a complete and timely overhaul. As usual, piecemeal patches and limited improvements have been the norm. You would think political authorities, especially since they're frequent flyers, would be up-to-date with updating the system for maximum efficiency in every way possible.

The following article provides some additional insight.

ARTICLE FOUND AT: www.wired.com/2015/02/air-traffic-control/
ARTICLE WRITTEN BY: Sara Breselor

DATE: FEBRUARY 24, 2015

TITLE: WHY 40-YEAR-OLD Tech Is Still Running America's Air Traffic Control

At any given time, around 7000 aircraft are flying over the United States. For the past 40 years, the same computer system has controlled all that high-altitude traffic—a relic of the 1970s known as the Host. The core system predates the advent of the Global Positioning System, so Host uses point-to-point, ground-based radar. Every day, thousands of travelers switch their GPS-enabled smartphones to airplane mode while their flights are guided by technology that pre-dates the Speak & Spell. If you're reading this at 30,000 feet, relax—Host is still safe, in terms of getting planes from point A to point B. But it's unbelievably inefficient. It can handle a limited amount of traffic, and controllers can't see anything outside their own airspace—when they hand off a plane to a contiguous airspace, it vanishes from their radar.

What does this mean? In ultrasimple, numeric-type terms, it means the seventeen-year-old kid sitting back in coach has more advanced electronics in his hand than the fifty-seven-year-old pilot has in his as he guides a 747 across the country.

Two items should be noted: Recently delivered airliners and other sophisticated aircraft have avionics that will accept and operate with forthcoming modern ATC systems. The second item is that the Federal Aviation Administration (FAA) has been working on a new system that should improve the current ATC system. The new system is referred to as a Next Generation Air Transportation System or NextGen. This new system has been in the works for some time. Today, phase one is in testing so bugs can be worked out. There have been problems and delays in the system testing. That's normal. NextGen won't be fully operational for many years, but at least an updated system is in the future. The cost will be many billions, but safety and economic benefits should far exceed the cost, and that's how it's supposed to work.

If NextGen is on the way, why mention ATC? Because politicians, unrelated to piloting, make left turns, then right turns, depending on the direction of the wind. That means they often slow-down important work in favor of other pet projects. Projects that attract voters.

Without detail, the following should be noted: considering the amount of electronic hacking in today's world, the NextGen system is a very important national security issue. It should be accelerated and strengthened.

Meanwhile, the old ATC system will continue to limp along, which means flyers are more than annoyed too often, businesspeople waste valuable time, the economy suffers, and the question of safety lingers.

Another comment draws an interesting comparison on what could happen when neglecting transportation infrastructure. This down-to-earth example may be amusing on the surface, but it should stand as a dire warning to those who depend on others for transportation. Article follows:

Article found at: transportation.house.gov/news/documentsingle. aspx?DocumentID=400364

Article written by: Paul Rinaldi, "The Hill"

Date: May 10, 2016

Title: Don't Let Our Air Traffic Control System Become the D.C. Metro of the Skies

> *For Washington, D.C., area residents, it was shocking to hear the U.S. Secretary of Transportation threaten to shut down the region's Metro subway system. When major portions of our nation's infrastructure are neglected, it can have devastating impacts. The same is true of the air traffic control (ATC) workforce and the technology they use. Now, imagine the reaction to headlines announcing air travel shutting down due to a shortage of air traffic controllers and system neglect. The U.S. air traffic control system is at a critical juncture. If we don't act soon, there could be dire consequences.*
>
> *If Metro officials had kept up with system improvements and proactive maintenance, things would be different. The same holds true for our ATC system....*

What does it take for officials to operate in such a way as to avoid problems, at least most problems, before those problems are making headlines? Maybe it's the headlines that are needed to get swift action. But isn't that a backward way to get things done? Doesn't everybody want everything running smoothly and efficiently and constantly?

It's more than the Metro. It's more than the ATC. It's all infrastructure in the United States. It all needs attention, and it needs it now.

Politicians, government authorities, and thus, the United States, have fallen well behind with upgrading infrastructure. Look at the grades provided by ASCE (American Society of Civil Engineers). It grades on an A-F system. That should be easy to understand. ASCE has assigned these designations to letters A-F:

A = Exceptional, B = Good, C = Mediocre, D = Poor, F = Failing.

The following list shows assigned grades to each category of infrastructure:

- Energy – D+
- Public Parks & Recreation – C-

- Roads – D
- Ports – C
- Bridges – C+
- Wastewater – D
- Levees – D-
- Drinking Water – D
- Schools – D
- Transit – D
- Rail – C+
- Inland Waterways – D-
- Aviation – D
- Solid Waste – B-
- Hazardous Waste – D
- Dams - D

Any student who received eleven Ds out of sixteen possible grades probably wouldn't make it to graduation. Why should it be any different with infrastructure? If the infrastructure grades don't improve, infrastructure is not going to make it. When infrastructure fails … we all fail.

A student can seek help, attend summer school, improve his or her grades, and graduate.

Infrastructure needs help, and $3.6 trillion by the year 2020. Will infrastructure improve enough to graduate?

New updated figures change the above sentence slightly. The cost figure is now $3.9 trillion and is needed by year 2025 to cure all infrastructure deficiencies. This timing comes from ASCE's 2017 national infrastructure report card. The eleven Ds are now twelve Ds. Not a good trend. Those results are well-known by government authorities and community leaders. The public … not so much.

The following paragraph is what ASCE says about infrastructure and would like everybody to know and understand:

> *Every family, every community and every business needs infrastructure to thrive. Infrastructure encompasses your local water main and the Hoover Dam; the power lines connected to your house and the electrical grid spanning the U.S.; and the street in front of your home and the national highway system….*
>
> *We know that investing in infrastructure is essential to support healthy, vibrant communities. Infrastructure is also critical for long-term*

economic growth, increasing GDP, employment, household income, and exports. The reverse is also true—without prioritizing our nation's infrastructure needs, deteriorating conditions can become a drag on the economy.

Our national infrastructure is usually not on people's minds as they go about their lives. Our politicians promise to improve everything up until Election Day. After that, they're off the hook. Add those thoughts together and America is behind a $4 trillion infrastructure eight-ball. Something has to change because deteriorating infrastructure doesn't cure itself.

All citizens use infrastructure, but for some, it can be much more intense. What about citizens who live near a hazardous waste facility? Or near a wastewater treatment plant? If a facility is old and operating poorly, are there dangers for a family? Do some facilities give off odors from time-to-time or often? What about a serious leak?

Serious hazardous waste leaks are not probable, but they do happen. Most are minor or very minor and may happen weekly. Many leaks are because of old or poorly functioning equipment. Many because of careless workers.

A worst case example is the Bhopal disaster in India. It's not US infrastructure, but it dramatically illustrates the seriousness of a hazardous waste leak or other similar problem.

ARTICLE FOUND AT: www.theatlantic.com/photo/2014/12/bhopal-the-worlds-worst-industrial-disaster-30-years-later/100864/

ARTICLE WRITTEN BY: Alan Taylor

DATE: DECEMBER 2, 2014

TITLE: BHOPAL: THE World's Worst Industrial Disaster, 30 Years Later

Thirty years ago, on the night of December 2, 1984, an accident at the Union Carbide pesticide plant in Bhopal, India, released at least 30 tons of a highly toxic gas called methyl isocyanate, as well as a number of other poisonous gases. The pesticide plant was surrounded by shanty towns, leading to more than 600,000 people being exposed to the deadly gas cloud that night. The gases stayed low to the ground, causing victims [sic] throats and eyes to burn, inducing nausea, and many deaths. Estimates of the death toll vary from as few as 3,800 to as many as 16,000, but government figures now refer to an estimate of 15,000 killed over the years. Toxic material remains, and 30 years later, many of those who were exposed to the gas have given birth to physically and mentally disabled children.

Much debate remains about the cause and effect of the disaster. Many claim the cause was deferred maintenance, and others say it was sabotage. Anytime there's legal and money matters associated with a disaster, the accusations and claims will be quite diverse.

The Bhopal disaster was horrible, and it's used here only as an extreme example. It doesn't mean there'll ever be a serious hazardous waste-plant problem in the United States. After all, the ASCE has given a grade of D (Poor) to hazardous waste infrastructure, not an F (Failing). Maybe next year.

The ASCE report lists many D grades, including two with a D-. Citizens should ask authorities what they think comes after a D- grade. Will authorities take full responsibility when there is an infrastructure failure and shutdown?

Citizens may not be in serious danger, but what about the psychological aspects of living in fear? It may be quite disconcerting for those families living near a poorly operating infrastructure facility or even fifty miles downstream from a dam. Dams received a grade of D (Poor).

The nation's spending habits often appear as odd. Politicians talk loudly about creating infrastructure jobs. At the same time, they promise more social benefits for those citizens who have failed to succeed in a normal lifestyle. Both are costly. Billions could be spent on infrastructure improvement, and billions could be spent on people improvement. Since there is little money for either, the politicians are forced to choose. We elect and pay them to choose wisely. But they choose what benefits them, which is rarely what benefits collective society. It's fairly simple. Thousands of infrastructure facilities or projects do not vote. Millions of government subsistence type people do vote. Who wins? Politicians for sure. Regular citizens for sure not.

If the nation's critical infrastructure is in poor condition then, it's a threat to all citizens. It's time to concentrate on necessities at home. The necessities that benefit all Americans.

Remembering the $20,000,000,000,000 debt … the "best for America" course of action is to reduce funds to unproductive citizens, collect minimum taxes from all, eliminate unneeded subsidies, eliminate US prisons, eliminate unneeded foreign aid, and use those funds saved to improve US infrastructure and security, which benefits all American citizens. It's as simple as that.

PART FOUR: THE DIRTY DOZEN
Changes for a Lifetime of Making Sense

Introduction to Part 4

DOES THE FOLLOWING fable say something to all American workers that they need to understand? It sure does ... especially in this highly competitive world.

> *Every morning in Africa, a gazelle wakes up. It knows it must run faster than the fastest lion or it will be killed. Every morning a lion wakes up. It knows it must outrun the slowest gazelle or it will starve to death. It doesn't matter whether you are a lion or a gazelle: when the sun comes up, you'd better be running.*

FABLE FOUND AT: quoteinvestigator.com/category/dan-montano/#return-note-2567-2

ATTRIBUTED TO: DAN MONTANO. "Lions or Gazelles?" *Economist.* July 6, 1985. p. 37. Verified on microfilm.

This fable may be very true for lions and gazelles, but American workers also need to heed the fable's message. Those words, if adapted, could change everything for American workers and America. World competition is chasing Americans out of their jobs. That trend must change direction and fast.

Tomorrow morning when the sun comes up, American workers need to be running faster and outpacing all other workers or ... they'll be eaten alive.

Running faster may not be enough. Other changes are needed as well. Some dramatic, some not so much. What if the gazelle could not only run faster but could change direction a split-second faster than the lion? That change would make all the difference in the world for the gazelle. The right changes in America would make all the difference in the world for America as well.

> *"Change is the law of life. And those who look only to the past or present are certain to miss the future."*
> — John F. Kennedy, US President (1917-1963)

Forget the past? No. Learn from the past. Change the present. Enjoy the future.

The "Dirty Dozen" represents a Baker's Dozen of familiar areas that should be changed. "Change" today's routine in order to benefit the country. The areas are quite diverse but the need for change is quite uniform.

Dirty Dozen #1

Are Taxes Too Low or Too High? Both. Ask Anybody.

WHAT ARE THE most popular phrases when it comes to taxes?

Tax the rich. Taxes are too high. Vote for me because I'll lower your taxes. Is there anything not taxed? Taxes are not fair. Everybody should pay taxes.

One of the above phrases actually stands-out more in today's fiscal debt predicament than the others. Most people are afraid to say it. It wouldn't be right. It's an unfair concept. But some people will say ... "Finally."

Unfortunately, the phrase is never mentioned by politicians because it's not politically correct for them to talk in such a way. Hardworking taxpayers wonder about it often, especially in April.

The phrase in question ... **"Everybody should pay taxes."**

The entire US tax system may need an overhaul, but here we'll speak only of one specific change. It's a relatively small change and a quite simple concept.

Everybody pays at least a minimum tax.

All people ... paying at least a minimum tax will help the United States financially, and people might even feel patriotic about it. Minimum tax payers will know they contribute to the country just like everybody else. Plus, they'll continue to receive all the regular benefits they get every day.

All citizens and non-citizens living in the United States use and benefit from services and infrastructure supported by federal income taxes. But the distribution of benefits or services from a wide variety of tax receipts is never exactly even. All people use roads, but not all use food stamps. All people are protected by law enforcement and the US military, but some never serve, use city-operated buses or receive free rent. People grumble about this inequity all the time, so a minimum federal tax, easiest to apply, may resolve most grumbling. It just makes sense: All people reap the basic benefits and all people pay the basic tax.

This is not about sales tax on merchandise or any of the numerous and ridiculous taxes attached to gasoline, hotel bills, phone bills, or real estate. Those taxes are another story, which makes little sense.

The minimum federal income tax should be 10 percent.

It should be paid by all citizens and non-citizens who collect a check or cash or other value for labor, services, awards, bonuses, or any type of support payments. The same minimum 10 percent tax should be paid on any type of interest, dividends, profit, or similar type funds received. If the funds are normally taxable, then they automatically qualify for the minimum 10 percent tax.

All receive services. All have rights. All enjoy protection. All pay taxes.

Most already pay 10 percent or much more. However, some citizens currently pay zero income taxes for any number of reasons. They would need to sharpen their pencils. April's rush would continue and may well intensify.

Again, for those who enjoy no income tax, regardless of reason, while enjoying use of US services such as roadways and bridges along with the privilege of knowing their homeland is safe because of our tax-supported military forces, a minimum tax of 10 percent would be collected.

In other words … **there are no exceptions.**

It should be remembered … some very hard-working citizens earn a great income and actually pay 50 percent of it in taxes. Along the way, they probably help create a few jobs.

Others work very hard supporting a spouse and two kids while earning $50,000 a year; they pay zero income tax and create zero jobs. Not creating jobs is okay, but paying a minimum tax needs to apply to all.

Interestingly, still others don't work at all, and some have never worked. They and their families might be receiving $50,000 a year in income or its equivalent. Income levels may be determined by family size or living location. Their income tax is zero. You could say they create jobs, but only at the local government assistance office because the office needs more and more bodies to continue handing out funds for the non-workers who are multiplying at a higher rate than the workers.

It's estimated there are 2,000 or more millionaires in the country who pay zero incomes taxes. They happily play the violin every April 15. Could they afford a minimum 10 percent tax?

Zero taxes? But, how many millionaires pay between 1 and 9 percent?

All of these examples represent citizens who enjoy living in our free country. They all receive the same ordinary and ongoing benefits.

A minimum 10 percent tax collected by our free country is not too much to ask from everyone. It's actually necessary before a financial collapse happens, and a minimum tax for all should be an easy "norm" to establish.

"All pay" is easy to understand.

"Ten percent" is easy to figure.

Considering the national debt is $20,000,000,000,000 and climbing, all citizens should feel proud to help the nation improve its financial position.

A minimum 10 percent income tax … preferably permanent.

Dirty Dozen #2

Who Can Argue with Charity?

Is ANYBODY AGAINST charity? No.

Is anybody against charity tax write-off? Doubtful.

Should most people be against a charity tax write-off? Maybe.

The beneficiaries of charity funds appreciate charity. For some, it feeds and clothes them. It helps them get back on their feet. It gives them hope for life. For others, it becomes a dependence.

The users of charity funds love charity. For some, such as grad students or researchers, the use of charity funds supports their insatiable quest for knowledge and discovery. For others, it simply pays their generous salary, which easily covers their BMW payment and much more.

The solicitors of charity funds say charity is good and necessary. For some of those solicitors, it fulfills an inner need to champion a worthy cause. For others, it's merely smiling at the public while conducting ruthless business planning behind closed doors before making steady bank deposits.

Once again: Should most people be against charity tax write-off? Yes.

Many regular citizens attend a religious service weekly. They drop $5 in the basket and feel good about it. The money usually goes to support the church or a local need. That need might be a needy family or some other cause. Everybody benefits in some way. Including the giver.

Would the citizen give the $5 if it was not a tax write-off? Yes.

Many regular citizens see sympathetic, usually professionally made, TV requests, or they receive enticing mail solicitations and then send money to any one of numerous charities. Those charities, such as the American Red Cross or St. Jude Children's Research Hospital, are generally thought of as doing good and important work. They are also businesses.

The donors to these charity-businesses, also known as non-profits, feel happy to do their part and their donations are tax deductible, which may or may not have some influence on the donor's reason to donate.

Most people are unfamiliar with the actual numbers of non-profit or charity organizations operating in the United States. The following information may be a surprise, and if so, perhaps it should be pondered:

INFORMATION FOUND AT: http://nccs.urban.org/data-statistics/quick-facts-about-nonprofits

DATE: No date

TITLE: QUICK FACTS About Nonprofits

Nonprofit Organizations

- **1,571,056 tax-exempt organizations**, *including:*
  - *1,097,689 public charities*
  - *105,030 private foundations*
  - *368,337 other types of nonprofit organizations, including chambers of commerce, fraternal organizations and civic leagues.*
- *In 2010, nonprofits accounted for **9.2 percent of all wages and salaries** paid in the United States.*
- *Nonprofit Share of **GDP was 5.3 percent** in 2014.*

Interesting statistics for the average citizen. One surprise should be that there are 1.5 million charity-type organizations in the United States. An even bigger surprise is that 9.2 percent of all wages and salaries paid in the United States are from nonprofits. It appears those individuals are enjoying their profits from nonprofits.

The question becomes: Is charity a business or is it a big business?

A lot of people are involved in "charity." People soliciting funds for a worthy cause, people donating as they wish, and people receiving help they need.

It sounds like a good deal all-around … but is it?

The following article sheds light on a sliver of the suggested "questionable-happenings" after the December, 2010, earthquake in Haiti:

ARTICLE FOUND AT: www.npr.org/2016/06/16/482020436/senators-report-finds-fundamental-concerns-about-red-cross-finances

ARTICLE WRITTEN BY: Laura Sullivan, NPR News Investigations

ARTICLE WRITTEN IN partnership with: Justin Elliott, ProPublica, an investigative journalism organization

DATE: JUNE 16, 2016

Title: Report: Red Cross spent 25 Percent of Haiti Donations on Internal Expenses

> *The American Red Cross spent a quarter of the money people donated after the 2010 Haiti earthquake—or almost $125 million—on its own internal expenses, far more than the charity previously had disclosed, according to a report released Thursday by Iowa Sen. Chuck Grassley.*

> *The report also says the charity's top officials stonewalled congressional investigators and released incomplete information about its Haiti program to the public. It concludes "there are substantial and fundamental concerns about [the Red Cross] as an organization."*

> *The report follows a nearly yearlong investigation by the Iowa Republican and his staff, launched after coverage by NPR and ProPublica of the Red Cross' Haiti response. The venerated charity raised nearly $500 million after the disaster, more than any other nonprofit, but an ambitious plan to build housing resulted in just six permanent homes, NPR and ProPublica found.*

Puzzling information especially considering the end result was six houses being built when thousands of people lost their homes.

Charity is a cherished concept, but sometimes greed or other motives become entrenched in the whole process from giver to solicitor to distributor to beneficiary.

United Way is another well-known tax-exempt charity and is generally thought to do good work. However, in the recent past, top leaders in the organization have been charged with fraud and mismanagement, and some have gone to prison.

Fraud and prison? Aren't those terms associated with unscrupulous criminals and shady businesses?

Is it possible big charities have become just another big business? Do some charities actually exist for the welfare, extravagant welfare, of top management and not the welfare of those who are suffering? There are indications that that is exactly true in many charities. Businesses are in business to make a profit. Charities are non-profit. But can't that, "no profit," be accomplished, at least in loose terms, by having no money left over at the end of the year? After all expenses are paid, the remaining funds are simply distributed to some needy cause. Or, more on the shady-side, the distribution figure is simply reduced by increasing expenses, which could be bonuses to management or paying down the mortgage on office real estate, which happens to be owned by management. It's only being speculated that this has happened or could happen. But there are many charities where the money figures really make little sense.

The following is a made-up charity name: Wishing for an Apple Charity. **But the operational figures below are nearly identical to many actual charities found when researching the subject.** Instead of dollar figures, percentages are used in both examples:

Wishing for an Apple Charity

Total Donation percentage = 100 percent

Total Overhead = 91 percent

Management & General Expenses = 11 percent

Fundraising Expenses = 80 percent

Benefit to the Needy = 9 percent

Looking at the figures, it doesn't appear that management is gouging the non-profit charity operation. But what is happening here? It appears this charity, which actually could be a one-man operation, is in the "business" of fund-raising. What if the charity brings in $10 million, has one or two managers, and pays wages to very friendly fund collectors? Little benefit goes to the needy, but something does, and that appears to make it legal.

It's as if a self-working job were created to collect donations. Maybe that is okay, but the end result doesn't seem worthy. It almost appears as if the charity exists only to conduct the activity of fundraising, pay management, and then distribute what's left to a cause. It doesn't add up as a wholesome operation.

Other actual charities have figures very similar to the Wishing for an Apple example, **except two percentage figures might be switched.** The same numbers are used for clarity. Looking at multiple charities, the percentage-figures can vary widely in all categories displayed. Second example:

Wishing for an Orange Charity

Total Donation percentage = 100 percent

Total Overhead = 91 percent

Management & General Expenses = 80 percent

Fundraising Expenses = 11 percent

Benefit to the Needy = 9 percent

Again, the above figures are very similar to many charity operations found when researching charities.

In simplistic terms ... a charity might feed and house people for a year, or for some unfortunate souls, it could be a lifetime. On the other hand, a charity could be a very lucrative lifetime job for the operator and other close associates.

Would it not be better for all concerned if the charity, instead of feeding and housing someone for years, would train that person to work? It wouldn't apply to all but to some. Those lucky people could then support themselves and be productive. The training would be short-term as opposed to feeding long-term.

Or would the charity's managers worry they could be out of business ... and a job?

Unusual questions concerning the donor, tax law, and the receiver of funds should be explored.

A taxpayer receives a tax write-off or deduction when a donation is made to a legitimate charity or any qualified organization. That's nice, but does it always make sense? Yes, for the donation's end use. Yes, for the donation solicitor. Yes, for the donor because the donor chose to donate, may feel good about it, and receives a tax write-off. No, often it doesn't make sense for the average citizen not involved in the transaction.

The average citizen should look at the donation as a loss. That is ... less tax money is paid by the donor to the government. The government is supposed to spend collected tax money wisely and to benefit all citizens. If the government is short for any reason, it borrows money or extracts more money from citizens. Donors pay less, non-donors or citizens pay more.

Two simple questions related to what was just said but concerning only the tax write-off aspect of a donation:

Should all donations be treated as equal?

Should donations be a tax write-off at all?

A donation could go to a charity, helping an area flattened by hurricane winds and rain, causing many citizens to be without electricity, food, or shelter. The people within the impacted area are often in a life-or-death situation.

A $500 donation to that hurricane area via a charity is worth a $500 tax write-off to the donor.

Another $500 donation ... could go to a university or museum that is operating perfectly. Even when it's raining.

The university has an endowment fund holding between $100 million and $25 billion. It charges students $40,000 to enter.

A museum may be holding an endowment fund worth millions of dollars, or it could be 100 times more. It charges people a museum entry fee of $10 or $15. The museum operates in a clean, quiet, and attractive setting.

A $500 donation to a peaceful museum is worth a $500 tax write-off.

A $500 donation to hurricane victims needing shelter is exactly the same.

Those two simple questions again: Should a $500 donation have the same tax write-off value whether it goes to a museum or to a desperate disaster area?

Should the $500 donation be a tax write-off at all?

Perhaps the best answer to the last two questions is … no and no.

Another aspect of the donation business needs mentioning. It's not widespread in numbers, but the numbers involved are big.

It's estimated that several hundred thousand millionaires live in the United States. There's also more than 500 billionaires. All are US taxpayers. Well, not exactly all. As noted earlier in Dirty Dozen #1, about 2,000 millionaires pay zero federal income tax. Several reasons may exist for this unusual zero tax blessing. But just knowing about such a zero tax bracket may be a contributing factor to many hardworking taxpayers fainting every April 15. The perfect remedy for this fainting spell was also mentioned in Dirty Dozen #1. Everybody, including the 2,000 laughers, must pay a minimum of 10 percent tax each and every year.

Some may think there should be additional tax guidelines beyond a minimum tax, especially when it concerns extremely high-wealth individuals. That's a different argument and shall not be covered here.

The 2,000 millionaires stand out in print because they pay zero tax. It's something for many to complain about at a cocktail party. Although, there may be a very small group at the party quietly snickering. But what about the other several hundred thousand millionaires? It might be shocking to learn their percentage tax rates. Some shockingly high … some shockingly low.

And, for those shockingly low rates, tax write-off donations may play a big part in tax amounts collected. It does appear high-wealth individuals can afford to do anything they please with their money, including, apparently, not pay taxes. But isn't that wrong for the country? Most taxpayers think so.

The following article may surprise many regular workers:

INFORMATION FOUND AT: www.huffingtonpost.com/2011/11/18/billioniares-taxes_n_1102234.html

INFORMATION FROM: THE *Huffington Post*

DATE: NOVEMBER 19, 2011

TITLE: SOME BILLIONAIRES Paying Less Than One Percent in Taxes

> *Despite making more than a billion dollars, some of the nation's super rich manage to pay an extremely low tax rate.*
>
> *The top 400 earners in the U.S. paid an average tax rate of 18 percent, according to a Bloomberg TV report noticed by Think Progress. And though that's a far lower rate than the 26.5 percent that many families making less than $100,000 pay annually in taxes, some of America's super-rich, have been able to whittle their tax bill down even more, paying a tax rate as low as one percent, according to Bloomberg.…*

These findings echo earlier reports, which suggest that the super rich may not be paying their fair share in taxes. More than 1,400 millionaires paid no U.S. income taxes in 2009, according to an August report from the Internal Revenue Service.

In addition, 25 percent of all millionaires pay a smaller percentage of their income taxes than millions of middle class households.

You might think the very wealthy in this country should pay a much larger percentage than they do. It appears many certainly should, but they will remind you that a small percentage of a very large dollar amount can be quite a sum. A one-billion-dollar income when taxed at the small 10 percent minimum tax amounts to $100 million dollars. Small percentage ... big dollars.

There are individuals in the United States with a net worth of $1 billion up to $100 billion. That's 1,000 to 100,000 ... million-dollar bills. Quite a stack.

What could a super-wealthy individual do with that kind of money?

He could expand his successful US business, creating many more jobs.

He could pay off debt in several of his ongoing businesses, which would reduce overhead and enable those businesses to produce products at a lesser cost, allowing the business to reduce selling price and consequently sell more product, creating more jobs. More jobs means more spending in the marketplace, which creates even more jobs. A welcome boost for the overall economy.

The super-wealthy could pay regular taxes on the money and then put the balance to work instead of hanging Monet artwork in the parlor.

Or they could give it all to charity in an attempt to avoid paying taxes—the same taxes most average citizens pay to the government every day.

Billionaires can usually do as they wish with their money, but what is best for them may not be best for the country or everyday citizens.

That statement is pertinent because some extremely wealthy individuals living in the United States have indicated they intend to donate nearly their entire fortune, tens-of-billions of dollars, to charities upon death. That sounds wonderful ... until you think about the tax ramifications for the government. The same government that collects taxes from regular working citizens in order to provide needed services for all citizens, including the very wealthy.

Billionaires can and do avoid paying substantial tax amounts by donating large sums to charity. It can be assumed that without a tax write-off, less would be donated. But substantial donations come from substantial wealth, and those donations may not substantially change because of a tax write-off. Often, those with their names on new hospital wings can afford it regardless of tax aspects.

The government, deeply in debt, and regular citizens take a hit when billionaires pay less taxes because of large donations. But the charities receive a windfall to use as they see fit, unless specific instructions go with the donation. Some regular citizens may benefit from such donations, but most do not.

Considering that a financial collapse because of our $20,000,000,000,000 debt would appear in physical terms, as a combination of earthquake, hurricane, and flood across the entire country … now is the time for a tax write-off change.

To cease or drastically change the tax write-offs will not end donations of any amount and of any kind.

It should be expected that churches would still receive donations from the congregation. Other well-known charities would still receive donations from those who feel good about giving.

Charity solicitors will still obtain donations after sudden disasters because people get emotionally involved. Donating is usually their only way to help.

Some charities, perhaps those not operated so well or so right, may fold, but other reputable charities would take up the slack. Charitable money would still flow, but not just for a tax write-off. That's good for the country and its citizens.

Dirty Dozen #3

Immigration and the Illegal Alien Problem: A Simple Fix

IMMIGRATION OR ILLEGAL-ALIEN immigration … either one qualifies as a modern national buzz topic. Both are whispered about early in the morning, and by evening, they're screamers.

Questions with short answer and comment:

1. If border-entry laws are broken … does it mean anything anymore?

   Not much. Laws must be respected and obeyed. Otherwise, there's societal breakdown. Unfortunately, illegal aliens and some Americans have forgotten this principle.

2. We need immigrants to do the work Americans won't do. Absurd?

   Yes. Tens of millions of Americans are out of work. Why? They're paid too much not to work. Change that and save the country billions of dollars.

3. Should immigrants be qualified with language, skills, and funds to live?

   Yes. Qualified immigrants could benefit the United States in many ways. Other countries, perhaps using common sense, qualify their immigrants.

4. Can immigrants easily assimilate into our neighborhoods and culture?

   Yes, most can. Europeans did well. Asians do well. Hispanics populate the West and Southwest and are important citizens in the United States. As might be expected, some cultures have more difficulty assimilating than others.

5. Do immigrants and illegal aliens work for practically nothing?

   No. Generally, immigrants are paid a "regular" wage. They work very fast, very hard, and require few breaks. The result is more work done for the same American dollar.

6. Round them up and ship them out?

   Not reasonable. Rounding up 12,000,000 illegal-alien immigrants and shipping them out would be very disruptive and next to impossible. At least a ten-year battle.

7. How do illegal-alien immigrants get into the United States?

   Most walk across the southern border. Most want work and a better life. Some bring drugs, guns, and death to America. It's all illegal. Seal the border.

The next paragraph … contains the super-secret method for successfully handling all future immigrants wishing to come to the United States. The popular catchall phrase is "immigration reform." This suggested method is directed at the US government, which needs direction in successful immigration.

Copy Canada and Australia's immigration policies. Simple.

That eliminates bureaucratic thinking, committees, studies, trials, and debating. Canada and Australia select immigrants who already read, write, and speak English (in Canada, also French), possess a "needed" skill, a certain level of education, and are employable. They must have money for certain fees and living expenses. Disregarding the millions of illegal entrants, the United States appears to accept anybody and then supports them. Where is the national benefit in that foolishness?

For those illegal-alien immigrants already residing in the United States … there's a simple way to deal with them.

It would be a little time-consuming, but it would also be peaceful, wise, reasonable, effective, legal, and most citizens would approve. It's amazing that politicians haven't thought of it before now.

Illegal aliens can't be rounded up and shipped out. They would first run and hide. Additional laws would be broken. Kids would cry. Disruptions would last ten years. Related chaos would be the norm in many regions of the country and required deportations would never be completed.

Nobody needs all that, nobody wants it, and nobody would put up with it.

It's a simple problem to cure. Tedious, frustrating, and tiring, but simple.

The Simple Plan (SP) starts at the border. That would be the southern border. But all borders and the coastline should be secure. That is … sealed shut.

Most American citizens understand that necessity. For those millions who double-lock their doors every night, but then fail to understand the big picture of secure borders, the following reasons should alert them as to why our porous border is an ongoing problem.

Secure our border because:

1. Terrorists enter our country and cause death and destruction.

2. Gang members enter our country and cause death and destruction.

3. Drugs enter our country and cause death, crime, and destruction.

4. Ordinary illegal aliens enter our country and may cause societal problems.

The SP starts with sealing the border. The two-step SP is outlined below:

SP-1: The military secures the border. Electronics assist. That can be accomplished as described in Part Two, Chapter Three. The process should start immediately and be operational in thirty days. Or 100 percent complete in ninety days.

SP-2: All illegal aliens, undocumented workers, illegal immigrants, or any immigrant unsure of his or her status while in the United States shall report to any Registration Station in any state in order to register. Numerous stations will be set up within ninety days and located in many government buildings currently in use for other services. The government will not need to build or rent separate buildings for registration. Post Offices with an empty room in the back or a similar government building would suffice. Homeland Security will handle processing.

Registration information shall be distributed via all possible distribution methods in both Spanish and English for a period of ninety days before registration begins and continuing during registration. Other languages added as required.

The list below contains information about registration and may be adjusted prior to or during the registration period. The list serves as a guideline for the registration process and instructions for compliance:

A.) All non-citizens must register to obtain legal status in the United States.

B.) Registration does not lead to deportation. Non-registration does.

C.) Registration will be according to first letter of last name and registration available for one calendar month only for particular letters.

The following month other letters called. "One month only" may need some trial and flexibility, including time extension for particular letters or late registration penalty.

D.) The first day of each month will have a random draw of three letters for the following month. Such as: February 1 drawing = H + K + R, which will be processed during month of March. March letters = H + K + R.

E.) Registration includes the following: All immediate family members provide full name, birth date and place, current address, employer, contact information, photo, fingerprints, and blood test. A short list of major assets and debts and their location, such as $1,000 in Bank of Name. Also included: From each adult one page handwritten in native language describing education, skills, work experience and travels.

F.) Registration document and photo ID to be mailed to address provided by each registrant. Do-not-forward mailing. The ID card provides evidence that the alien-immigrant has registered and is a probationary legal resident with resident human rights but without voting privileges.

G.) Voting privileges start twenty-five years from registration date.

H.) Other social services for newly legal immigrant residents as compared to regular citizens TBD; they may be limited for some period of time.

I.) Ongoing registration process shall be extensively publicized in order to demonstrate to all residents, but especially immigrants, that registration is not deportation and the process is simple and proceeds very well. The entire registration process is designed to alleviate any fears within the alien-immigrant community, thereby speeding-up registration.

J.) Registration is the *only way* to be legal for those in the United States illegally. No registration means illegal-resident and mandatory deportation.

K.) All registrants will be required, minimally, to read and understand basic English over a TBD period of time. It's important for understanding laws, signs, documents, correspondence, and other interactions.

L.) Registration goal: 100 percent compliance. In front door, processed, out back door in thirty minutes or as fast as possible.

All information required in item E is necessary and important. Example: Blood test not only registers blood type but may also disclose infectious diseases. Second example: Hand written page in native language should yield information that can be verified and a handwriting sample on record for the named applicant.

Registration of all will take some time but it can be accomplished in an orderly and as expedient as possible manner. Information forms should be obtained and filled out by immigrant applicants prior to registration day.

The ID card solves some potentially sticky problems for all immigrants such as dealing with police, schools, employers, hospitals, or any situation where proper ID is needed.

The ID card will verify the holder as a legal US resident allowing the previously illegal alien to live more easily a regular life, obtain work, and pay taxes. It allows the employer to employ without fear of government reprisal.

Those who refuse to register or provide a photo, fingerprints, blood sample, or any requirement may have good reason for remaining as anonymous as possible. At some point, they will be detained and then deported. Returning into the United States across a secure border will not be easy.

A sealed border along with immigrant registration should bring a decrease in crime and other social problems. A welcome change for any large city.

Registration with an ID card provides legality, which will improve the immigrant's overall life and alleviate the concerns of American citizens.

Dirty Dozen #4

The Underground Cash Society Hurts No One ... Really?

EVERYBODY'S HEARD OF the black market. It sounds like something illegal, dangerous, and hidden from view. And only shady characters are involved with it. If that's what you think ... you'd be wrong. At least wrong about the shady characters. It's probable that we've all participated in the black market. Knowingly or unknowingly and, over time, maybe both.

The following words or phrases are similar in meaning and might substitute for black market: underground market, informal economy, unrecorded economy, untaxed economy, cash market, illegal market, unreported economy, or shadow economy.

Anyone who has paid cash to a babysitter or the neighborhood grass cutter has inadvertently contributed to the "unreported economy," unless the babysitter reported earnings to the government. Is that a problem? Probably not.

Many citizens who have shopped at a small individual-owned store or eaten at the local diner may have noticed when paying cash that the owner-clerk made change without ringing up the transaction. The same thing could happen at a barbershop or any similar place. Is that a problem? Probably so.

These transactions don't necessarily mean you did something illegal. But there's a good chance the owner-clerk did so when he failed to register the sale in the cash register. It's probable no tax will be paid on that income. And if your cash-paid bill included state sales tax, there's a very good chance the sales tax never reached the state.

When a homeowner calls the local tree-remover to have a tree removed and the owner-estimator says the cost is $330, including 10 percent sales tax, then that should be the cost regardless of payment type. But a better deal may be offered to the homeowner by the tree cutter. Such as: If the homeowner pays cash, he'll save some money. Namely, the sales tax. If the homeowner agrees, he'll save $30. Maybe a little more. Quite tempting because everybody wants a deal, and most people think the state wastes tax money anyway. If the home-owner takes the deal, he'll save at least $30, but the tree-cutter will probably save a lot more.

What just happened is a "questionable transaction" that affects the entire US economy. It could be called a black market or a cash-economy transaction. The homeowner knowingly saves $30, and the government unknowingly loses $30 worth of sales tax. And it's also very probable the government doesn't re-ceive the regular income tax due on the $300 as it goes totally unreported.

The homeowner saves money, but he ends up skirting the law by not pay-ing the correct tax due. Again, in one's opinion, the tax money may be squan-dered by the state, but paying it is the law. The tree-cutter, a small business man, is breaking the law. He does what he does every day … cuts trees and collects cash as often as possible, and then he pays a lot less in taxes than he's supposed to pay. Is any of this a problem? Yes, for everybody, including the government and regular citizens.

Tree-cutters are just an example. Exactly how many tree-cutters could there be? Millions. That is, when you include those many people who clean houses, paint houses, or do any number of small jobs, side jobs, and after-hours jobs. You can also include numerous repairmen who work for themselves. Let's just say their "bookkeeping" may demonstrate considerable forgetfulness.

Another common scenario: It's not terribly unusual to see several young men, often they're unemployed or illegal residents, standing outside a large builder-supply store in the morning. They're waiting for a contractor who's looking for day-laborers to work that particular day. These guys are picked up, do some work, are paid in cash, and that's it. No taxes, no paperwork, no benefits, and it's all part of the underground cash economy. Is that a problem? Yes, and it could be more of a problem than just paying a guy for some dirty work. What if the day laborer is collecting unemployment benefits or welfare support? He might not be interested in a regular job. By working several days a week for cash and collecting government benefits at the same time, he's do-ing financially well. He's not paying taxes on income while he's collecting gov-ernment money and that comes from taxes collected from working citizens. Maybe the contractor pays these guys $10 per hour but his regular men earn $20 per hour and pay taxes. The contractor might even deduct $1 out of the $10, telling the cash worker it's for taxes, and then the money stays in his pock-et. Who's going to snitch?

Will the above examples continue without much change? Probably so.

What does all of this mean? It means a typical hard-working citizen is pay-ing a little bit more in taxes than is necessary. Maybe it's more than a little bit.

That little extra being paid is because some smiling entrepreneur is paying less in taxes. Same for the laborer. That's costly for all taxpayers and our country.

The IRS estimates the country is losing about $500 billion in taxes not paid to the treasury because of the "cash economy" that continues to flourish.

It should be noted that examples discussed refer to relatively minor activity, a bending of the rules, which is all very common in our society.

Other serious criminal activities fall under the terms of black market or shadow economy. Using cash and paying no taxes is dominant in the drug, prostitution, and the counterfeit goods marketplace. These are serious matters for law enforcement and shall not be discussed here.

The relatively tame matters discussed here in Dirty Dozen #4 should be cleaned up by government and by society. A plan needs to be put in place to allow small business owners, individual repairmen, and all cash-paid workers to change any fraudulent business practices into regular, accepted, and legal practices "without repercussion." **That means a complete change to operating above-board without exception.** No questions asked. Start paying regular taxes. Going straight, with no setbacks or second chances allowed. Attached to this "open plea to cash operators" to forgo any cash transactions will be stringent laws with stiff penalties. The government would be saying, "We'll forget the past if you remember the future ... by paying all taxes due without fail."

Why this change-of-heart enforcement policy now? Because the United States is $20,000,000,000,000 in debt and close to a financial collapse, and the whole world knows it. Every little bit of financial effort helps. That includes citizens and entrepreneurs paying the correct amount of tax due.

Dirty Dozen #5

Voting Is Always the Answer

VOTING IS A great tradition in the United States. Everybody votes. Everybody should vote. Voting is always the first Tuesday in November. Citizens show purposeful effort by leaving their houses on voting day in order to vote. Changing the voting age from twenty-one to eighteen was a smart move. You must be out-of-town or bedridden if voting an absentee ballot. It's important to vote even if you have no comprehension ability. Military personnel votes are always on time and counted. One citizen, one vote is certain. All voting pole observers and workers are above reproach. Voting in the United States is the purist system in the world. Vote integrity is equal in cities and rural areas. Chicago is the epitome of voting.

It won't be easy but the above paragraph needs some change. It's imprecise.

If voting is such a US tradition, why do only about 50 percent of citizens vote? Would the country be better off with even fewer voters? Maybe it depends on exactly who votes. Not who they are by name, but who they are by brain.

Who votes and what is needed to vote in the United States? Answer … in some cases, anybody and nothing. The more popular answer suggests only registered citizens vote. In reality, you don't even need to be able to read. There's always some totally unbiased voter who would laughingly assist with the X.

This may be an exercise in futility, but an "intelligent voter qualification" list has been be printed out below, regardless of appearing absurd to the average citizen.

Isn't it probable the country would be better off with sensibly-qualified voters voting? The numbered entries below should be explicit enough to be noticed and criticized by most readers. And really … shouldn't voting be done by citizens possessing some knowledge of a candidate's background and a basic understanding of the effect that candidate's policies would have on the entire country?

Qualifications to vote should be as follows:

1. US citizen

2. Successful one-time completion of short literacy test written in English

3. Minimum age – twenty-one years unless serving or have served in military

4. Minimum education – high school graduate

5. Voter is not currently accepting government welfare

6. Voter has never been involved in any kind of voter irregularity

7. Voter registered one year in advance with verifiable photo ID

8. Voter votes "absentee ballot" with specific verifiable reason only

9. Voter votes between 6 a.m. and 11:59 p.m. one day only

10. Voter provides immediately verifiable photo ID at voting pole

Of course, some of the above qualifications will be problematic such as the voting exclusion for those receiving government welfare. But politicians, looking for entire family votes, will preach to welfare recipients that their welfare paycheck and entitlements will be protected or increased. It's almost as if some politicians prefer more people on welfare just for their votes. Instead, they should be promising their help in initiating a local job training program that will enable welfare recipients to find work and then recover their voting privilege.

Doesn't it make more sense to ensure legal and sensible voting at all times?

Doesn't it make sense to improve the average quality of the US voter?

Doesn't it make sense to improve the overall quality of the final vote?

Doesn't it make sense for politicians to help people get off of any kind of assistance?

All controversial? Yes. But what is best for the country at this time?

Tighten up the voters and loosen up the politicians. That makes sense today. Politicians should readily disclose their political history and background. Fully explain their positions and why those positions will be better for all citizens after election. Isn't that all-important? Politicians need to offer a thorough explanation of policies instead of offering incomprehensible promises.

Voting day used to be an important day. In the past, people have walked ten miles just to vote. Make voting day that important again. Make voters important again. All citizens should be striving to be well-informed voters. That's better than striving to qualify for government benefits.

Informed voters would demand exceptional candidates, and thus, all citizens would benefit. So would the country.

Dirty Dozen #6

Regulations … to Die For?

YES, THAT HAPPENS. But usually it's the business that dies. Regulations are put in place to help. Or so they say. But the usual questions pop up … help who, what, when, where, why, and how?

Regulations are often put in place by politicians because they feel the need to act as if they're protecting something. That something is often talking-points for their next campaign or it could be the associated workers, ordinary citizens, the regulation-issuing government department, or even the lowly minnow. Who or what really gets the unchecked protection? Often it's the minnow.

Often, the safety issue is front and center. That sounds fine, except, in many ways, regulations are actually hurting citizens and, therefore, the whole country. The old adage, "There's safety in numbers" is not working very well when it comes to government regulations. Too many regulations usually add too much cost and the costs are rarely affordable. That should be obvious to anyone who looks at the cost figures for overburdening regulations being enforced at the same time the country continues to deteriorate financially. Some regulations are just not affordable at this time. Some never. The number of regulations and their cost are detailed below and sum up the country's "regulatory problem":

ARTICLE FOUND AT: https://www.fiscalnote.com/2016/04/07/the-trillion-dollar-cost-of-regulations-in-the-united-states/

ARTICLE WRITTEN BY: Belinda Lei

DATE: APRIL 7, 2016

SOURCE: HTTPS://WWW.AMERICANACTIONFORUM.ORG

TITLE: THE TRILLION-DOLLAR Cost of Regulations in the United States

> In the past eight years, sweeping changes to healthcare, environmental, labor, and energy policies have resulted in huge changes to the way these industries do business—with staggering costs.

Since 2008, 25,155 new regulations have been issued under the Obama administration. The economic impact, according to American Action Forum, was $727 billion with 460 million new hours of paperwork required.

Annual costs of all current federal regulations are estimated at $1.88 trillion, or 11 percent of the US GDP. If the cost of regulation was a country, it would rank as the world's 10th largest economy.

Who in the world is trying to run America out-of-business?

The most popular answer is China. Everybody knows it has cheap labor and its workers work fast. Mexico is another good answer. Mexico is undercutting our business operations the same as China, and it's much closer to the United States. Politicians yell, "They're not playing fair." But business isn't a fair game to play. It's business, and business is often a survival-of-the-fittest exercise, and that refers to making tough but smart business decisions. All American team members must make smart decisions. All refers to … all.

Besides Chinese and Mexicans working hard … who or what else could run American workers and American industry out of business?

Well, exactly who comes up with idiotic anti-business nonsense ideas and turns those ideas into almighty regulations? And then badgers decent people and businesses into regulatory submission. Could that be an American team member? Yes, it could, and it's the American government.

If proof is needed … read some regulations below that make little sense but big trouble for workers trying to move ahead:

ARTICLE FOUND AT: www.businessinsider.com/ridiculous-regulations-big-government-2010-11

ARTICLE WRITTEN BY: Michael Snyder, The Economic Collapse

DATE: NOVEMBER 12, 2010

TITLE: 12 RIDICULOUS Government Regulations That Are Almost Too Bizarre to Believe

Even with all of the massive economic problems that the United States is facing, if the government would just get off our backs most of us would do okay. In America today, it is rapidly getting to the point where it is nearly impossible to start or to operate a small business.

The federal government, the state governments and local governments are cramming thousands upon thousands of new ridiculous regulations down our throats each year. It would take a full team of lawyers just to even try to stay informed about all of these new regulations.

Small business in the United States is literally being suffocated by red tape. We like to think that we live in "the land of the free," but the

truth is that our lives and our businesses are actually tightly constrained by **millions** *of rules and regulations.... The following are 12 examples of ridiculous regulations that are almost too bizarre to believe....*

As you read on, you may wonder exactly who is running America out of business. Is it China, or is it Mexico, or ... is it us?

#1 Private Investigator's License

The state of Texas now requires every new computer repair technician to obtain a private investigator's license. In order to receive a private investigator's license, an individual must either have a degree in criminal justice or must complete a three year apprenticeship with a licensed private investigator. If you are a computer repair technician that violates this law, or if you are a regular citizen that has a computer repaired by someone not in compliance with the law, you can be fined up to $4,000 and you can be put in jail for a year.

#2 Business Privilege License... For Bloggers

The city of Philadelphia now requires all bloggers to purchase a $300 business privilege license. The city even went after one poor woman who had earned only $11 from her blog over the past two years.

#3 Funeral Director License for Monks

The state of Louisiana says that monks must be fully licensed as funeral directors and actually convert their monasteries into licensed funeral homes before they will be allowed to sell their handmade wooden caskets.

#4 Teeth Brushing Regulation

In the state of Massachusetts, all children in daycare centers are mandated by state law to brush their teeth after lunch. In fact, the state even provides the fluoride toothpaste for the children.

#5 D.C. Tour Guide License

If you attempt to give a tour of our nation's capital without a license, you could be put in prison for 90 days.

#6 Raw Milk License

Federal agents recently raided an Amish farm at 5 A.M. in the morning because they were selling "unauthorized" raw milk.

#7 Pumpkin and Christmas Tree Vendor License

In Lake Elmo, Minnesota farmers can be fined $1,000 and put in jail for 90 days for selling pumpkins or Christmas trees that are grown outside city limits.

#8 Untangling Whale Restriction

A U.S. District Court judge slapped a $500 fine on Massachusetts fisherman Robert J. Eldridge for untangling a giant whale from his nets and setting it free. So what was his crime? Well, according to the court, Eldridge was supposed to call state authorities and wait for them do it.

#9 Interior Design License

In the state of Texas, it doesn't matter how much formal interior design education you have—only individuals with government licenses may refer to themselves as "interior designers" or use the term "interior design" to describe their work.

#10 Additional 1099s to File

Deeply hidden in the 2,409-page health reform bill passed by Congress was a new regulation that will require U.S. businesses to file millions more 1099s each year. In fact, it is estimated that the average small business will now have to file 200 additional 1099s every single year. Talk about a nightmare of red tape! But don't try to avoid this rule—it is being reported that the IRS has hired approximately 2,000 new auditors to audit as many of these 1099s as possible.

#11 License to Close a Business

The city of Milwaukee, Wisconsin makes it incredibly difficult to go out of business. In order to close down a business, Milwaukee requires you to purchase an expensive license, you must submit a huge pile of paperwork to the city regarding the inventory you wish to sell off, and you must pay a fee based on the length of your "going out of business sale" plus a two dollar charge for every $1,000 worth of inventory that you are attempting to sell off.

#12 Labeling Products with Calorie Counts

The U.S. Food and Drug Administration is projecting that the food service industry will have to spend an additional 14 million hours every single year just to comply with new federal regulations that mandate that all vending machine operators and chain restaurants must label all products that they sell with a calorie count in a location visible to the consumer.

The twelve regulations above are examples of silly or outrageous regulations. Nevertheless, politicians or some government authority put the regulations in place. Apparently, being shortsighted or not understanding the business downside of some regulations isn't of much concern to many government officials. They smile as if they're the almighty.

Presumably, or hopefully, the most ridiculous regulations get changed over time.

The overwhelming problem lies in the sheer numbers of regulations. Businesses can't keep up with them, and the costs kill business. Since 2008, more than 25,000 regulations have been put on the books. Our business competitors in China and Mexico can operate without much of the regulatory cost necessary in the United States. That difference in cost is like night and day.

If you're in a war zone and you hear someone say, "We're getting some R & R," it usually means you're going to get some Rest and Relaxation. Sounds good.

If you're working for an American company and you hear someone say, "We're getting some R & R," it might mean your job's now in jeopardy because the company's being slapped with more costly Ridiculous Regulations. Sounds bad.

But, of course, in either case you may get some time off. Maybe that's how the government looks at it. More ridiculous regulations … more rest and relaxation.

Dirty Dozen #7

The Writing's on the Wall

SPEAKING TO AMERICA'S working citizens:

Graffiti … have you seen any?

Or have you been blind since birth? A shut-in for the last fifty years? Live self-sufficiently in a cabin 1000 miles from nowhere?

Speaking to America's playful youth:

Graffiti … do you worship at a wall?

Do you feel your personal visionary thoughts must be laid down on a solid surface for posterity? Do you think your nearly senseless hand-wit expressions will lead to a Hollywood career? Do you see yourself as a gift to humanity, and you believe civilization will marvel at your monstrous landscapes?

What can be said of such genius? How about this:

"Get lost and take your crayons with you."

If you're incapable of serious thought and you refuse to fade into oblivion … we suggest you pick one or all four of your bedroom walls and scribble until your heart's content. Awake or passed-out, you can be surrounded by your coloring-book of juvenile drawings.

Cavemen didn't have crayons or coloring books. They scratched on their cave bedroom walls. But at least their cave scrapings serve as enlightenment about our distant past since they help us understand how early humans lived and what they were thinking.

Modern day street-graffiti-junkie … we already know how you live and we don't care what you're thinking. You live in a nice house and Daddy drives a nice car. Or you live in a housing project and Daddy watches a lot of widescreen TV. Different sides of town but similar mentality.

What we care about is you destroying our property and costing us money and embarrassment removing your "bogus-art." You crow about your graffiti drawings, but they're meaningless nonsense to the civilized world.

We would like you to finish evolving as soon as possible and join us in today's world ... not revert back to elementary caveman expression.

Young graffiti artists ... supposedly, the world is yours to enlighten, but not with crayons, chalk, or spray paint. The following article may assist your understanding of the real world:

ARTICLE FOUND AT: www.nytimes.com/roomfordebate/2014/07/11/when-does-graffiti-become-art/graffiti-is-always-vandalism

ARTICLE WRITTEN BY: Heather MacDonald

DATE: DECEMBER 4, 2014, last updated

TITLE: GRAFFITI Is Always Vandalism

> *Anyone who glorifies graffiti needs to answer one question: If your home were tagged during the night without your consent, would you welcome the new addition to your decor or would you immediately call a painter, if not the police?*

> *No institution that has celebrated graffiti in recent years—like the Museum of Contemporary Art in Los Angeles or the Museum of the City of New York—would allow its own premises to be defaced for even one minute. Graffiti is something that one celebrates, if one is juvenile enough to do so, when it shows up on someone else's property but never on one's own.*

> *The question "When does graffiti become art?" is meaningless. Graffiti is always vandalism. By definition it is committed without permission on another person's property, in an adolescent display of entitlement....*

Graffiti is a crime. A crime against taxpaying citizens. Graffiti seems to be everywhere. Tomorrow there will be more than there is today. How do you stop it here in the United States?

It's quite simple. You adapt strong, not weak, laws and publicize the execution of the punishment. That should curb 90 percent of graffiti.

If anyone doubts the immediate effectiveness of simplicity and strong laws, they should check with Singapore authorities. Their laws control "graffiti-crime" because they're strong, highly publicized, and simple to remember.

Perhaps the US should treat graffiti-crime as a crime and the punishment should be swift and severe. The offenders, graffiti vandals, would end-up curbing their graffiti activity for at least three years.

There is no doubt about that ... in Singapore.

Graffiti-crime punishment in Singapore consists of a $1,500 fine, three years in jail, and eight strokes of caning. The $1,500 fine almost sounds like fun. The three years in jail lasts three years. The scars from the caning ... last a lifetime.

If the United States continues with little effective enforcement of weak graffiti laws, perhaps the government should arrange to remove graffiti regularly with available free labor. It's unfortunate, but that free laborer may feel more punished than the graffiti vandal.

Welfare collectors, already being paid not to work, could remove graffiti and clean walls, which would benefit property owners. Minimum compensation between the owner and the government, not the graffiti remover, could be arranged. The same work would be needed for defaced government property, such as walls along roads. This would not remedy all situations because some surfaces need expert work to repair while others do not.

Generally, welfare recipients do not work for welfare benefits. Occasionally, cleaning or removing graffiti would be a small change. Recipients would still collect the welfare benefit, and they would be assigned only limited work. No additional money. Only additional but limited work. The government receives money compensation from the private property owner if the owner uses government services for graffiti removal.

The whole process seems so unnecessary, but something must be done, and the above scheme is something.

It should be expected welfare souls would look upon this task as forced-labor. Other problems may present themselves as well. It's unfortunate, but welfare costs and graffiti scribblings are both increasing and both need to be curtailed.

Usually, anti-graffiti laws or regulations are weak in the United States and not readily enforceable. More effort seems to be devoted toward prevention, along with suggestions for easier cleanup. Not surprisingly, graffiti continues to increase.

Owners are asked to remove graffiti as soon as possible, put up fences, grow vines on buildings, use security cameras, paint walls with protective coatings, or use sacrificial (removable) surfaces. If a budding graffiti artist smears dirty-words across your wall, you can just peal the damaged wall off and present a new canvas for the beaming brat. Sadly, the remedies mentioned are real and being suggested today.

Wishy-washy prevention methods must change. Weak enforcement of anti-graffiti laws must change. Authorities should call Singapore for advice. Simple.

Dirty Dozen #8

Welfare ... the Best Money-Job You'll Never Have

WHY WOULD ANYONE want to be on welfare?

Several smart-aleck answers come to mind: Hump-day is Wednesday, which means workers start looking ahead to a fun weekend. For those living on welfare, there is no hump-day ... only weekends. Free rent, free food, free phone, free heat, and free doctor visits free the welfare recipient's mind from that dreaded "first of the month due-date." Being on time for work or rushing to get somewhere is unnecessary. Take all day. Welfare ... almost sounds as if it's a better life.

One of these days, someone will start welfare benefits at age one and continue them until death at 101 years of age. That would establish a record for the longest uninterrupted career. Unfortunately, the recipient would miss his or her own retirement party.

Earlier in Part One, Chapter One, it was shown that welfare dollars paid in some states amounted to higher wages than many workers received for working a full-time job in that same area. An example might be Washington, DC, where welfare recipients receive the equivalent of an hourly job rate of $13.99. In some states, the hourly equivalents are even higher. The stupidity of that equation produces a "worthless-to-the-country" outcome: a potential American worker staying home, never progressing off welfare, because he or she feels there's no money-reason to do so. "Stay home and relax" pays the same as "Get out of bed and go to work." That needs to change for two critical reasons: our money and our country.

In the beginning of Dirty Dozen #1 it stipulates that a minimum tax of 10 percent should be applied to all income, including welfare income. The following scenario reinforces the minimum tax on welfare proposal, especially when comparing work pay rates to welfare pay rates.

If you're living in Washington, DC, and working a job for $13.99 per hour, there's a very good chance you're paying taxes on your income. Those taxes could be all or any one of: city, state, federal, FICA, or other fees. That doesn't include property, sales, gas, or all those leech-taxes printed on your phone bill. If the worker making $13.99 per hour is paying only part of those taxes, his hourly net wage might be $13, but it's probably closer to $12 per hour. That brings up a silly question: Why get out bed in bad weather to work for $12 an hour when you can stay home and watch TV for $13.99 an hour?

Welfare recipients, having considerable spare time, should attend "life-improvement" classes. Such classes could be implemented within the welfare program to save the government money over time and benefit the welfare recipient. That benefit would be the "management of and improved care" for the welfare family while the family is living off another person's paid-in tax money.

The government should use part of the minimum 10 percent tax money collected from welfare checks to teach those living on welfare how to live a better life. That doesn't mean buying a newer vehicle to replace an older one.

It should be mandatory for welfare recipients first to attend classes and then implement what is taught in those classes in order to remain in the welfare program. At least that should be the inference. The classes could be administered at the local welfare office, which is familiar to the recipient.

Most classes would cover everyday commonsense behavior. Something all citizens could use from time to time. Classes would demonstrate how to operate a household more efficiently, thereby saving the welfare recipient time and money. Another aspect of life most citizens could use.

One of the reasons for these "everyday commonsense classes" being taught to welfare recipients is the hope that children in the home will be better prepared to function well at home, school, and in all aspects of their young lives.

What would that mean to the individual, family, neighborhood, and in general, all of American society?

It should mean all-around improvement within the family and neighborhood atmosphere. That would be an exceptional benefit to the welfare recipient. Fewer problems at school. Fewer doctor visits. Improved community-police relations. And less overall cost to society.

The classes or studies being referred to are similar to those listed in Part Three, Chapter Three of this book. They were listed under Groups A, B, and C. There the reference was about the need for high school students to be prepared as broadly as possible before entering the working world. What's being suggested here for welfare recipients is not a whole lot different.

Welfare recipients need to improve themselves and their households by learning and understanding certain behavior, just like everyone else. Perhaps the class should be referred to as a reminder or refresher course.

Welfare recipients should be forced to take classes in order to learn or be reminded of the following subject matters:

1. How to budget money so household needs are met as best as possible.

2. How to be frugal with money and utilities.

3. How to best react to or deal with police matters.

4. The benefits of good manners.

5. The benefits of good grooming.

6. The benefits of common courtesy.

7. The benefits of proper appearance.

8. The benefits of discipline.

9. The benefits of and understanding of taking responsibility.

10. The benefits of and meaning of good morality.

Welfare recipients mastering the above common-sense areas would generally find everyday life much improved. That's a benefit for the entire family. It may even help or enable the recipient to progress from welfare existence to being gainfully employed. A welcome change that should be cheered by all.

Getting off welfare is the target. Getting paid to work is the way.

Dirty Dozen #9

Unions ... It's Your Country and Your Country Needs Your Help

SPEAKING DIRECTLY TO Union Men and Union Women of the United States:

Can you double production in the same amount of work time? Can you match or exceed the product quality of any competitor in the world? Can you agree some work rules previously insisted upon by union bosses, need to change drastically or be eliminated completely?

It won't be easy. You'll have to work faster, harder, and smarter. You'll have to change some work rules that are very favorable, too favorable, to workers. Take fewer breaks. You'll have to cross-train and then cross-work for efficiency and expediency. You'll have to start working at the exact starting time and stop working at the exact quitting time. Start a minute early, quit a minute late is even better. It's not for you or your company. **It's for your country. It's for your country. It's for your country.**

Union members, you should also understand it will do little good for your country if you bust your butt for one, two, or three years and then strike for one, two, or three months. Foreign competitors around the world love long American work stoppages. They provide those competitors an opportunity to assure customers of an uninterrupted supply and sell them more product. Competition is a business and production contest to see who's still standing at the end. A survival-of-the-fittest game ... except it's not a game. It's a struggle for business-life over business-death.

Union workers work in companies. Companies are managed by management. If the workers increase production as stipulated above, management will be thrilled. Managers may even appear to have exceptional management skills because the company greatly increased output. That's fine. But management should not profit monetarily unless the workers do so equally. What management should do is prepare to work late. Maybe very late.

The extra hard work commitment by *all personnel* is to help stabilize and save the country ... not the company. Remember ... "It's for your country."

If that concept, country not company, is not recognized by all ... then foreign competitors will continue to lead America to the whipping shed.

The article below, "5 Reasons Unions Are Bad For America," sums up fairly well what has happened on a wide scale in the United States. It's not a pretty picture. The article dumps a load on unions. It presents information that should be known and understood by all. All ... being union members, company leaders, government leaders, and ordinary citizens. It doesn't mean one group is all wrong and another group all right. Usually, there are two sides to every story. Sometimes three sides.

What is needed is for all concerned to focus on saving the country from financial ruin. Some will give more and some will give up more than others. Nevertheless, if there's victory in reaching the objective, all would celebrate equally. And that objective is: Saving the country from financial ruin and creating very good jobs well beyond current employment. The opposite would be intolerable and especially so for regular working citizens. They probably wouldn't be working at all.

Serious anti-union, but pro-taxpayer, reasons follow:

ARTICLE FOUND AT: townhall.com/columnists/johnhawkins/2011/03/08/5_reasons_unions_are_bad_for_america
ARTICLE WRITTEN BY: John Hawkins
DATE: MARCH 08, 2011
TITLE: 5 REASONS Unions Are Bad for America

> At one time in this country, there were few workplace safety laws, few restraints on employers, and incredibly exploitive working conditions that ranged from slavery, to share cropping, to putting children in dangerous working conditions. Unions, to their everlasting credit, helped play an important role in leveling the playing field for workers.
>
> However, as the laws changed, there was less and less need for unions. Because of that, union membership shrank. In response, the unions became more explicitly involved in politics. Over time, they managed to co-opt the Democratic Party, pull their strings, and rewrite our labor laws in their favor.
>
> As Lord Acton noted, "Power tends to corrupt," and that has certainly been true for the unions. Unions have become selfish, extremely greedy, and even thuggish in their never-ending quest to take in as much as they can for themselves, at the expense of everyone else who crosses their path.
>
> That's why today, unions have changed from organizations that "look out for the little guy" into the largest, most rapacious special interest

group in the entire country. Where unions go, disaster usually follows. Just to name a few examples:

*1) **Unions are severely damaging whole industries:** How is it that GM and Chrysler got into such lousy shape that they had to be bailed out? There's a simple answer: The unions. The massive pensions the car companies paid out raised their costs so much that they were limited to building more expensive cars to try to get their money back.*

They couldn't even do a great job of building those cars because utterly ridiculous union rules prevented them from using their labor efficiently. America created the automobile industry, but American unions are strangling it to death. Unions also wrecked the steel and textile industries and have helped drive manufacturing jobs overseas. They're crippling the airline industry and, of course, we can't forget that...

*2) **Unions are ruining public education:** Every few years, it's the same old story. The teachers' unions claim that public education in this country is dramatically underfunded and if they just had more money, they could turn it around. Taxpayer money then pours into our schools like a waterfall and....there's no improvement. A few years later, when people have forgotten the last spending spree on education, the process is repeated.*

However, the real problem with our education system in this country is the teachers' unions. They do everything possible to prevent schools not only from firing lousy teachers, but also from rewarding talented teachers. Merit pay? The unions hate it. Private schools? Even though everyone knows they deliver a better education than our public schools, unions fight to keep as many kids as possible locked in failing public schools. In Wisconsin, we've had whole schools shutting down so that lazy teachers can waste their time protesting on the taxpayers' dime. Want to improve education in this country? Then you've got to take on the teachers' unions.

*3) **Unions are costing you billions of tax dollars:** Let's put it plain and simple: Government workers shouldn't be allowed to unionize. Period.*

Why?

Because you elect representatives to look out for your interests.

It's obviously in your interest to pay as little as possible to government workers, to keep their benefits as low as possible, and to hire as few of them as possible to do the job. However, because the Democratic Party and the unions are in bed with each other, this entire process has been turned on its ear. Instead of looking out for your interests, Democrats try to hire as many government workers as possible, pay them as much as possible, and give them benefits that are as generous as possible, all so that union workers will do more to get them re-elected.

In other words, the Democratic Party and the unions are engaged in an open conspiracy to defraud the American taxpayer. There's no way that the American people should allow that to continue.

4) Unions are fundamentally anti-democratic: *How in the world did we get to the point where people can be forced to join a union just to get a job at certain places? Then, after they're dragooned into the union, they have no choice other than to pay dues that are used for political activities which the unwilling dues-paying member may oppose.*

Add to that the fact that the Democrats and the government unions collaborate to subvert democracy at the expense of the taxpayer and it's not a pretty picture. Worse yet, unions have gotten so voracious that they even want to do away with the secret ballot, via card check, so they can openly bully people into joining unions. The way unions behave in this country is undemocratic, un-American, and it should trouble anyone who cares about freedom and individual rights.

5) Government unions are bankrupting cities and states: *Government unions have bled billions from taxpayers nationally, but the damage they're doing on the local level is even worse. We have cities and states all across the country that are so behind on their bills that there have been genuine discussions about bankruptcy. There are a lot of irresponsible financial policies that have helped contribute to that sorry state-of-affairs, but unquestionably, the biggest backbreakers can be directly traced back to the unions.*

As the Washington Times has noted, union pensions are crushing budgets all across the country.

Yet it comes as little surprise that the same profligacy that pervades the corridors of federal power infects this country's 87,000 state, county and municipal governments and school districts. By 2013, the amount of retirement money promised to employees of these public entities will exceed cash on hand by more than a trillion dollars.

So, what happens when these pensions can't be paid? They will come to the taxpayers with their hands out. When they stroll forward with their beggar's bowl in hand, the American people should keep their wallets in their pockets. That may not seem fair, but the public sector union members have gotten a great deal at everyone else's expense for a long time and if somebody has to take a haircut, and they do, it should be the union members instead of the taxpayers they've been bilking for so long.

Was the article too harsh on unions? Maybe so. Maybe no.

The article was reprinted in full because it is a major wakeup call for all taxpayers. It should be the same for government leaders, and even union members.

Government unions have often been too harsh on taxpayers and industry unions have often been too harsh on companies.

All collective bargaining negotiators should first review these words: foresight, common sense, good judgement, reasonable, and end-result. Then negotiate.

Government union bosses and other assorted government cronies can start by focusing on the increasing number of city bankruptcies. Industry union bosses can start the return-to-glory production increase by agreeing to eliminate asinine work rules.

Company executives should then find great excitement in higher sales and higher profits. Great excitement is fine. Higher profits should bring excitement to workers as well as owners. That means workers, especially when they are company share owners, should be rewarded with added financial benefits along with an expansion of jobs in the domestic workplace.

Common sense bargaining … let's light it up in bright lights: "The country has returned to fiscal responsibility and manufacturing greatness, which was achieved because of sacrifice and extra hard work from the Unions of America."

Dirty Dozen #10

Made in the USA

"MADE IN THE USA" used to be stamped on everything. American workers were busy. American citizens were happy. People around the world appreciated our ingenuity while at the same time they were envious of our manufacturing ability. And that was fine until over the years it all changed. Many would say … reversed.

Detroit is a glaring example. Are Detroit citizens happy? Is Detroit buzzing with factory activity? Just listen. Walk down any busy street and listen. Can you hear citizens singing and automobile manufacturing plants humming that old familiar jingle? How did it go? "See the USA in your Chevrolet," and back in those happy days, the jingle could have continued this way: "See the USA in your Chevrolet, made in the USA."

The United States somehow needs to bring back the longer version of that catchy jingle. If that happened, you can be assured the workers in Detroit and across the country would be singing in the streets.

But today, you can't sing the jingle. It just wouldn't sound right because it doesn't rhyme. Try it yourself. 'See the USA in your Chevrolet, made in Japan.' Or it could be China or Mexico or Canada or Germany. At the very least, parts in the Chevrolet are made here and there and everywhere.

What happened? As a general example, here's what happened: We, the United States, used to sell little parts to China; then we sold bigger parts to China; then we sold trucks to China; then we laughed and sold our emerging competitor a whole truck factory so we wouldn't have to be bothered with frequent shipping; then we sold "know-how" to China; then China stole advanced know-how from us.

Now there's today. China continues to steal advanced know-how technology from the United States. China manufactures trucks and sells them to

Chinese citizens and anyone else who will listen. You can apply a similar scenario to Japan, except it sells its trucks to Americans and everybody else.

Especially damaging to the United States is the theft of advanced-anything by anybody at any time. As always, the usual suspect continues to be China, but others help themselves as well. When the United States loses trade secrets or modern technology by theft, or in any other way, it shouldn't be a surprise when fewer and fewer products are marked "Made in the USA."

Something else happened that has little to do with China directly or with other mass-producers of product. But it does have to do with our Detroit example.

Reinforcing what was said in Dirty Dozen #9 ... over the years, the union group UAW (United Auto Workers) got too big for its britches. It packed on a 100 pounds of burdensome work rules. You might say all those unnecessary rules caused vehicle production's backside to split-out. The cost of labor in Detroit went through the roof. Vehicle costs went up and sales went down.

It wasn't just auto manufacturers but many industries that suffered the same fate. Union work rules and higher costs were damaging, but they can't be blamed for all manufacturing problems in the United States. There's plenty of blame to go around. And, maybe "blame" is the wrong word.

The overall point is ... the United States is losing jobs. China, Mexico, and many others are gaining jobs. "Made in the USA" is fading. That trend must reverse, and union members could lead the charge. Not union bosses ... union members.

Union members could sound the battle cry, "Made in the USA. Made in the USA. Made in the USA." Citizens should answer ... with buying action.

As noted below, the current trend in manufacturing is not good for the country or the labor unions:

INFORMATION FOUND AT: www.citizen.org/documents/manufacturing-job-loss.pdf

ARTICLE PRODUCED BY: Public Citizen

DATE: NO DATE

TITLE: RESOURCES TO Track Trade-Related Job Loss for Your State and District

> *Nearly 5 million U.S. manufacturing jobs—one out of every four—have been lost since implementation of the North American Free Trade Agreement (NAFTA) and the World Trade Organization (WTO). Since NAFTA took effect, more than 55,000 American manufacturing facilities have closed.*

Other estimates suggest a higher number of closings, depending on how manufacturers are classified such as to size. That trend, if not reversed, will end badly for the United States.

While labor unions forced detrimental rules into the workplace, thus pushing costs higher, sales slowed, and most wages in the country stagnated.

At the same time, China was introducing workers to the concept of working hard, very hard, for a few dollars a day and then living a better life. Labor-favorable work rules were few. The end result was low cost.

Perhaps you've noticed ... buy anything today, check the country of origin, and it says, "Made in China." Whose fault is that?

China is so busy, it's subbing work out to Viet Nam. Viet Nam nearly disappeared a few decades back, but it is now winning the manufacturing war. Who would've ever guessed Viet Nam would be out-manufacturing the United States in anything.

Earlier in this book, China's manufacturing of vehicles and aircraft was discussed. An apparent bright future for China.

America needs that same bright future. It would mean more jobs, a better lifestyle, and continued mobility for American citizens. More cars, buses, trains and planes. Mobility, all over the place. But ... how comfortable would Americans be, sitting back in their cushy seats, seeing the phrase "Made in China" stamped on their modes of transportation?

What does it say to American citizens when they enter any big store such as Target and the labels say, "Made in China, Made in China, Made in Viet Nam, Made in China, Made in Mexico, Made in India, Made in China, etc.?"

Even in grocery stores, more and more, we find edible products from foreign countries. They are grown there, processed there, shipped here, and then finally sold in the local grocery store. A number of grocery store items are even from China. China, mentioned again, because that country is literally on the other side of the world, and it still supplies us with ... everything.

Everything? Most would say, "It can't supply us with everything. Obviously, we still must go to the local barbershop. That will never change, right?" Perhaps "obviously" is a bit strong. The same might be said of "never."

The average men's haircut in a big city is approaching $30, including tip. Some cities are higher. How long will it be before a sign shows up announcing Chinese haircuts in ten minutes for $10? Does that sound farfetched and impossible? Don't bet on it. Someday it will just be a matter of pricing and equipment availability. Don't laugh. Read on.

It's now possible to have your brain "operated on" in Fargo, North Dakota by a Chinese doctor from Hong Kong who is physically working in a London hospital. Farfetched? Yes. Impossible? No. Has it happened? Probably, or definitely in some types of surgery. It's a remote type of surgery and it's done every day. The doctor is usually close-by, but not necessarily.

Haircuts could be done in the same way except for two problems. The equipment is still too expensive and the price of haircuts is still too low. It's possible, perhaps probable, the Chinese are working on both right now.

United States citizens must get back to buying products stamped "Made in the USA." An extremely simple concept, but extremely difficult to implement.

Three very basic reasons why it's difficult for many Americans to buy American-made goods:

1. Some buyers must consider cost. China is less expensive.

2. Some buyers never check labels. Labels read China.

3. Sellers stock what sells. Regardless of origin.

American citizens need to be aware of and concentrate on all three reasons because those reasons explain what shoppers must overcome at any large store. Buying goods marked "Made in the USA" is no longer an easy task.

The interesting article referenced below lists ten good reasons to buy American-made goods as opposed to foreign-made goods when the goods are found together.

Listed in reverse order below:

ARTICLE FOUND AT: madeinusaforever.com/toptenreasons.html

ARTICLE WRITTEN BY: Todd Lipscomb

DATE: NO DATE

TITLE: TOP TEN Reasons to Buy American

> *"Buy American!" might sound like nothing more than a slogan advanced by American manufacturers to sell products made in the USA, but the truth is that there are many reasons to consider buying American-made clothing, American-made toys, and other US-manufactured goods. We've listed just a few of the benefits of buying American below:*

> *Top Ten Reasons to Buy USA Made Products:*

> *10) Foreign labor standards allow unsafe worker conditions in many countries. When you buy American you support not only American manufacturers but also American workers, safe working conditions, and child labor laws.*

9) Jobs shipped abroad almost never return. When you buy goods made in the USA, you help keep the American economy growing.

8) US manufacturing processes are much cleaner for the environment than many other countries; many brands sold here are produced in countries using dangerous, heavily polluting processes. When you purchase American-made product, you know that you're helping to keep the world a little cleaner for your children.

7) Many countries have no minimum wage restrictions, or the minimum wage is outrageously low. When you choose products made in the USA, you contribute to the payment of an honest day's wages for an honest day's work.

6) The growing lack of USA ability to manufacture many products is strategically unsound. When you seek out American-made goods, you foster American independence.

5) The huge US trade deficit leads to massive, unsustainable borrowing from other countries. Debt isn't good for you and it isn't good for America.

4) Foreign product safety standards are low. For example, poisonous levels of lead are in tens of millions of toys shipped to the USA. When you buy toys and other goods made in the USA, you can be confident that American consumer protection laws and safety standards are in place to protect your family.

3) Lack of minimum wage, worker safety, or environmental pollution controls in many countries undermines the concept of "fair and free trade". No Western nation can ultimately compete on price with a country willing to massively exploit and pollute its own people. When you buy only American-made products, you insist on a higher standard.

2) Factories and money are shifting to countries not friendly to the USA or democracy. When you avoid imported goods in favor of American-made items, you help ensure that the United States doesn't find its access to vital goods impacted by political conflict.

1) As the US manufacturing ability fades, future generations of US citizens will be unable to find relevant jobs. Buy American and help keep your friends and neighbors—and even yourself—earning a living wage.

Some strong reasons? Yes. Some easy to change? No.

It makes no difference. US citizens need to change by buying more products marked "Made in the USA." US manufacturers must do their part as well.

American products of good quality and a competitive price will sell well in the United States and in foreign markets. That "quality and price" must be achieved.

What if a buyer can't find certain products "Made in the USA"? Obviously, he or she must buy what is needed. If Americans have a vast choice of similar products from many countries, then the preferred selection that best serves the United States is in this order: Buy products made in the USA, then Canada, and then Mexico. There's reason for that order. Canada imports the most goods from the United States. Mexico is close behind. And they're both close neighbors. Exports and imports between the United States and Canada and between the United States and Mexico are nearly equal.

US imports from China are more than four times the amount of US exports to China. However, the figures do fluctuate considerably with the price of petroleum. Even though the United States and China are very large trading partners, anyone can see there's a large imbalance. That's not good for the United States. It's as if we are at the mercy of the Chinese. Sooner or later, the United States will need some special product from China, and China will be in a position to increase the price drastically or even terminate supply. What if China was the only supplier of titanium, which is used in high-performance aircraft? Could that interfere with our security?

All Americans need to relearn … and then start humming this tune again "See the USA in your Chevrolet made in the USA." Or, at least, the last four words.

Dirty Dozen #11

Post Office or Any Government-Owned or Rented Building

"Excuse me, could you tell me where the post office is located?"

"Yes, just go two blocks that way, turn right, go past two abandoned commercial buildings and it's on your right. You can't miss it. It's the largest and newest building in town. Some people around here refer to it as the town's Taj Mahal."

What's wrong with that picture?

Too often it's accurate. Not necessarily the Taj Mahal part, but the idea that in many towns the post office happens to be a sizable, attractive, and newer building. Sometimes the post office is the largest and newest place in town. It just doesn't seem necessary. It's as if the average citizen, the local government, and the federal government forgot the country is $20,000,000,000,000 in debt. Is that massive debt figure forgettable? Apparently, yes. When will financial commonsense return to the United States? It must be soon or it will be too late.

In the above scenario, a stranger driving through a small town is directed to the post office and passes two abandoned buildings. Would it have been less expensive to remodel one of the abandoned buildings into the post office?

Every town has buildings, very often vacant, suitable for an updated post office. Or for many other government functions. It's very probable the cost would be less and often substantially less.

A fair argument might be made against remodeling in favor of purchasing a lot in the perfect area and building an attractive building that will serve the public for many years. But those fair arguments are not remotely close to matching the extreme need to reverse the $20,000,000,000,000 national debt. That debt reduction must start immediately and be applied to every aspect of government. Why not start with something as simple as maintaining or expanding current post offices or at least refraining from going overboard by making any new post office the town's Taj Mahal?

Some important aspects about post office buildings must be considered before passing judgement on this area of the government's operation.

1. Today, post offices are supposed to fund all operations from their own income generated by the sale of stamps and other services. No tax collected funds are "supposed" to be used.

2. Post offices lose billions of dollars in most years. In 2012, post offices lost about $16 billion. In 2013 and 2014, the loss was $4-5 billion.

3. Post offices receive huge government direct and indirect subsidies every year.

4. Other unusual methods are used to prop up post office operations, and those methods indirectly remove potential tax money from normal government income, which then affects regular citizens. Examples: post offices pay no property taxes, no toll fees, and vehicles are exempt from registration fees. Post offices borrow money at extra low interest rates, which means others pay a tiny fraction more to make up the difference.

5. Post office workers belong to very strong unions and receive very good wages, great benefits, and, as with other government employees, early and lucrative retirement benefits. If post office workers' retirement benefits compared to private sector benefits … stamps would be less expensive.

6. About 30,000 post office buildings are in this country, but only about 10 percent of them are owned by the Post Office.

There may be some surprises listed above for the average citizen. Many think the Post Office is strictly a federal government operation, but the government says the Post Office stands on its own. You'll have to judge for yourself on that one, considering the billions in government subsidies paid to operate post offices.

One surprise appears to stand out more than the others. Post office buildings are mostly not owned by the government. Who readily thought that?

On the surface, many citizens would think that is good. Somebody else is building these elaborate places for postal operations and spending his own money, not taxpayer money, for a building that upon occasion is referred to as the town's Taj Mahal. But citizens need to remember that when someone provides a building for another, rent is paid and rent tends to increase over time. One reason for that is the almost constant increase in real estate value. Buildings can double in value over time. Rents can also double over time.

What does this mean for the government, the building owner, and the average tax-paying citizen?

It means the government will miss out on any value appreciation of the building. It means government rental costs will constantly increase. Other building maintenance costs may also flow through to the government.

It means the building owner will receive the financial benefits of real estate ownership instead of the government. Usually a building's mortgage is paid-off over time, but rents and rent increases continue forever.

It means the average citizen will pay more and more for stamps. Stamps used to cost one or two pennies. Now they're about fifty cents. Long distance phone calls used to cost $10. Now they're about fifty cents. Those estimates aren't exact, but the figures do say something about government versus private industry business sense.

The Post Office was used only as an example because all citizens are familiar with their post office. The local Social Security office, Department of Motor Vehicles, and most government buildings could have substituted for the Post Office. It makes little difference whether the building is owned or leased. All are supported by taxpayer funds. All have banker's hours which is curious.

New, elaborate, or fancy buildings, often in a high rent district, are *not* necessary when numerous vacant buildings are available for a fraction of the cost.

Often when the government needs, or thinks it needs, another government building, it contracts to build it new. The government buys land, often but not always, in a high-cost area, contracts to build, and before long old and new employees occupy the building.

To clarify that … employees generally occupy the expensive new building during the hours of 8 a.m. to 5 p.m.

That's exactly one-third of a day, disregarding lunch hour, breaks, and empty weekends. It's costly to average taxpayers, but especially so in newer or more expensive buildings. Few hours used for work, many hours used for heat and air conditioning. Additional waste.

What's this all about? It's simple. The federal government and the citizens of the United States owe $20,000,000,000,000 and that debt may end the decent lifestyle most Americans enjoy.

So why don't politicians who run the government stop building or renting expensive buildings for general or routine government work? Millions of vacant or abandoned structures exist and are dying for a sale. The majority are houses. But tens of thousands of empty buildings would be suitable for much of the government's work. "Suitable" includes an okay location and a sound structure. The buildings would need limited to moderate rehabilitation, but the cost would not be comparable to finding a building lot, arguing about permits, and building new. The same contractors can probably be used for new or rehab work. Contractors would be busy either way. The cost saved could be enormous and the immediate area revitalized. Cost savings should be the objective. Area improvement a bonus.

Adopting used buildings for government operations will save money for taxpayers. Building sellers will have money to put into circulation. The government could do the same thing with vehicles. It buys new vehicles by the thousands every year. Why not buy two-year old cars and trucks? Huge discounts. Regular citizens do it all the time. Smart. Saves money by eliminating early depreciation. The same new-car sellers sell used vehicles. Over time, manufacturers would manufacture about the same number of vehicles since the same number of vehicles would be needed across the country regardless of age or use. The government saves money. Regular citizens save money. The vehicle sellers make money, and the government workers have a fairly new car to ride around in during the work day.

This kind of change in thinking is needed before politicians drive the country over the debt cliff. Surely, most people would agree. But still, we accelerate toward the financial abyss.

And, what about that 8 a.m. to 5 p.m. work time? Government workers make good money and retire earlier than most. Assign some of them to a second shift. What are they going to do ... quit? A second shift would be meaningful.

It would save money and increase service. Government buildings rehabbed or built new could be much smaller. Same for parking lots. First shift workers' vehicles drive out at 4:01 p.m. and second shift vehicles drive in at 4:59 p.m. Isn't that about the way many government workers operate anyway? That attitude has to change as well. Arrive anytime, but start exactly on time. Finish work exactly at quitting time. Not fifteen minutes early so you can wash your clean hands.

Many government workers love to say, "We're here to serve the public." Well, often the public is busy from 8 a.m. to 5 p.m. during the week. They can't easily get to the government department during typical government working hours. But if the government department was open for second shift hours, including Saturday morning, then government workers could truly serve the public much better. Smaller building, less overhead costs, and better service to the public. All needed changes. Who could argue with that?

Avoiding a national financial collapse will take a team effort. All government buildings, and all government workers, need to economize in any way possible. Government caused the $20,000,000,000,000 problem. Government should fix the problem, or at the very least, government should set an example that at least goes in the direction of fixing the problem.

The Post Office is very visible to the public so it was used as an example. That example should be carried to every government building and operation.

Dirty Dozen #12

The Russians are coming … the Russians are coming.

WELL, IT'S ABOUT time. Why have they waited so long?

When will we get some peace in the world? American citizens are tired of the frightening headlines we see day after day. It's as if the Russian government and the United States government constantly do things that end up in headlines. It's absolutely maddening. Do they both want a world war that could end civilization? These federal governments … what good are they anyway?

Federal government leaders should concentrate on national security and whatever is best for all citizens today, tomorrow, and twenty-five years from tomorrow. Instead, they generate anxiety about matters that threaten the lives of citizens every day. Damning headlines are damaging to the psyche.

Special note: This section, in referencing "headlines," disregards the media's glaring role in grandiose headlines.

Too many headlines very closely resemble the following phrases: Russian planes flew within a few feet of an American war ship, Russian hackers hacked into State Department computers, Russia launches super-secret submarine, Russia unveils Satan-2 missile able to wipe out Texas, Russia is trying to hide something from the CIA, Norway hosting US troops will upset Russia, Russian bombers fly a few miles off California coast, US intercepts Russian bombers near coast of Alaska, US Army chief suggests US will win war with Russia, Russia gains by re-opening bases in Cuba and Viet Nam. Are we doomed? Sounds like it.

Those phrases are all similar to actual and recent national headlines. A hundred more could have been used. All suggest the possibility of armed conflict for American and Russian youth. Surely there is a better way forward.

What if American citizens traded places with Russian citizens?

The heading above, "The Russians are coming," could be thought of as a true welcoming phrase for Russians coming to this country. It sounds a whole lot better than the noise about Russian planes buzzing our ships. That's an explosive international incident waiting to happen. And then what?

While the US and Russian governments play chess with each other, perhaps an intelligent group of leaders could get together and establish an exchange program focusing on "average middle-class families." At this point, the guess is middle-class families would be more suitable than very poor or very wealthy families regardless of whether they reside in Russia or the United States.

The program's desired purpose would be to demonstrate to each other and the rest of the world that regular citizens from different countries are very, very similar to each other in most ways. In this case, we are speaking of Russians and Americans. If a family from each country passed the other on the sidewalk and each smiled or nodded at the other, neither family would guess the other is a foreign family. So what is the problem? No problem … with regular citizens.

If US and Russian citizens are so similar, why are we always pointing fingers at each other and arguing about something?

The answer to that question is quite simple. We're not.

Only the two governments are stinking each other up … not the people.

Regrettably, if the two governments get into a serious squabble, such as shooting at each other, only regular citizens from each country will be in the line of fire. Both federal governments will be sitting on big soft cushions moving their chess pawns around. The only noise in the room will be the jingling of ice.

Here's a better way to mate: several leaders from business, education, community, government, and an exchange-program advisor meet together as a committee and formulate a family-exchange program. Representatives from each country attend. This is done all the time, but on a much narrower basis such as business or student-exchange. There may be many student-exchanges, but that's one student, not a family unit. Exchange students are high school or college age. Their agenda is quite different.

Families could apply for the program by offering certain criteria needed for selection and approval. Start with several families in different areas of each country and strive to reach hundreds and then thousands in the future. The individual experiences and outcomes could be covered by media and distributed as widely as possible in each respective country. Problems will always exist such as income for the family and schooling for children. Those matters can be worked out and may not be perfect. Perfect is rarely normal.

The privately operated program could be called, "The Russians Are Coming," which would generate attention in itself. The program would arrange for Russian families to come to the United States for six months. They would stay in another exchange-family's house and live life as similar to an American family's life as possible. Houses within the entire program would be fungible. The Russian family or the American family, would do as it pleased and be responsible for all living expenses in its host country with the exception of rent. The rent or the monthly house payment would be paid by the actual home-owner. The Russian family would still be responsible for its own rent or house payment back in Russia. It's an exchange-family swapping houses with another family. This family-exchange program would amount to an exploration of typical family lifestyles in each host country. That aspect of the program is key. **The end result should be to demonstrate that everyday life for a Russian family is very similar to that of an American family. Both eat, drink, dance, study, sleep, work, play, kiss, and raise kids. Regular citizen family life. "Regular citizens" have little interest in pointing missiles at each other.**

Each family would need some initial assistance in such a new setting. Respective governments would have knowledge of the program and specific requirements might need to be followed, but it would be a private program. Government involvement would lead to unnecessary interference and the usual added cost that would hamper the program and its intent.

Even a very large scale family-exchange program doesn't mean the scary headlines would immediately change. But over time the attitude of the population in each country would change. More and more citizens would understand it's strictly the federal governments, through their actions, who propagate scary headlines for their own amusement and everybody's confusion.

Regular citizens in both countries, through a family-exchange program, would have a better understanding and appreciation of each other and could remain at peace … forever. Politicians be damned.

Dirty Dozen #13

Volunteers ... the Difference Between Failure and Success?

VOLUNTEERS ... WHAT good are they?

They help those in need, they get the job done, they save money for others, and they feel good about all of it. Measure those values against those clamoring for another raise or else.

Volunteering withstands the usual questions all the time. Those questions may be very basic, but their answers are quite varied. About 300 million variations. That's about the number of people in the United States excluding those who spend much of the day in bed. The very young and the very old.

Who ... should be a volunteer?

That's easy. Every man, woman, and child who is a citizen or resident of the United States. There's nothing like "100 percent participation" to get the job done.

Is that possible? Yes. Probable? No. Easy? No. Silly? No.

What ... would volunteers do?

That's easy. Volunteers could pick up a paper-wad from the sidewalk or urgently travel to a disaster site and work with the Federal Emergency Management Agency (FEMA) to save lives and assist the area in returning to normal. And anything and everything in between those two extremes.

When ... would volunteers volunteer?

That's easy. Every single day is available. Volunteering doesn't have to be every day for every volunteer. But there are a lot of paper-wads lying around, so someone walking down the street could spot-a-speck at any time.

Disasters are fewer than paper-wads. Trained volunteers are often needed with little warning. They could be away from home for several days, and they could make a difference in the outcome of a disaster situation.

Where … would volunteers volunteer?

That's easy. Volunteers are needed everywhere. Paper-wad duty. Disaster duty. Local senior center. Neighborhood beautification. Front yard clean-up.

Everywhere means as close as their own front yard. Volunteers could walk out the front door and volunteer to maintain their own yards. That would benefit them, their neighbors, their community, and their country.

Why … be a volunteer?

That's easy. Unless you want all the many personal reasons. Easy … if you just want general reasons that apply to almost any volunteering. Those reasons are listed below. They come from the University of California at San Diego and they're listed as "reasons to do community service":

ARTICLE FOUND AT: https://students.ucsd.edu/student-life/involvement/community/reasons.html

DATE: AUGUST 2, 2016

TITLE: COMMUNITY SERVICE: Top 10 Reasons to Volunteer

REASONS, WITH SOME explanation listed in reverse order:

> **#10: *It's good for you.***
>
> *Volunteering provides physical and mental rewards. It:*
>
> - **Reduces stress:** *Experts report that when you focus on someone other than yourself, it interrupts usual tension-producing patterns.*
> - **Makes you healthier:** *Moods and emotions, like optimism, joy, and control over one's fate, strengthen the immune system.*
>
> **#9: *It saves resources.***
>
> *Volunteering provides valuable community services so more money can be spent on local improvements.*
>
> - *The estimated value of a volunteer's time in California is $26.87 per hour based on the* Corporation for National & Community Service.
>
> **#8: *Volunteers gain professional experience.***
>
> *You can test out a career.*
>
> **#7: *It brings people together.***
>
> *As a volunteer you assist in:*
>
> - *Uniting people from diverse backgrounds to work toward a common goal*
> - *Building camaraderie and teamwork*

#6: *It promotes personal growth and self esteem.*

Understanding community needs helps foster empathy and self-efficacy.

#5: *Volunteering strengthens your community.*

As a volunteer you help:

- *Support families (daycare and eldercare)*
- *Improve schools (tutoring, literacy)*
- *Support youth (mentoring and after-school programs)*
- *Beautify the community (beach and park cleanups)*

#4: *You learn a lot.*

Volunteers learn things like these:

- **Self:** *Volunteers discover hidden talents that may change your view on your self worth.*
- **Government:** *Through working with local non-profit agencies, volunteers learn about the functions and operation of our government.*
- **Community:** *Volunteers gain knowledge of local resources available to solve community needs.*

#3: *You get a chance to give back.*

People like to support community resources that they use themselves or that benefit people they care about.

#2: *Volunteering encourages civic responsibility.*

Community service and volunteerism are an investment in our community and the people who live in it.

#1: *You make a difference.*

Every person counts!

The above reasons demonstrate that volunteering yields many personal benefits for the volunteer.

There are also nationalistic reasons to volunteer.

The country faces a monstrous national deficit. It's been mentioned numerous times in previous chapters. It's also been stated that all citizens must participate in reducing the deficit. Volunteering, in certain ways, can save money and actually help reduce government spending.

Adventuresome citizens could volunteer for critical, tedious, dirty and even dangerous jobs. Volunteering to help FEMA is a very good example.

There are thousands of employed FEMA workers at this time. They rush into disaster zones and work long hours to stabilize an area hit by hurricanes, floods, tornados, and other happenings judged to be disasters. Their work is critical during difficult times. At least, that is the common belief.

But what about the slow times? Those times in-between disasters. Surely, there are light-work times that can't compare to the rush for hurricane preparation and then the agonizing recovery efforts.

Slow times at FEMA require less than half the number of employees as do the frantic times after a major disaster. Isn't that the perfect time to have volunteers at-the-ready. Just a phone call away. Or today, another type signaling device that provides all information needed.

In small towns, fire departments are often volunteers. A signal goes off alerting volunteers to report immediately. Volunteer firemen, already trained, arrive at the station and respond to a local fire. It does help that fires in small towns are infrequent.

The system works because people have volunteered, received training, and desire to serve their community.

These volunteers are not paid, but there may be expense reimbursement. Any pay would change the volunteer to an employee.

Volunteers save their community a lot of money compared to a fire department with full-time employees who spend much of their time sitting around the firehouse. The volunteer fire department works well in small towns, but not in bigger cities because more residents and structures produce enough fires to require a full-time fire department.

Fires occur frequently in cities. Disasters occur infrequently. Disasters might be equated with fewer fires in small towns, thus requiring fewer full-time employees. Volunteers can fill that important need exactly when needed.

If disasters are infrequent, then FEMA could learn something from small town fire departments. FEMA should have *many* trained volunteers who are ready, willing, and able to respond when needed. That time being just before, during, and after a disaster. That's a time when people readily come together to help one another. Americans do it all the time. If offered the chance to volunteer officially, they would surely do so during any disaster affecting fellow citizens.

So what about FEMA? FEMA is part of the newest, one of the largest, and one of the most expensive departments of our federal government, namely, the Homeland Security Department.

Why doesn't FEMA use volunteers?

FEMA might say that it does use volunteers. It just doesn't call them volunteers. It calls them Reservists. They're called up when there's a disaster, and they might work for thirty days. That sounds great ... right up until

the time you find out the Reservists are paid fairly well and they get transportation and housing plus a large stipend for food.

True volunteers from around a disaster area would help without pay. They could help FEMA, but they'd be called volunteers not reservists. True volunteers would assist fellow citizens and yield true savings for taxpayers.

They would have to be trained in advance and would need specific type clothing identifying them as FEMA volunteers. They would work near home.

The volunteer system to help FEMA might start in this way:

1. Volunteers are background-selected from around the regional area.

2. They are initially trained for a week.

3. They attend a one-day refresher meeting every three months.

4. They are assigned general type disaster work, not technical.

5. They have a specific supervisor and monthly email training updates.

Much of volunteer disaster work would be general support work, but also very necessary work. These volunteers would serve their own communities.

Someone has to perform the grunt work such as cleanup, moving supplies, directing site traffic, and assisting full-time FEMA personnel with fulfilling their jobs. The work might be labor intensive and not very exotic, but it has to be done. Volunteers can do that work, especially working in their home area or region.

Over the years, FEMA has had its share of criticism. Much of it deserved. Using citizen volunteers will not eliminate all the usual criticisms, but at least the overall cost could be substantially less. That aspect, less cost, for any government operation, should be forever praiseworthy.

Something to ponder: Could it ever be that volunteers actually perform better than some FEMA personnel? Volunteers are working for personal reasons and would likely prefer to be remembered for a job well done.

FEMA employees are government employees who may see their jobs as just jobs to obtain as much money as possible while en route to one of those early and lucrative government pensions.

Consequently, a curious divergence may exist between true volunteers for FEMA duty and actual FEMA employees or Reservists called into action to work a disaster.

The volunteer, working for his or her own satisfaction and no pay, probably wants to finish the job as soon as possible and get home. The FEMA employee, working a job for very good pay, plus overtime-pay during disasters, plus daily perks, may hope the work stretches out longer rather than shorter. Volunteers working faster while employees are working slower? Does that make any sense?

Not long ago, an individual working for FEMA wrote an article that could be referred to as an "inside job." Effort was made to select limited paragraphs and sentences from the article, but the article being peculiarly interesting, thorough, and quite enlightening deserved to be reprinted in full.

ARTICLE FOUND AT: www.dailykos.com/story/2013/4/9/1200363/An-Insider-s-Critique-of-FEMA

ARTICLE WRITTEN BY: John Aloysius

DATE: APRIL 9, 2013

TITLE: AN INSIDER'S Critique of FEMA

> For three months I have worked 60 hours a week for FEMA, witnessing first-hand the inner-workings and organizational mentality from a wide range of inside perspectives. My initial placement was on a mobile, language-needs strike team that was based out of the Joint Field Office (JFO) in Forest Hills, Queens. I was later reassigned to a base in the field, visiting damaged homes and assisting with recovery efforts on the Rockaway Peninsula. Throughout it all I was shocked at what seemed to be an intentional inefficiency that aggressively discouraged questioning aimed at improving the speed and effectiveness of the relief effort.

> FEMA has three categories of workers: a small permanent staff; several thousand "reservists" who are deployed only during disasters; and "local hires," which are sourced from disaster areas and stay on after many of the reservists have gone home. I never interacted with any permanent staff, and as far as I could tell, the recovery from Superstorm Sandy was run and managed by reservists.

> While generally weary of government, I naïvely assumed that FEMA would attract a staff motivated by a desire to help others. My first interactions with local hires showed more pragmatic motivations, often just unemployed workers happy to have found a job, but it was also nearly universally mixed with empathy and altruism. The quality of the local hires varied, many seemed well suited for a professional workforce while others seemed incompetent. It's hard to believe that there were not better applicants willing to assist with disaster relief, so the first problem is poor hiring but that is relatively minor, the real issue is the work environment. Despite my initial misgivings about this group, I later realized that almost all the quality workers were in fact local hires.

My first day on the job I went out with a reservist who was also my direct supervisor and visited faith-based organizations. Our task was to collect data, assess needs and ultimately help the larger recovery effort. About half the numbers we turned in for the day were completely made up. We drove by churches and guessed the size of the congregation, its language needs and overall damage. Even with the gross exaggeration of the work that we did, even if those numbers were all real, it would still be less accomplished than I would have expected during our ten-hour shift. Almost all the reservists I encountered had mastered the art of wasting time. When I was at the JFO we sat around for an hour or two before we left on any assignment. In the Rockaways, we did not linger quite as long at the command post but like clockwork, every day we ate a leisurely breakfast at two separate places. We got coffee at one restaurant then breakfast sandwiches in another, it was all just a way to waste time.

A significant part of any day was spent sitting in a car. When I worked out of the JFO, my team would sometimes have assignments that required a lot of driving, necessitating visiting both Nassau and Manhattan in the same day for example. In hindsight, I believe that up-per management (also reservists) did this intentionally, as part of the overall strategy to waste time and extend their own deployment. When we did arrive at our destination we often sat in the car for half an hour or more before exiting. Sometimes the supervisor would be on a personal phone call, sometimes sorting papers, sometimes not doing anything at all but wasting time.

The reservists had a good salary and impressive perks, such as a $70 a day food stipend that is added to their pay, and tried very hard to not work themselves out [of] a job. There was an acute awareness that the more efficient we were—in this case the faster we helped affect-ed communities recover—the shorter our job would be. So we worked slowly, and we intentionally worked inefficiently. This was not isolated to the level just above me but widespread throughout the organization. It went beyond wasting time though. Many of the decisions and direc-tion given from above were illogical. We spent a week visiting busi-nesses to ask if we could leave fliers there, though we did not have any actual fliers to leave, nor did we ever return with any. Another day was spent writing consent forms out by hand that we would never use. Many of the local hires were surprised and frustrated. There were also some that were happy with a lazy system and everyone at least em-braced parts of it. For example, I gladly went home early nearly every day—as did everyone else.

There were some small attempts at improvement, but they never lead [sic] anywhere. When my team did street canvasing I stepped out of the vehicle immediately and stood outside, thinking it would encourage others. One reservist on my team would often step outside with me, but our supervisor never followed and no one else from the two or three car loads of workers ever stepped outside until she did. It changed nothing but made my accomplice and me frustrated and cold—this was in early February—so we soon stopped trying and waited in the car with everyone else. The reservist who tried to encourage a better work ethic choose [sic] to leave the FEMA mission early, she was the first person to leave my team in Rockaway. When we were handwriting consent forms another team member questioned the logic of it and was shouted down with comments such as "Where can you get a job that pays you for doing so little and then lets you go home early? Don't ruin this for the rest of us." That team member was let go the following week. He was the second person to leave our Rockaway team.

The worst aspect of FEMA is not the general incompetence of the decision makers, nor the intentional waste, it is the workplace culture. Any suggestion for efficiency, any questioning of the modus operandi is greeted with hostility. I've never encountered a job that guarded its own misgivings so fiercely. As the job progressed, almost all local hires, myself included, acquiesced to the situation and eventually grew close with it. The ones who embraced the inefficiency most, the ones who were the happiest to collect a pay check for sitting idle, were rewarded. Most reservists begin as local hires and the local hires that embraced the waste and sloth are the most likely to apply and eventually advance within the organization. In essence, negative behavior is rewarded.

Workers will always take as much as they can, the difference with FEMA is that encouraging inefficiency is not hurting the bottom-line of a still profiting faceless millionaire, its [sic] hurting working families who were devastated by a natural disaster. Volunteers (occupy sandy, etc) worked much harder than FEMA and other paid workers I interacted with. The paid workers seemed to be working for a paycheck while the volunteers had no other motivation but to help people and tried to maximize their efforts and effectiveness.

Yes, there were exceptions and good workers but that's all they were, exceptions. My critique is limited to my own narrow experiences with the organization, beginning in December and ending in late March but it seems clear that everything I witnessed was part of an organizational pattern. At the end of the day, FEMA has a very worthy mission and *actually does significantly contribute to disaster recovery, but it can be so much better.*

Assuming that government should provide a safety net and help overwhelmed communities recover from natural disasters, FEMA needs to exist. The way that it has evolved—the willful inefficiency and extreme hostility toward constructive criticism—is appalling and needs to be torn down and replaced. I worked as a Field Operations Supervisor during the 2010 census and was happily surprised with the quality of the other managers and the general work environment, and there are volunteer relief organizations that work well so it is possible. There are successful templates that exist. Disaster survivors deserve so much more from us.

Another eye-opener concerning government employees? It seems so.

It appears many, or at least some government employees, even when working on what amounts to a tragedy for American citizens, can't quite bring themselves to work long-and-hard even to help their brethren. As the article suggests … unpaid volunteers might do more efficient work. At least, their hearts would be in the job. If it wasn't … they wouldn't be there.

How many government departments would do a much better job for American taxpayers if the lazy, only the lazy, were weeded out and replaced with volunteers? The answer … all of them.

Generally, volunteers feel better because they gave something of themselves. The sidewalk is cleaner. The neighborhood appears more attractive. A lonely person has a visitor. There's less cost for clean-up after a minor or major disaster. And, disaster clean-up is completed sooner rather than later. Volunteers can make the difference between success and failure.

Drive down any street and unkempt properties are noticeable. Somebody needs to remind those owners to become their own volunteers—to clean up their properties and increase neighborhood value. Call it neighborhood-patriotism.

It's possible to drive out of one town and directly into another. Back-to-back towns. Sometimes there's no need to see a sign or village boundary marker. That's because there's a noticeable change with cut grass, flowers, no debris or an attractive welcome sign. That town's leadership cares about the town or … they just have good volunteers. The other town or its citizens may care little. Uncut grass and numerous paper-wads. Which town would you rather claim as home?

The point is … citizen-volunteers can make a difference across the entire country. Their attitude improves the whole country, and their work creates value for the whole country. Volunteers should rise up from the nation's youth, its home-makers, workers, and retired citizens. Volunteers can matter in small, unseen ways, or in very large scale projects. They can improve a neighbor-hood or save a city. Both improve the country. More volunteering ... a welcome change.

Remember the hopeful words of a famous president some fifty years ago:

"And so, my fellow Americans: ask not what your country can do for you, ask what you can do for your country."
— John F. Kennedy, US President (1917-1963), inauguration address

A nation of volunteers, all for one, one for all ... wouldn't that be something?

Conclusion

America Must Choose

"**The End**" ... of the American way of life?

Or, shall it be ...

"**The Beginning**" ... of the return to the American way of life?

More simply ... shall it be death, or shall it be life?

"The American way of life." What is that?

Here's how Wikipedia defines it.

INFORMATION FOUND AT: https://en.wikipedia.org/wiki-American_way

DATE: NO DATE, current

> The **American way of life**, or simply the **American way**, is the *unique lifestyle, real or imagined, of the people living in the United States of America. It refers to a nationalist ethos that purports to adhere to principles of "life, liberty and the pursuit of happiness." At the center of the American way is the American Dream, the idea that upward mobility is achievable by any American through hard work. This concept is intertwined with the concept of American exceptionalism, the notion that the American way is only possible in the U.S. because of the unique culture of the nation....*

More than half a century ago, a well-known social philosopher published his definition of what is meant by "the American way of life." It's still quoted today after many decades:

INFORMATION FOUND AT: https://en.wikipedia.org/wiki-American_way

SOURCE: *PROTESTANT, CATHOLIC, JEW: An Essay in American Religious Sociology.* Garden City, NY: Doubleday, 1955.

WRITER: WILLIAM HERBERG (1901—1977) intellectual, scholar

The American Way of life is individualistic, dynamic, and pragmatic. It affirms the supreme value and dignity of the individual; it stresses incessant activity on his part, for he is never to rest but is always to be striving to "get ahead"; it defines an ethic of self-reliance, merit, and character, and judges by achievement: "deeds, not creeds" are what count. The "American Way of Life" is humanitarian, "forward-looking," optimistic. Americans are easily the most generous and philanthropic people in the world, in terms of their ready and unstinting response to suffering anywhere on the globe. The American believes in progress, in self-improvement, and quite fanatically in education. But above all, the American is idealistic....

Would all American citizens recognize the American Way of Life today?

Would all American citizens feel they're living the American Dream today?

All ... is rarely possible, but the choice is, in fact, presented to all.

Shall it be death, or shall it be life?

Dear American citizen ... souls all, your choice should be easy ... but it will not be, as pain is within either choice and pain brings hesitation and hesitation can lead to eternal damnation.

For those American citizens, who for whatever reason, choose *not to sacrifice* in any way, choose *not to work* harder than ever before, choose *not to serve* your country ... then you'll be offering to stand witness to the death of the American Way of Life.

You'll have become the "I" in the phrase uttered by J. Robert Oppenheimer after he witnessed the first atomic bomb blast at White Sands, New Mexico, on July 16, 1945:

"Now, I am become death, the destroyer of worlds."

Oppenheimer, part of a group of distinguished intellectuals who gathered to watch the ultimate in modern man-made destruction, also remarked, *"We knew the world would not be the same. A few people laughed, a few people cried, most were silent."*

Would saying, "a few people laugh, a few people cry, most are silent," accurately reflect our American society today?

Those quiet words have the potential to haunt our country until dust.

For those American citizens, hopefully all, who choose to seize the moment, being determined to make American life great again ... it will not be easy, it will not be fast, and it cannot be the other guy. It must be you. And you must reach far and wide.

You will need to find from within yourself the fortitude of Maximillian Kolbe and, at the same time, be determined to be as fortunate as Franciszek Gajowniczek. A tall, tall order for any mere mortal.

The life-struggles of Kolbe and Gajowniczek should be known to every American citizen. If … the same inner fortitude is demonstrated in America … good fortune will surely follow. It could be an American success story about how hard work, sacrifice, dedication, and persistence is always worthy.

Below is a description of Kolbe and Gajowniczek's time together. It's not a story but only a snapshot of their short but dramatic life-changing meeting … long ago in Poland.

INFORMATION FOUND AT: https://en.wikipedia.org/wiki/Maximilian Kolbe

> ***Maximilian Maria Kolbe***, *O.F.M. Conv. (Polish: Maksymilian Maria Kolbe; 8 January 1894 – 14 August 1941) was a Polish Conventual Franciscan friar, who volunteered to die in place of a stranger in the German death camp of Auschwitz, located in German-occupied Poland during World War II….*
>
> *Kolbe was canonized on 10 October 1982 by Pope John Paul II, and declared a martyr of charity. He is the patron saint of drug addicts, political prisoners, families, journalists, prisoners, and the pro-life movement. John Paul II declared him "The Patron Saint of Our Difficult Century"….*
>
> *After the outbreak of World War II, which started with the invasion of Poland by Germany, Kolbe was one of the few brothers who remained in the monastery, where he organized a temporary hospital. After the town was captured by the Germans, he was briefly arrested by them on 19 September 1939 but released on 8 December. He refused to sign the Deutsche Volksliste, which would have given him rights similar to those of German citizens in exchange for recognizing his German ancestry. Upon his release he continued work at his monastery, where he and other monks provided shelter to refugees from Greater Poland, including 2,000 Jews whom he hid from German persecution in their friary in Niepokalanów…. On 17 February 1941, the monastery was shut down by the German authorities. That day Kolbe and four others were arrested by the German Gestapo and imprisoned in the Pawiak prison. On 28 May, he was transferred to Auschwitz as prisoner #16670.*
>
> *Continuing to act as a priest, Kolbe was subjected to violent harassment, including beating and lashings, and once had to be smuggled to a prison hospital by friendly inmates. At the end of July 1941, three prisoners disappeared from the camp, prompting SS-Hauptsturmführer Karl Fritzsch, the deputy camp commander, to pick 10 men to be starved to*

death in an underground bunker to deter further escape attempts. When one of the selected men, Franciszek Gajowniczek, cried out, "My wife! My children!", Kolbe volunteered to take his place.

> *According to an eye witness, an assistant janitor at that time, in his prison cell, Kolbe led the prisoners in prayer to Our Lady. Each time the guards checked on him, he was standing or kneeling in the middle of the cell and looking calmly at those who entered. After two weeks of dehydration and starvation, only Kolbe remained alive. "The guards wanted the bunker emptied, so they gave Kolbe a lethal injection of carbolic acid. Kolbe is said to have raised his left arm and calmly waited for the deadly injection. ...*

> *On 12 May 1955, Kolbe was recognized as the Servant of God. Kolbe was declared venerable by Pope Paul VI on 30 January 1969, beatified as a Confessor of the Faith by the same Pope in 1971 and canonized as a saint by Pope John Paul II on 10 October 1982. Upon canonization, the Pope declared St. Maximilian Kolbe not a confessor, but a martyr...*

The information presented shows Maximillian Kolbe to have led a short life of compassion, determination, persistence, and courage ... right up until the time of his death.

How many souls can do that?

Can Americans do that? They've done it before.

Can today's Americans do it? They'll have to ... or they'll never be as fortunate as Franciszek Gajowniczek.

Francis, a caring man of decency and good fortune. A man, who until his death, would love and honor and cherish Maximillian Kolbe.

A history of Francis' auspicious life follows:

INFORMATION FOUND AT: https://en.wikipedia.org/wiki/franciszek_Gajowniczek

> ***Franciszek Gajowniczek*** *(November 15, 1901 – March 13, 1995) was a Polish army sergeant whose life was saved by priest St. Maximilian Kolbe, who volunteered to die in his place. Gajowniczek had been sent to Auschwitz concentration camp from Gestapo prison in Tarnów.... Gajowniczek and Kolbe met as inmates of Auschwitz in May 1941.*

> *Franciszek Gajowniczek, a Roman Catholic, was born in Strachomin near Mińsk Mazowiecki. He lived in Warsaw since 1921, and had a wife and two sons.... He was captured by the Gestapo in Zakopane. He arrived at Auschwitz on October 8, 1940. When a prisoner appeared to have escaped, Sub-Commandant Karl Fritzsch ordered that ten other prisoners die by starvation in reprisal. Franciszek Gajowniczek (prisoner number*

5659) was one of those selected at roll-call. When the Franciscan priest, Kolbe, heard Gajowniczek cry out in agony over the fate of his family, he offered himself instead…. Kolbe's exact words have been forgotten, but one version records his words as, "I am a Catholic priest from Poland; I would like to take his place, because he has a wife and children." The switch was permitted; after all his cellmates died, Kolbe (prisoner 16670) was put to death with an injection of carbolic acid.

Gajowniczek was sent from Auschwitz to Sachsenhausen concentration camp on October 25, 1944. He was liberated there by the Allies, after spending five years, five months, and nine days in German concentration camps in total. He reunited with his wife, Helena, half-a-year later in Rawa Mazowiecka. Though she survived the war, his sons were killed in a Soviet bombardment of German occupied Poland in 1945, before his release.

Gajowniczek was a guest of Pope Paul VI in the Vatican, when Maximilian Kolbe was beatified for his martyrdom on October 17, 1971. In 1972, Time magazine reported that over 150,000 people made a pilgrimage to Auschwitz to honor the anniversary of Maximilian's beatification. One of the first to speak was Gajowniczek, who declared "I want to express my thanks, for the gift of life." His wife, Helena, died in 1977. Gajowniczek was in the Vatican again as a guest of Pope John Paul II when Maximilian Kolbe was canonized by him on October 10, 1982.

In 1994, Gajowniczek visited the St. Maximilian Kolbe Catholic Church of Houston, where he told his translator Chaplain Thaddeus Horbowy that "so long as he … has breath in his lungs, he would consider it his duty to tell people about the heroic act of love by Maximilian Kolbe." Gajowniczek died in the city of Brzeg on March 13, 1995 at the age of 93. He was buried at a convent cemetery in Niepokalanów, slightly more than 53 years after having his life spared by Kolbe.

Dear America … to avoid the pitfalls of the world past and in the future, you, as a nation, must capture the inner strength of Maximillian Kolbe. And from that time on … you'll rise to the good fortune of Franciszek Gajowniczek.

Who will sit in judgment of that? Only one. History.